REFL

SUNDAYS

YEAR **A**

REFLECTIONS
FOR
SUNDAYS
YEAR **A**

ANGELA ASHWIN	PAUL KENNEDY
JEFF ASTLEY	JOHN KIDDLE
ALAN BARTLETT	BARBARA MOSSE
JOHN BARTON	DAVID MOXON
SARAH DYLAN BREUER	ROSALYN MURPHY
ROSALIND BROWN	GORDON MURSELL
JOANNA COLLICUTT	NADIM NASSAR
GILLIAN COOPER	MARK OAKLEY
STEPHEN COTTRELL	HELEN ORCHARD
STEVEN CROFT	MARTYN PERCY
ANDREW DAVISON	JOHN PERUMBALATH
MAGGI DAWN	SUE PICKERING
PAULA GOODER	JOHN PRITCHARD
PETER GRAYSTONE	BEN QUASH
MARY GREGORY	SARAH ROWLAND JONES
JOANNE GRENFELL	TIM SLEDGE
MALCOLM GUITE	TOM SMAIL·
HELEN-ANN HARTLEY	ANGELA TILBY
LINCOLN HARVEY	GRAHAM TOMLIN
CHRISTOPHER HERBERT	KEITH WARD
SUE HOPE	MARGARET WHIPP
EMMA INESON	CATHERINE WILLIAMS
JOHN INGE	JANE WILLIAMS
MARK IRELAND	CHRISTOPHER WOODS
CHRISTOPHER JONES	JEREMY WORTHEN

Church House Publishing
Church House
Great Smith Street
London SW1P 3AZ

ISBN 978 0 7151 4735 1

Published 2016 by Church House Publishing
Copyright © The Archbishops' Council 2016

The opinions expressed in this book are those of the
authors and do not necessarily reflect the official
policy of the General Synod or The Archbishops'
Council of the Church of England.

Liturgical editor: Peter Moger
Series editor: Hugh Hillyard-Parker
Designed and typeset by Hugh Hillyard-Parker
Copy edited by Ros Connelly
Printed by Ashford Colour Press Ltd, Gosport, Hants

What do you think of *Reflections for Sundays*?

We'd love to hear from you – simply email us at

publishing@churchofengland.org

or write to us at

Church House Publishing, Church House,
Great Smith Street, London SW1P 3AZ.

Visit **www.dailyprayer.org.uk** for more information
on the *Reflections* series, ordering and subscriptions.

Contents

About the authors   1

About *Reflections for Sundays*   7

An introduction to Matthew's Gospel   9

ADVENT   20

CHRISTMAS SEASON   35

EPIPHANY SEASON   48

THE PRESENTATION OF CHRIST   63

ORDINARY TIME BEFORE LENT   66

LENT   81

PASSIONTIDE   97

HOLY WEEK   100

EASTER SEASON   111

ASCENSION DAY   142

PENTECOST   150

ORDINARY TIME   155

ALL SAINTS   249

ORDINARY TIME: ALL SAINTS TO ADVENT   252

DEDICATION FESTIVAL   264

HARVEST THANKSGIVING   268

About the authors

Angela Ashwin travels widely as a retreat leader and speaker on prayer and discipleship. She has written several books, including *Faith in the Fool: Risk and Delight in the Christian Adventure*.

Jeff Astley is an Anglican priest, and currently Alister Hardy Professor of Religious and Spiritual Experience, Glyndŵr University, Wales, and an honorary professor at Durham University and York St John University.

Alan Bartlett is Vicar of a Durham City parish and two former pit village churches. He was formerly on the staff of Cranmer Hall (teaching Church History, Anglicanism, Spirituality and Practical Theology).

John Barton retired as Professor of Old Testament at Oxford University in 2014 and is now a Senior Research Fellow of Campion Hall, Oxford. He is an Anglican priest and assists in the parish of Abingdon-on-Thames.

Sarah Dylan Breuer is a public theologian, someone called to help others to claim their gifts as theologians in our varied contexts. She has served on the Executive Council of the US Episcopal Church and travels extensively as a preacher, retreat facilitator and worship leader.

Rosalind Brown is Canon Librarian at Durham Cathedral with oversight of the Cathedral's public ministry. A town planner before ordination, she has written books on ministry and several published hymns.

Joanna Collicutt is the Karl Jaspers Lecturer in Psychology and Spirituality at Ripon College Cuddesdon and Advisor on the Spiritual Care of Older People for Oxford Diocese. She also ministers in a West Oxfordshire parish.

Gillian Cooper is a writer, teacher and Old Testament enthusiast. She has worked as a theological educator, a cathedral verger and an administrator.

Stephen Cottrell is the Bishop of Chelmsford. He is a well-known writer and speaker on evangelism, spirituality and catechesis. He is one of the team that produced *Pilgrim*, the popular course for the Christian Journey.

Steven Croft is the Bishop of Sheffield and writes widely on scripture, leadership and mission.

Andrew Davison is the Starbridge Lecturer in Theology and Natural Sciences at Cambridge University, Fellow in Theology at Corpus Christi College and Canon Philosopher of St Albans Abbey.

Maggi Dawn is Associate Professor of Theology and Literature, and Dean of Marquand Chapel, at Yale Divinity School in the USA. Trained in both music and theology, she was ordained in the Diocese of Ely, and holds a PhD from the University of Cambridge.

Paula Gooder is Theologian in Residence for the Bible Society. She is a writer and lecturer in biblical studies, author of a number of acclaimed books, and a co-author of the *Pilgrim* course. She is also a Reader in the Church of England.

Peter Graystone works for Church Army, developing projects that take Good News to people who have no real experience of church. He edits the website Christianity.org.uk and reviews theatre for the *Church Times*.

Mary Gregory is Team Rector of Ashby de la Zouch and Breedon on the Hill in the Diocese of Leicester. She is an amateur quilter and a passionate retired-greyhound owner.

Joanne Grenfell is Archdeacon of Portsdown in the Diocese of Portsmouth.

Malcolm Guite is Chaplain of Girton College, Cambridge. An acclaimed poet, he lectures widely on theology and literature. His many books include *Sounding the Seasons: Seventy Sonnets for the Christian Year*.

Helen-Ann Hartley is the 7th Bishop of Waikato in the Diocese of Waikato and Taranaki, New Zealand. She was ordained priest in the Diocese of Oxford and served as Director of Biblical Studies at Ripon College Cuddesdon.

Lincoln Harvey is Assistant Dean and Lecturer in Systematic Theology at St Mellitus College, London. He has written numerous books and articles, including *A Brief Theology of Sport*.

Christopher Herbert was ordained in Hereford in 1967, becoming a curate and then Diocesan Director of Education. He was an incumbent in Surrey and, later, Archdeacon of Dorking and then Bishop of St Albans. He retired in 2009.

Sue Hope is the Vicar of St Paul's Shipley and an Adviser on Evangelism for the Diocese of West Yorkshire and the Dales.

Emma Ineson is the Principal of Trinity College Bristol. Before that she was Chaplain to the Bishop of Bristol and has also been Chaplain to the Lee Abbey community in Devon.

John Inge is the 113th Bishop of Worcester. He is Lead Bishop on Cathedrals and Church Buildings, and Chair of the College of Evangelists.

Mark Ireland is Archdeacon of Blackburn and co-author of six books on mission-related themes, most recently *Making New Disciples: Exploring the paradoxes of evangelism* and *How to do Mission Action Planning*.

Christopher Jones was widely respected across the Church of England, spending eight years as Home Affairs policy adviser for the Archbishops' Council until his death in 2012.

Paul Kennedy is Rector of East Winchester and Area Dean. He is also a Benedictine oblate at the Anglican Alton Abbey and blogs at http://earofyourheart.com/wp/

John Kiddle is Archdeacon of Wandsworth and was previously Director of Mission in St Albans Diocese after parish ministry in Watford and Liverpool. He is passionate about resourcing churches for mission.

Barbara Mosse is a writer and retired Anglican priest. She has worked in various chaplaincies, and has taught in theological education. Her books include *Welcoming the Way of the Cross*.

Sir **David Moxon** KNZM is the Archbishop of Canterbury's Representative to the Holy See and Director of the Anglican Centre in Rome. He was formerly Archbishop of New Zealand.

Rosalyn Murphy is vicar of St Thomas' Church, Blackpool. She is a writer in biblical studies, often bringing a liberation and womanist theological perspective to her research.

Gordon Mursell was Bishop of Stafford until his retirement in 2010. He now lives in south-west Scotland and is a writer on Christian spirituality and keen hillwalker.

Nadim Nassar is an Anglican priest, and is the Director and Co-Founder of the Awareness Foundation and co-author of the Awareness Course. He was born and raised in Lattakia, Syria.

Mark Oakley is Chancellor of St Paul's Cathedral, London, and a Visiting Lecturer in the Department of Theology and Religious Studies, King's College London. He writes on the relationship between faith, poetry and literature.

Helen Orchard is Team Vicar of St Matthew's Church in the Wimbledon Team. She was previously Chaplain-Fellow at Exeter College, Oxford and before ordination worked for the National Health Service.

Martyn Percy is the Dean of Christ Church, Oxford. From 2004 to 2014 he was Principal of Ripon College Cuddesdon, and prior to that was Director of the Lincoln Theological Institute.

John Perumbalath is Archdeacon of Barking in Chelmsford Diocese. He has served as a theological educator and parish priest in the dioceses of Calcutta (Church of North India) and Rochester.

Sue Pickering is a spiritual director, retreat leader and writer. A clerical Canon of Taranaki Cathedral, Sue finds inspiration in family, friends, 'ordinary' life, contemplation, creation, gardening and quilting.

John Pritchard has recently retired as Bishop of Oxford. Prior to that he has been Bishop of Jarrow, Archdeacon of Canterbury and Warden of Cranmer Hall, Durham.

Ben Quash is Professor of Christianity and the Arts at King's College London, the author of the 2013 Lent Book *Abiding*, and Canon Theologian of Coventry and Bradford Cathedrals.

Sarah Rowland Jones was a mathematician, then a British diplomat, before ordination in the Church in Wales. After 11 years as researcher to successive Archbishops of Cape Town, she returned to the UK to run Cardiff's city centre church.

Tim Sledge is Vicar of Romsey Abbey and Area Dean. Prior to this he was Mission Enabler in the Peterborough Diocese. He is author of a number of books including *Mission Shaped Parish* and *Youth Emmaus*.

Tom Smail was a leading Scottish theologian, preacher and writer. He was Vice-Principal and Lecturer in Doctrine at St John's College, Nottingham.

Angela Tilby is the Diocesan Canon at Christ Church Cathedral, Oxford. A former BBC producer she was Tutor and Vice-Principal of Westcott House, Cambridge for ten years and then vicar of St Bene't's Church, Cambridge.

Graham Tomlin is Bishop of Kensington and President of St Mellitus College. He was formerly Vice Principal of Wycliffe Hall, Oxford and the first Principal of St Mellitus.

Keith Ward is a Fellow of the British Academy, Emeritus Regius Professor of Divinity, Oxford, a Canon of Christ Church Cathedral, Oxford, and Senior Research Fellow at Heythrop College, London.

Margaret Whipp is the Lead Chaplain for the Oxford University Hospitals. She has served in parish ministry, university chaplaincy, and most recently as Senior Tutor at Ripon College Cuddesdon.

Catherine Williams is an Anglican priest working as a Selection Secretary for the Ministry Division of the Archbishops' Council. Her ministerial priorities are vocational discernment, prayer and spiritual direction.

Jane Williams lectures at St Mellitus College, London and Chelmsford, and is a Visiting Lecturer at King's College London. She taught previously at Trinity Theological College, Bristol.

Christopher Woods is a vicar in Stepney, East London, also working in the Stepney Training and Development office. Before that he was Secretary to the Church of England's Liturgical Commission and National Worship Adviser.

Jeremy Worthen is the Secretary for Ecumenical Relations and Theology at the Church of England's Council for Christian Unity. His publications include *Responding to God's Call* (Canterbury Press).

About *Reflections for Sundays*

Reflections for Daily Prayer has nourished tens of thousands of Christians with its insightful, informed and inspiring commentary on one of the scripture readings of the day from the Common Worship lectionary for Morning Prayer. Its contributors over the years have included many outstanding writers from across the Anglican tradition who have helped to establish it as one of today's leading daily devotional volumes.

Here, in response to demand, ***Reflections for Sundays*** offers thoughtful engagement with each of the *Common Worship* principal service readings for Sundays and major holy days. Reflections are provided on:

- each Old Testament reading (both Continuous and Related)
- the Epistle
- the Gospel.

Commentary on the psalm of the day can be found in the companion volume, ***Reflections on the Psalms***.

In addition, Paula Gooder provides a specially commissioned introduction to Matthew's Gospel, while contributions from 50 distinguished writers ensure a breadth of approach.

Combining new writing with selections from the weekday volumes published over the past ten years, ***Reflections for Sundays*** offers a rich resource for preaching, study and worship preparation.

An introduction to Matthew's Gospel

Each of the Gospels has a 'flavour': something that makes their particular telling of the story characteristic of that Gospel, something that makes you know that this is unmistakably Matthew (or Mark, Luke or John). Indeed, one of the glories of having four Gospels is that we have the one story told four ways – ways that bring out different emphases about Jesus, who he was and what he said and did. Through these differing emphases, we get a deeper, more profound insight into the life, death and resurrection of Jesus.

The problem is that it is all too easy to miss these emphases, either because we become too familiar with them or because we read our Gospels in such short chunks that we forget to look for and experience the repeated accents to which our Gospel writers draw attention throughout the story. In this short introduction to Matthew's Gospel, I want to draw your attention to some of the most important of these accents in this Gospel, so that as you read the Gospel during this lectionary year, you are able to notice more easily the key elements of how Matthew tells his story.

Judaism and Matthew's Gospel

There is no doubt at all that the key 'flavour' of Matthew's Gospel is Judaism; its language, its structure, its allusions, its references all have an Old Testament or Hebraic feel. Matthew's story about Jesus is a Jewish one, told from a Jewish perspective, with a largely Jewish audience in mind; it therefore portrays Jesus very much as the fulfilment of Old Testament expectation.

This Jewish flavour comes through in many different ways. The most obvious, of course, are the phrases that introduce direct quotations from the Old Testament: 'for so it has been written by the prophet' (e.g. Matthew 2.5) or 'Then was fulfilled what had been spoken through the prophet' (e.g. Matthew 2.17). These phrases seek to show that Jesus was the one that had been long expected in Hebrew tradition. At first glance Jesus appears to come in unexpected form, because he was born in poverty, refused the option of military might and proclaimed a new way of being. What Matthew sought to do, however, was to demonstrate that, though in unexpected form, Jesus had been long expected – you just needed to look carefully and know your Old Testament well to see that he was, in fact, the one for whom Jews had waited so long.

These are not, however, the only Hebraic aspects of Matthew's Gospel. One of the striking features of Matthew is that he included phrases or ways of speaking that seem to suggest that they were taken directly from Hebrew or Aramaic (a Semitic language closely connected to Hebrew which was widely spoken in the Ancient Near East at the time of Jesus). Phrases dotted through the whole of Matthew, which were translated in the King James Version as 'And it came to pass' but which are smoothed in modern translations to something along the lines of 'Now when Jesus...' (see for example Matthew 7.28), seem to be a translation from Hebrew or Aramaic via Greek.

Indeed, modern readers are not the first to notice the Hebraic tone of Matthew's Gospel. One of the earliest writers about the Gospels, Papias, declared that Matthew had collected the words of Jesus 'in the Hebrew language'. The problem with this statement is that, although there are a few phrases, such as 'and it came to pass', that seem to have jumped straight out of the Hebrew language, this is not true of most of the Gospel. Scholars have tried, with only minimal success, to reconstruct an original Hebrew or Aramaic version. Despite the Gospel's Jewish feel and the few Hebraic-type phrases, the Gospel appears to have been written first in Greek, but by someone who spoke Hebrew or Aramaic, and so introduced a few turns of phrase into an otherwise very Greek text. It is possible then that what Papias meant was that Matthew had collected the sayings in a Hebrew style, i.e. so that the Gospel was – as it certainly appears to be – thoroughly steeped in Jewish theology and thinking.

Jesus as the new Moses

The Jewish feel of the Gospel is not just restricted to a few phrases or even to a wide range of Old Testament quotations. One of the most important features of the Gospel is that it tells its story of Jesus with the Old Testament firmly in mind. Right from the start it is clear that Jesus is the new Moses, come to give the new law to God's people. This emphasis on Moses begins as early as the birth narratives, in which various details are clearly reminiscent of Moses' infancy. So, for example, at Moses' birth Pharaoh killed all the other baby boys leaving only Moses (Exodus 1.22-2.10) as happened too for Jesus with Herod (Matthew 2.13-18) and when Moses' life was in danger he fled from Egypt to Israel (Exodus 2.15), when Jesus' life was in danger he fled from Israel to Egypt (Matthew 2.13-21). In case we are in any doubt of the connections between the two accounts, Matthew 2.15 quotes from Hosea 11.1 – 'Out of Egypt have I called my Son' – which alludes to yet another Moses story – that of the Exodus.

The connections with Moses do not stop there. Just as Moses fasted for 40 days and nights in the wilderness (Exodus 34.28); so Jesus also fasted for 40 days and nights at his temptation (Matthew 4.2). Probably most important of all is the emphasis in Matthew on Jesus' Sermon on the Mount: just as Moses went up Mount Sinai to receive the law, so Jesus went up a mountain to deliver the new law in the Sermon on the Mount (Matthew 5–7). Jesus even makes specific reference backwards to the Mosaic law with the formula: 'You have heard that it was said ... but I say to you' (Matthew 5.21; 27; 33; 38; 43).

It is important to recognize these deep connections between Moses and Jesus for what they are and not to be troubled by what they are not. To our modern eye, these typologies drawn by Matthew could suggest that Matthew was either 'making up' the story or indeed massaging it to fit the details. This does not seem to me to be what is happening here. In all three synoptic Gospels Jesus fasted for 40 days and nights; in Luke's Gospel we find many of the 'new laws' proclaimed by Jesus in the Sermon on the Mount. Matthew is not so much making up the stories as seeing in the events that happened deep theological patterns. What Matthew was doing was providing us with a lens through which to observe what Jesus said and did so that we could make more sense of – see more truly – who he really was. This Jesus, this new Moses, had come to show us how to live: how to welcome and live fully within the Kingdom of God.

Jesus and mountains in Matthew

It is probably worth noticing at this point that the mountain at the Sermon on the Mount is not the only mountain to be found in Matthew. There are five others, making six in all:

- The first mountain is found in the temptation narrative where Jesus was tempted to worship the devil (Matthew 4.8).
- The second is the Sermon on the Mount (Matthew 5.1).
- The third is the mountain where Jesus healed many sick people (15.29).

● The fourth is the mountain of transfiguration (Matthew 17.1).

● The fifth mountain is the Mount of Olives, where Jesus taught about the end times (Matthew 24).

● The sixth and final mountain is the setting for the encounter between the disciples and the risen Jesus where Jesus commissioned them to make disciples of all nations (Matthew 28.16).

It is easy to make too much of motifs like this. Various scholars have argued extensively for there being only five mountains, like the five books of Torah, as that would have been pleasing and would have fitted the connections with Moses. The problem is that in order to arrive at just five mountains, you have to miss one out. This challenge suggests that we need to be cautious lest we place unwarranted emphasis on such motifs. Nevertheless, it is interesting to note that the events which took place on each of the six mountains – a temptation to worship the devil; teaching; healing; transfiguration; exploration of the end times and the commission to make new disciples – make a neat summary of who Jesus was and what he came to do. In an aural culture, it would have been easy to listen out for the six key mountain motifs and through them to understand the centre of Matthew's message.

The fivefold structure of Matthew

It is often said that beauty is in the eye of the beholder. This is certainly true. It is also true that the structure of a book can also be in the eye of the beholder. You only need to glance at many commentaries on the Bible to observe that there are nearly as many proposed structures for the books of the Bible as there are people proposing them. Matthew's Gospel is different. Although not everyone agrees on the precise details, many scholars discern a fivefold pattern to the Gospel. What is particularly striking is that the majority of the material that is specific to Matthew's Gospel (and not to be found in Mark's Gospel) can be identified as five discourses that provide teaching on narratives about what Jesus did. It is even more striking to observe that Matthew 7.28, 11.1, 13.53, 19.1, and 26.1 all contain a phrase such as '...when Jesus had finished saying these things', a phrase that appears to provide the bridge from one section of the Gospel to another.

If we take these formulaic phrases as a guide then the structure of the Gospel would look like this:

- Prologue: genealogy, nativity and infancy narratives – Matthew 1–2
- First narrative (the baptism of Jesus) and discourse (the Sermon on the Mount) – Matthew 3–7
- Second narrative (stories of miracles interwoven with stories of discipleship) and discourse (focusing on mission and suffering) – Matthew 8–10
- Third narrative (conflict with Jesus opponents) and discourse (a series of parables) – Matthew 11–13.52
- Fourth narrative (increasing opposition to Jesus) and discourse (preparation of the disciples for Jesus' absence) – Matthew 13.53–18
- Fifth narrative (Jesus travels to Jerusalem) and discourse (the coming end) – Matthew 19–20
- Epilogue: the last week of Jesus' life, death, resurrection and great commission – Matthew 21–28.

Unlike with Matthew's mountains, this outline does seem to have a genuine fivefold structure and might well have been influenced by Matthew's concern to present Jesus as the new

Moses, and to present his Gospel as the new fivefold Torah for the new people of God.

Matthew and the Pharisees

The only jarring note in Matthew's otherwise profoundly Jewish Gospel, is the apparent distance that Matthew seems keen to establish between Jesus and the Jews of his day, especially the Pharisees. Chapter 23 of the Gospel contains a long list of sayings (found only in Matthew) condemning the Pharisees for bad advice, bad practice and for generally missing the main point of the worship of God. The repeated phrase 'Woe to you, scribes and Pharisees...' throughout the chapter only serves to drive home the point of Jesus' anger. Added to this is the fact that throughout the Gospel, synagogues are referred to as 'their synagogues' (Matthew 4.23; 9.35; 10.17), so the distance between Jesus and his fellow Jews in Matthew's Gospel seems quite extensive.

This seems odd given the clearly Jewish emphasis of the rest of the Gospel. One explanation for this, offered by some though not all scholars, is that Matthew's Gospel was written into a Jewish Christian community that was struggling with a conflict between themselves and their fellow Jews. Matthew therefore offered a picture of Jesus – and of the following of Jesus – that was profoundly Jewish but at the same time offered a strong critique of the Judaism practised by their close neighbours.

In other words, Matthew might have been offering the story of Jesus as a genuine way of expressing Jewish faith and belief through the following of Jesus, while at the same time seeking to put distance between the Jewish Christian community and those with whom they were in conflict.

The dating and authorship of Matthew's Gospel

This brings us to when the Gospel might have been written and by whom. This is a question that is hard to answer but one that matters to many people, so it is worth sketching out some of the key issues that might help us to begin to construct an answer.

Who was Matthew?

A good place to begin is with the question of who Matthew was. The Gospel was attributed to Matthew quite early in its life. The Papias who noted that the Gospel was a collection of stories about Jesus in the Hebrew style also attributed the authorship to Matthew possibly as early as 125 AD; this was repeated by Irenaeus around 50 years later. By the end of the second century AD, this Matthew was firmly associated with the Matthew who was one of the Twelve and was a former tax collector (Matthew 9.9; 10.3).

One of the problems here is that although Matthew is named and identified as a former tax collector in Matthew's Gospel, he does not appear in either Mark or Luke, where the former tax collector was called Levi. One possible answer to this conundrum is that Matthew was known by two names; either that, or there were two former tax collectors one mentioned by Matthew and one by Mark and Luke.

When and where was the Gospel written?

Christian tradition identifies Antioch as the place where Matthew's Gospel was written. Although there is little concrete evidence to support this, it would be as good a location as any. As we observed above, when reflecting on Matthew's Gospel and the Pharisees, the Gospel may reflect a situation in which there was a growing conflict between Matthew's Jewish Christian community and their Jewish brothers and sisters. We know from Acts that such a conflict did take place early on in the Christian life in Antioch, so there is no reason to assume that it suddenly resolved later in the first century. There is certainly evidence – even if it is slightly sketchy – that the Jewish War (66–72 AD) and the fall of the temple in Jerusalem (70 AD) contributed to heightened tensions between Jews and a number of groups, including followers of Christ.

Another factor that might nudge us to this date would be that Matthew, like Luke, contains a lot of material that overlaps with Mark, suggesting that Mark had already been written when Matthew was composed. Scholars often date Mark to the late 60s AD or very early 70s, so if Matthew knew Mark, then this might suggest a date for Matthew of the mid-70s AD (though it could have been slightly later or slightly earlier).

Concluding reflections

People react to Matthew in widely differing ways. For some, Matthew is their favourite Gospel; for others their least favourite. Others still are more lukewarm in their response, neither loving nor hating it. Matthew's is a profoundly practical Gospel. Probably more than any of the other gospels, Matthew's Gospel shows what it is like to live in the Kingdom: the Sermon on the Mount, the Kingdom Parables and the other discourses of Jesus all reveal profoundly practical insights into how we, who seek to follow Jesus, should live. The 'new law' of Jesus is in many ways even more taxing than the 'old law' of Moses, requiring not only right action but right thought and attitude too.

Matthew also appears to reveal the gritty reality of life in the Kingdom. The Gospel reveals that conflict existed for those who read it: whether from inside that community when disagreements took place (see 'If another member of the church sins against you, go and point out the fault when the two of you are alone', Matthew 18.15) or from those who were not followers of Jesus ('Beware of them, for they will hand you over to councils and flog you in their synagogues', Matthew 10.17). Matthew holds out no utopian vision of life in the Kingdom; his is a stark depiction of life as it really was – and, for many Christians around the world, still is.

As we meet the Jesus of Matthew's Gospel, however – through the new law he brought, the parables he told, the discourses he unfolded, the miracles he did, indeed simply through the way he lived his life and faced his death – we are reminded that, no matter what the cost, Jesus is the one truly in whom we can find rest for our souls (Matthew 11.28); the one worthy of our worship (Matthew 28.17); and the one who sends us onwards to take the message of this good news to the ends of the earth (Matthew 28.19). This Jesus still calls 'come, follow me' (Matthew 4.18-19) as he did to the very first disciples. If we hear his voice and answer his call, we can be sure that our lives will never be the same again.

Introduction by **Paula Gooder**

First Sunday of Advent

Isaiah 2.1-5
Psalm 122
Romans 13.11-end
Matthew 24.36-44

Isaiah 2.1-5

'Nation shall not lift up sword against nation' (v.4)

The famous and very encouraging passage that foretells the end of war, with swords beaten into ploughshares, leads into yet another prediction of doom for those who displease God ('The haughty eyes of people shall be brought low, and the pride of everyone shall be humbled, v.11) – salvation and judgement always occur together in Isaiah, for whom there is no 'cheap grace'. Pride and self-satisfaction are the essence of what he condemns – people worshipping gods 'their own fingers have made' (v.8). In other words, their apparent worship of God is really a form of self-worship. God, however, is merciful, and verses 2 to 5 foresee a time when all people on earth will follow his ways and so be at peace with each other.

A powerful image of this transformation can be found in the Sainsbury African gallery at the British Museum, where there is a 'tree of life' made from parts of guns. It is a monument to an initiative by a Catholic bishop in Mozambique, which was taken up and developed by Christian Aid. During the Cold War, millions of weapons flooded into Mozambique, and their continued existence gravely threatened the country's peace as they came to be used for settling internal disputes. Under the 1995 initiative 'Transforming Arms into Tools', people can bring their guns to a collecting point and receive agricultural implements in return. The tree of life celebrates this venture, by which instruments of death have been replaced with instruments of life.

Reflection by **John Barton**

Isaiah 2.1-5
Psalm 122
Romans 13.11-end
Matthew 24.36-44

Romans 13.11-end

'... the day is near' (v.12)

'Wake up and smell the coffee!' the saying goes. Pull yourself together, pay attention and get a grip before it's too late!

Paul's warning is not that we avoid disaster, but should make the most of the good news. 'Salvation is nearer to us now than when we became believers' (v.11). We have the capacity to experience more fully all that salvation brings, as we mature in faith, and 'put on the Lord Jesus Christ' (v.14) ever more fully. With this comes the responsibility of sharing the riches of salvation with others, as the day ahead dawns.

In Paul's time, the hours after dawn were generally the busiest and most productive. In our society, the rhythm of the day can be a little different. I live and work in a city centre that wakes up slowly. Most shops only open at 10 am, and it can take hours more for the streets to feel alive.

But what those who come into town later in the day fail to see is quite how much work goes on before opening time. In fact, the pedestrian precinct is open from midnight for vehicles bringing in all that is necessary for businesses to be ready by opening time. The day then runs smoothly for customers because of the hard work put in beforehand.

Are we equally prepared and ready to serve those whom God sends our way?

Reflection by **Sarah Rowland Jones**

Isaiah 2.1-5
Psalm 122
Romans 13.11-end
Matthew 24.36-44

Matthew 24.36-44

*'But about that day and hour no one knows,
neither the angels of heaven, nor the Son ...' (v.36)*

When it comes to the date of the coming of the Son of Man, ignorance may indeed be the door to bliss, and it could be very great folly to be wise!

If you think that you know the date of the second advent, these verses testify against you that such privileged information is reserved for God the Father alone.

Moreover, if we knew exactly when the train would arrive, we would not need to be on the platform until a minute or two before. The gospel, by contrast, requires not last-minute preparations but continual, alert readiness for Christ's appearing.

But how do you remain alert and expectant when, after 2,000 years, he still has not come? The answer is that the promise of his ultimate coming to claim his kingdom remains credible because, in the meantime, he keeps coming in many other, if still less than ultimate, ways. In his word, in his sacraments, in his daily providences, in the love of his people, he goes on coming. As we remain alert to receive him in all these ways, our hope will grow that, in his own good time, he will come in all his glory.

Reflection by **Tom Smail**

Isaiah 11.1-10
Psalm 72.1-7,18,19*
Romans 15.4-13
Matthew 3.1-12

Isaiah 11.1-10

'... the lion shall eat straw' (v.7)

In a world where genetic modification becomes more and more easy, and more and more widespread, we have rightly become nervous about the many ways in which we interfere with 'wild nature'. But it's something we have done for centuries, and continue to do even without the help of the latest scientific technology. Sometimes it will be to make our dogs more dangerous, sometimes less, depending what more or less self-serving need we have for such changes. Sometimes it will be to make our leeks bigger or our roses more fragrant.

Perhaps this vision of God's holy mountain seems like a travesty of wild nature in the service of a human dream. What sort of a lion eats straw? Wouldn't such a lion have lost its 'lion-ness' to such a degree that it hardly merits the name? But this may not be a prediction of what awaits lions at the end of time, so much as a proclamation of the ultimate invincibility of the peace which passes all understanding. It passes all understanding, so we need pictures like these to help us approach a conception of it. Nevertheless, it's a real peace, and it is surely coming, just as it pre-existed the creation of the world and that world's fall. For it is the peace of God, and we look forward to it not in a genetically modified future so much as a messianically modified one. Lions will experience it in their own proper way, according to God's plans for them, as we will experience it in ours.

Reflection by **Ben Quash**

Isaiah 11.1-10
Psalm 72.1-7,18,19*
Romans 15.4-13
Matthew 3.1-12

Romans 15.4-13

'Welcome one another' (v.7)

The importance of hospitality runs through both Old and New Testaments. Abraham received bread and wine from the mysterious priest-king Melchizedek (whom the writer to the Hebrews sees as prefiguring Jesus Christ: Genesis 14.18 ff; Hebrews 7). Later, Abraham offered food and drink to the Lord, or three men, or whoever it was that came to him at the oaks of Mamre with the promise of a son by his wife Sarah (Genesis 18).

This hospitality works both ways, with God himself offering and receiving human hospitality. We see Jesus Christ most profoundly accepting human hospitality in his mother's womb, and offering himself, his body and blood in the bread and wine, at the Last Supper. Jesus knew everyday hospitality too, eating and drinking with everyone from Pharisees and religious scholars to tax-collectors and society's outcasts.

he challenge comes: do we prefer to offer hospitality, to be in the superior position of host, to retain control? Or are we ready equally to be welcomed by others, trusting ourselves into their hands? Mutuality is once again implicit in Paul's exhortations, and essential to the harmony in which he tells us to live. Whether we are equally at home giving and receiving hospitality can be a good touchstone for diagnosing the insidious influence of pride in our relations with others. It may even be worth asking whether we find it easier to relate to Christ as host or guest in our lives.

Reflection by **Sarah Rowland Jones**

Isaiah 11.1-10
Psalm 72.1-7,18,19*
Romans 15.4-13
Matthew 3.1-12

Matthew 3.1-12

'... with unquenchable fire' (v.12)

Matthew strongly underscores the parallels between Jesus and John the Baptist. Both start out in the wilderness. They proclaim the same gospel of the closeness of God's rule, and both insist on a radical turning around as the right response (v.2; cf Matthew 4.17).

John is only the herald (Matthew 11.10), however, whose role it is to prepare the way for the Lord's coming (v.3), and his preaching seems to be wholly focused on judgement. Forgiveness comes only in the words and actions of Jesus. We might suspect that John later began to doubt Jesus' status – perhaps because he didn't seem radical enough (see Matthew 11.2-3). It could be that Jesus' power was not the sort of power that John expected; maybe it wasn't fiery enough for this rough prophet (vv.11-12).

Jordan River had been the crossing point for Israel's conquest of their Promised Land. It therefore marked the final gateway at the end of their long journey of redemption. Where will it end for us? The Baptist expects repentance revealed in good fruits, and prophesies a burning judgement at the harvest. Jesus' condemnation of his enemies is voiced in similar language (Matthew 7.16-20; 12.33-37). But the 'unquenchable fire' is an image of destruction rather than of everlasting punishment; some will prefer to view it as a fire of purification, reminiscent of T. S. Eliot's allusive, paradoxical words in *Little Gidding*: that our only hope and choice is being 'redeemed from fire by fire'.

Reflection by **Jeff Astley**

Third Sunday of Advent

Isaiah 35.1-10
Psalm 146.4-10
or *Canticle:* Magnificat
James 5.7-10
Matthew 11.2-11

Isaiah 35.1-10

*'A highway shall be there, and it shall be called
the Holy Way' (v.8)*

To modern ears, a highway in the desert may not sound like good news. We are glad of motorways when we need to get somewhere, but if you have ever crawled round the M25 on a Friday afternoon or languished in gridlocked highways around Los Angeles, a highway in the desert is the stuff of nightmares.

What did Isaiah have in mind? Not all the exiles returned to Judah, but first a large group, and later some smaller groups really did walk some 800 miles home through the desert to Jerusalem. In contrast to the 40 years of the Exodus, with their circuitous desert wanderings, Isaiah paints a picture of a safe, straight way home. It is a way through the desert laid about with oases of water to save them from the confusion of mirage and the beating sun; an immense pilgrimage on which no traveller would go astray; a road along which they would sing all the way home.

Troubled neither by the standstill of gridlock nor by wandering around in circles, the road home after a long, lonely exile is a way forward not backward, a way towards a future and a hope, a way towards re-discovered identity and recovered dignity. This is the Holy Way, the highway God makes in the desert.

Reflection by **Maggi Dawn**

Isaiah 35.1-10
Psalm 146.4-10
or Canticle: Magnificat
James 5.7-10
Matthew 11.2-11

Third Sunday of Advent

James 5.7-10

'The farmer waits for the precious crop from the earth' (v.7)

This passage presents us with a conundrum. It suggests that prayer is answered in real and tangible ways. 'The prayer of the righteous is powerful and effective,' the letter goes on to say (v.16). But the prelude to this claim is an injunction to learn from those who are especially patient – those who are models of how to wait. Be like a farmer, the passage says; be like a prophet; be like Job.

This is to capture two aspects of the experience of prayer, both of which are well and widely attested to in the Christian Church. There are very many Christians who will testify with joy to the fact that they have known their prayers to be answered and felt the effectiveness of God's grace powerfully in their lives. But there are others who have dwelt in a dark night of the soul, questioning where God is and what God's will might be.

I am not sure that the Letter of James wants to resolve the apparent tension between these two aspects of prayer; equally, it does not want to deny either type of experience. Christians are to pray with a patience that sets no ultimatums. And yet... they are to pray in the real expectation of an answer. The waiting that strains forward needs accompaniment by a straining forward that knows how to wait.

Reflection by **Ben Quash**

Isaiah 35.1-10
Psalm 146.4-10
or Canticle: Magnificat
James 5.7-10
Matthew 11.2-11

Matthew 11.2-11

'And blessed is anyone who takes no offence at me' (v.6)

There is almost a humorous tone to this phrase of Jesus, because he knows all too well that it is impossible for humans not to, at least occasionally, take offence at other human beings. Human relationships frequently falter because we think we have caused offence, or we think that someone else has taken offence at us, when quite often this is not the case at all. When we think someone is offended, we become defensive, angular and cold, instead of learning the self-awareness to realize when we need to apologize or when in fact we have misread someone else entirely. Jesus himself may have been defensive at times, especially when challenged by the Pharisees, but his defensiveness would always have been forgiving and merciful.

Many people do, of course, take offence at Jesus and he knows it, but the test is whether people can see him for who he really is – the Messiah, the Word made flesh, not just an ordinary rabbi. Then they need not be offended, but feel blessed that God has come near to them and that God has become flesh and blood. Jesus is encouraging people who hear his teaching to take it seriously, to strip away arrogant self-obsession and to receive the blessings of the Father.

Reflection by **Christopher Woods**

Isaiah 7.10-16
Psalm 80.1-8,18-20*
Romans 1.1-7
Matthew 1.18-end

Isaiah 7.10-16

'Look, the young woman is with child and shall bear a son'
(v.14)

Hardly any verse in the Bible has been more discussed than verse 14. Who is this young woman? Is she the wife of Isaiah? Or of Ahaz? Or is this a more general reference? Is there a single or a double fulfilment in the birth – that is, an immediate birth and the birth of the Messiah? Matthew 1.23 and countless nativity plays have concluded that the Hebrew 'alma' refers to a virgin, whereas strict translation renders the word 'a young woman'. 'Alma' must include women who are virgins, but not only those.

Here is a promise that has echoed down the centuries. Immanuel will be born as 'God with us' and our confidence will forever be able to rest in that greatest of all fulfilments. There is no moment and no place that will be outside God's presence. 'God with us' is always with us. However, God needed a young woman to go along with this great vision. God found such a person in young Mary from a little Galilean village called Nazareth (pop. 200?). Mary made space for God in her womb, just as Joseph of Aramathea made space for God in his tomb. Without the co-operation of human beings in the purposes of God, God has allowed himself to be limited in what he can do, a truth that applies to prayer as well as providence. What a responsibility rests on every believer every day! Like Mary, we are the co-operative agents of God's loving action in the world. Saying 'yes' is a daily decision. How will we say 'yes' today?

Reflection by **John Pritchard**

Fourth Sunday of Advent

Isaiah 7.10-16
Psalm 80.1-8,18-20*
Romans 1.1-7
Matthew 1.18-end

Romans 1.1-7

'... declared to be Son of God' (v.4)

The baby whose birth we celebrate during the coming days was the Almighty God, walking and talking (or rather, helpless and crying) among us. We are so familiar with this central Christian belief that we sometimes forget how astounding it is.

Jesus' first followers were Jewish. This means it was abhorrent for them to think that a man could be divine. One of the reasons the Jews were so utterly revolted by being conquered by the Romans was that the emperor Tiberius Caesar was a man who claimed to be a god. Jews were prepared to go to their deaths rather than worship Caesar.

Jesus never made a direct statement that he was God. Perhaps if he had, people would have been so angry that he might have been murdered in a backstreet. Instead, he fascinated and provoked people by saying, 'The Father and I are one,' (John 10.30) or by telling them that their sins were forgiven, which is something only God can do (Mark 2.5).

It must have seemed wrong in every imaginable way for Jesus' first followers to begin to see him as divine. Every bone in their body must have resisted it. But they came to believe it because what they had seen and heard didn't have any other explanation (v.4). It left them with no choice.

So they worshipped him as God – and Christianity was born.

Reflection by **Peter Graystone**

Isaiah 7.10-16
Psalm 80.1-8,18-20*
Romans 1.1-7
Matthew 1.18-end

Fourth Sunday of Advent

Matthew 1.18-end

'...they shall name him Emmanuel,
which means, "God is with us."' (v.23)

Whether you take it literally or not, Matthew's narrative of Joseph's dream conveys a rich spiritual meaning. Perhaps the most important point is that Jesus is born of the Spirit. He is filled with the Spirit from the first moment of his life, so that he has an intimate sense of the inner presence and power of God. His life is a perfect manifestation of the loving action of God. Jesus is by nature and from the first what we hope to become eventually by grace – Spirit-born, Spirit-filled and Spirit-led. Being a disciple of Jesus is to seek to be wholly dependent on the Spirit each day, to have a sense of the inner presence of the Spirit, and to express the healing, reconciling and forgiving love of God in all our actions.

That is only possible if God fills us with the power of the divine life, makes the presence of the Spirit known to us, and enables us to manifest the divine love that was fully expressed in Jesus. That is 'salvation', liberation from all that separates us from God. And that is why the child is to be called Jesus (the Greek form of Joshua, 'Yahweh saves'). God saves us by making us one with the divine life through the action of the Spirit, so that we too may be Spirit-born.

Reflection by **Keith Ward**

Christmas Eve

24 December

2 Samuel 7.1-5,8-11,16
Psalm 89.2,19-27
Acts 13.16-26
Luke 1.67-79

2 Samuel 7.1-5,8-11,16

'... the Lord will make you a house' (v.11)

The trouble with inspired and powerful leaders is their tendency to think they are omnipotent, and King David is a case in point. Later in his story he will assume he has the right to take the woman he wants and murder her husband, with tragedy the inevitable result, but for now he has the best of intentions. He has defeated his enemies and rules over a peaceful kingdom. He knows he owes it all to God. He has a palace, so now God must have one too, a temple for the ark of the covenant, the symbol of God's presence.

God has other ideas, however. If there is to be any house building, it is God who will do it. The house God has in mind is not a building, but a dynasty, a succession of faithful rulers for God's people. 'Your house and your kingdom shall be made sure forever before me,' God tells David (v.16).

Historically, we know, David's dynasty came to a sad end when the kingdom was overrun by the Babylonians. However, God's promise did not come to an end, because its fulfilment was not dependent on any achievements of David's inadequate successors but rather on God's own reliability. There would be a new and surprising fulfilment.

And so today we await the birth of another descendant of David, the one in whom God's promise finally comes to fruition, whose throne is indeed established forever.

Reflection by **Gillian Cooper**

2 Samuel 7.1-5,8-11,16
Psalm 89.2,19-27
Acts 13.16-26
Luke 1.67-79

Acts 13.16-26

'So Paul stood up and with a gesture began to speak' (v.16)

This is a breathtaking overview of salvation history from Paul. You can tell he was trained in the Tarsus school by Gamaliel, that great Mediterranean Jewish scholar. You can also tell that all of this training and all of this command of the story of God's redeeming grace through Jewish history was itself utterly transformed and reinterpreted by Paul's experience of the risen Christ on the road to Damascus.

Paul now sees that his dramatic encounter with God in resurrection life was, in fact, the life of God, who had created the journey of the people of Israel. This life had been moving through all of the history of the world and, in particular, in and through the consciousness and destiny of the ancestors of Israel. This life was present in their liberation from Egypt, in their wilderness time in the desert, in their settlement of Canaan, in the judges and kings – and now decisively and ultimately foretold by John in the arrival of a saviour once and for all. This has to be good news. There can be no greater goodness than the goodness that this news comes to bring.

The resurrection of Jesus is all about the overcoming of the powers of sin and death. It is all about freedom from 'all those sins from which you could not be freed by the law of Moses' (Acts 13.39), meaning their death-dealing power, 'for God did not give us a spirit of cowardice, but rather a spirit of power and of love and of self-discipline' (2 Timothy 1.7).

Reflection by **David Moxon**

Christmas Eve

24 December

2 Samuel 7.1-5,8-11,16
Psalm 89.2,19-27
Acts 13.16-26
Luke 1.67-79

Luke 1.67-79

'Zechariah was filled with the Holy Spirit ...' (v.67)

Expectant parents often spend many months thinking about what their child will become – and by what name it will be called. Often the name chosen has a wealth of thoughts, longings, desires and hopes attached to it. This is important because our name plays a part in helping us define who we are and what we will become. In naming his child, John's father, Zechariah, speaks out and takes a risk for God.

Zechariah's song – the *Benedictus* – praises God who is acting in history to bring about liberation and salvation for the people of Israel. Unlike the crowds, Zechariah knows what his child will become; Gabriel told him in the Temple. Zechariah proclaims it from the rooftops: '... you, child, will be called the prophet of the Most High' (v.76). This child's vocation is to prepare the way for the Messiah. He is destined to help the people of Israel back into a right relationship with Yahweh. He will lead them to a point of repentance so that they can acknowledge their Saviour who is coming. This child, filled with the Holy Spirit, bursts through societal norms – even his name, John, breaks with family tradition. He is a new sign from God, and he points the way to God's fresh beginning.

What will you become? Who is God calling you to be for him and for others? Some are called, like John, to be a signpost enabling others to find their way to faith in Christ. Is that your calling?

Reflection by **Catherine Williams**

[1] *Set I readings:*
Isaiah 9.2-7
Psalm 96
Titus 2.11-14
Luke 2.1-14[15-20]

Christmas Day

25 December
Principal Feast

Isaiah 9.2-7

'The people who walked in darkness have seen a great light'
(v.2)

These verses are well known from Christmas carol services. They are read as a promise, looking forward to the coming of Christ and God's kingdom. However, their original intention was not prophetic.

The passage contains no references to the prophet or God's inspiration. It also contradicts the previous oracles, predicting disaster, and is written so as to avoid a timeframe. These verses are here not to prophesy but to encourage hope from the resources of faith.

Existential despair has fallen upon Judah, and, in the darkness of despair, reliance upon God grows. Jerusalem is not going to save itself; it needs miraculous deliverance or 'the zeal of the Lord of hosts' (v.7) as when Gideon overthrew Midian. The people have a messianic hope of God's personal deliverance when all traces of bloody conflict are burnt. This is similar to the alcoholic who, in the pit of addiction, calls upon a higher power to deliver. Freedom comes from God, but it often takes a crisis before we turn to God and no longer rely upon ourselves. The names proclaimed before God are throne names: 'Wonderful Counsellor, Mighty God, Everlasting Father, Prince of Peace' (v.6). The hope proclaimed is that we enthrone God, not despite our despair, but because of it.

Reflection by **Paul Kennedy**

[1] *There are three sets of readings for use on Christmas Night and Christmas Day. Set III should be used at some service during the celebration.*

Christmas Day

25 December
Principal Feast

Set I readings:
Isaiah 9.2-7
Psalm 96
Titus 2.11-14
Luke 2.1-14[15-20]

Titus 2.11-14

'For the grace of God has appeared, bringing salvation to all' (v.11)

God's unmerited love – what the Bible calls 'grace' – shines out today through the child in the manger. God gives himself to us in and through the child Jesus. Yet this outshining of grace is also curiously hidden. God refuses to manifest himself in a way that would bludgeon us into belief. Nor does he bypass the 'matter' of ordinary life. We have to look hard at the child in the manger to see who he really is. We are invited to exercise faith, a faith that leaves us free, a faith that gives us lots of space for exploration, for wonder.

Yet this faith does not allow us to stop there, kneeling in the straw of the stable. Because we too are to be an 'outshining' – imperfect, yes; flawed, yes; cracked vessels through which the light of Christ can be seen. There's a long journey ahead, to allow the gospel of Jesus to percolate through us and to have its full effect. It means a lifetime's work, and it is, again, a work of grace. We can become 'self-controlled, upright, and godly' (v.12) only because Jesus Christ has purified us (v.14). Indeed, we do not know what true holiness looks like, apart from Christ, and human attempts to personify it always founder. Far better to soak ourselves daily in the grace of God and to allow him to train us (v.12) in the way that we should live. 'Training' implies 'learning', and learning suggests the possibility of mistakes. The struggle to live out our faith in this present age, while waiting for the full glory of God (v.13) has always been an authentic Christian experience.

Reflection by **Sue Hope**

Set I readings:
Isaiah 9.2-7
Psalm 96
Titus 2.11-14
Luke 2.1-14[15-20]

Christmas Day

25 December
Principal Feast

Luke 2.1-14[15-20]

'... to you is born this day in the city of David a Saviour' (v.11)

Luke tells the nativity story with great economy. In just seven verses, history is made. The true Saviour of the world is set against the Roman Emperor, a self-proclaimed god. Jesus' origins are humble, and the story human and earthy. However, there are extraordinary elements within the everyday. Labourers meet with angels. The baby is called 'Saviour ... Messiah ... Lord' (v.11), and the story of his birth brings together the whole of creation. Angels, shepherds, straw, animals and stars are represented. Everyone and everything is there. Heaven comes together with earth; past, present and future are held in tension. Prophecy, which has been dormant for centuries, bursts forth from both angels and people.

The good news that the shepherds bring causes amazement. Mary treasures the words about her new son. She ponders them, taking them out and turning them over – thinking things through. Jesus, born in the city of David, is the chosen one whom all have been waiting for to come and make all things new. Treasuring Jesus and the words about him makes Mary a new person also.

Mary's obedience to God's calling has led her on an extraordinary adventure, which is far from over. There will be many more words about Jesus for her to treasure and ponder in the years ahead. Vocation is never a one-off event, but a lifelong journey of challenge and discovery. As we celebrate Christ's birth let's remember there is always more of Jesus to ponder and treasure.

Reflection by **Catherine Williams**

[1] *Set II readings:*
Isaiah 62.6-end
Psalm 97
Titus 3.4-7
[2] Luke 2.[1-7]8-20

Isaiah 62.6-end

'See, your salvation comes' (v.11)

For Christmas Day, we are given a prophetic word of praise for those who look out and shout out for the victory of God, and a word of hope for justice.

The sentinels (watchmen) are posted on the walls of the city by the prophet, or by God, to observe round the clock who is coming and to arouse its inhabitants. 'You who remind the Lord' (v.6) – who are probably royal officials – should also not allow themselves any sleep. Their task is to ensure that God gets 'no rest' either: not until the Lord fulfils his promise that his people will at last profit from their own harvest, in dramatic contrast to the dismal years of foreign devastation and occupation. God's silence – his apparent negligence and inactivity – must be challenged by the insistence of these 'reminders', so that he remembers his promises to his people. The anticipated fulfilment of those assurances is expressed in verse 10, in which the people of God prepare a great highway on which the Lord may come close, the redeemed return from exile, and all the nations tread a pilgrim way to Zion.

This is a vivid prophetic appeal to encourage the people of Israel to hold fast to the promises of God, and to hold those promises before God. For Christians, it addresses our own belief in the supreme fulfilment of God's promises on this holy day.

Reflection by **Jeff Astley**

[1] *There are three sets of readings for use on Christmas Night and Christmas Day. Set III should be used at some service during the celebration.*
[2] *For a reflection on Luke 2.[1-7]8-20, see page 37.*

Year A • Christmas Season

Christmas Day

25 December
Principal Feast

Titus 3.4-7

'... the goodness and loving-kindness of God our Saviour appeared' (v.4)

Exactly twelve months ago there was a sign in the window of the flat below mine. It had a picture in red crayon of a bearded face. In suspiciously adult handwriting were the words: 'Dear Santa. Please stop here. I have been good. I am Evie, aged four.' A similar message might be there today. I'm not sure at what age children these days realize that Mum or Dad is intercepting Santa's mail.

Evie *is* good, of course, and very charming. But my prayer is that one day she will encounter 'the goodness and loving-kindness of God our Saviour' (v.4). On that day she will discover that she's not just the daughter of a splendid mother and father, but heir to an indescribably rich treasure – the hope of eternal life (v.7). It has nothing whatever to do with how good she has been. It's unreservedly the gift of God, whose nature is to be merciful.

If I were to put a message in my window this Christmas Day, I would paraphrase the slave trader who was transformed by encountering God, John Newton: 'I'm not what I ought to be, but I'm not what I once was. And it's by the grace of God that I am what I am.'

So shall I close by wishing you the joyful Christmas you deserve? No! Because of the wonderful mercy of God, I am anticipating that it will be infinitely better than that (v.5).

Reflection by **Peter Graystone**

Christmas Day

25 December
Principal Feast

[1] *Set III readings:*
Isaiah 52.7-10
Psalm 98
Hebrews 1.1-4[5-12]
John 1.1-14

Isaiah 52.7-10

'How beautiful upon the mountains are the feet of the messenger who announces peace' (v.7)

Singing is an appropriate vehicle to mark the unalloyed joy of Christmas Day. Indeed, in this passage from Isaiah, the look-outs are already singing as they see the Lord returning to the holy city, and even the city ruins are breaking into song (vv.8,9). Nor will the exiles leave captivity with their tail between their legs. Isaiah says they won't make a dash for it, but will leave with dignity, the Lord at their head (52.12).

It's wonderful to be the bearer of good news. It's been said that the gospel is something that can be shouted across the street, like 'The baby's arrived!' or 'Simon's out of danger!'. When we hear good news, we too probably want to shout it out. How brilliant, then, to be able to announce the good news of peace to a world so long at war. 'Peace at last!' is an authentic gospel shout.

The only problem then is that we have to justify that great announcement by the way we try to embody that peace and share it with others. However, if we believe that Christ truly has made peace on the cross and reconciled all things to himself (Colossians 1.20), the least we can do is tell people about it and invite them into that reconciled space. That's quite a task, but at least it makes daily discipleship interesting.

Reflection by **John Pritchard**

[1] *There are three sets of readings for use on Christmas Night and Christmas Day. Set III should be used at some service during the celebration.*

Set III readings:
Isaiah 52.7-10
Psalm 98
Hebrews 1.1-4[5-12]
John 1.1-14

Christmas Day

25 December
Principal Feast

Hebrews 1.1-4[5-12]

'... he has spoken to us by a Son' (v.2)

There is no prologue or introduction to Hebrews and no named author. The writer simply edits himself out, allowing his message to burst upon us from the very first verse. It is as sudden and unexpected as the coming of the Son of God to this world, which we celebrate today.

The message is majestic in its simplicity and scope. God spoke through the prophets to our ancestors. This means that God has always been a communicating God. He has spoken through the prophets to our ancestors in faith. But now, in these 'last days', God has spoken to us in a more intimate way, by a Son. This inaugurates a new level of God's engagement with us.

Like most people in the ancient world, those who received this letter believed in invisible powers, both evil and good. Through a skilfully crafted medley of texts, mostly from the psalms, the writer sets out to prove that the authority of the Son is final. He is not a mere angel, but a Son. He not only conveys God's will; he is the imprint of his being.

As we enter into the wonder of Christmas Day, our reading calls us afresh to put God first, to listen to his voice and today, as every day, to seek his reflection in the face of Christ.

Reflection by **Angela Tilby**

Christmas Day

25 December
Principal Feast

John 1.1-14

'And the Word became flesh and lived among us' (v.14)

Many of us will be spending time at home over the Christmas period. Unlike a summer holiday, when we might travel to more exotic places, this is a time when we often stay put. We venture out only towards that which is familiar, perhaps visiting loved ones, family, old friends. Christmas is domestic – that is one of its joys.

Yet amid our domesticity, today's reading challenges us. It presses and agitates our thinking, demanding that we face up to the almost unimaginable identity of the child born in Bethlehem. This is not any old child. Nor is this simply a saviour. He was 'in the beginning' (v.2), 'without him not one thing came into being' (v.3), and – as John the Baptist testifies – 'he was before me' (v.15). There is something irreducibly odd about Christmas. This child is our maker, the Word become flesh.

Yet for all its mind-bending re-imagining of eternity and time, this passage still paints a domestic scene. This is the Son who is 'close to his Father's heart', as John goes on to say in verse 18. This is the Son who is close to his Father's bosom. Despite its metaphysical complexities, we are simply invited into the tender embrace that is the identity of God. Christmas really is domestic: a family in Bethlehem, a Father's Son.

Reflection by **Lincoln Harvey**

Isaiah 63.7-9
Psalm 148*
Hebrews 2.10-end
Matthew 2.13-end

First Sunday of Christmas

Isaiah 63.7-9

'... no messenger or angel but his presence' (v.9)

The prophet celebrates the memory of God's interaction with his people. It is a story of 'mercy' and 'steadfast love', of God as loving parent and bringer of salvation. The key to the story lies in verse 9: God was himself with his people, the prophet recalls, acting for them, travelling alongside them.

The Old Testament tells many stories of angels and messengers sent by God, explaining, helping and proclaiming good news. But they are not enough, Isaiah suggests. If we read on in chapter 63, we find that the people are feeling the lack of God's own presence. 'Look down,' they plead, 'turn back'. They long for a return to the good old days, the time of the ancient stories of battles fought and seas divided, and God at the head in a pillar of fire. Those days are long, long ago, the stuff of legends. The reality for God's people is much more prosaic, but still the longing remains.

In this season we celebrate the fulfilment of that longing, a fulfilment that is both expected and surprising. When God is present this time, it is the same but different. Seas are not divided but walked on. The battles are not against human enemies. Yet there is no less mercy and steadfast love. There is salvation, too, and this time it does not end.

Reflection by **Gillian Cooper**

43

First Sunday of Christmas

Isaiah 63.7-9
Psalm 148*
Hebrews 2.10-end
Matthew 2.13-end

Hebrews 2.10-end

'... the pioneer of their salvation' (v.10)

God's purpose is to bring 'many children to glory' (v.10). We are called to share in the family likeness of Jesus Christ.

The author of Hebrews urges us to contemplate the coronation of Jesus, recognizing that it is the consequence of his willingness to share our humanity to the very end, to death itself. Hebrews is noted for its stress on the humanity of Christ. Christ shares our condition, we are his brothers and sisters. This is why the author describes him as the 'pioneer' of salvation, the one who goes ahead and marks the way so that we can follow. We can trust him as our pace-setter in the race of life. As long as we keep focused on him, we will keep going towards the goal. When we lose heart, we need to recall what he has achieved for us by sharing our flesh and blood. He has made us holy, liberating us from the fear of death and so destroying the hold that death has over us.

At this point, the author introduces another image to help us understand what Christ can mean to us. His mediating role is a priestly role; he offers the sacrifice that sets us free. As a faithful priest, he knows what it is to be tested and tempted. His encouragement to us comes from his own experience.

Reflection by **Angela Tilby**

Isaiah 63.7-9
Psalm 148*
Hebrews 2.10-end
Matthew 2.13-end

First Sunday of Christmas

Matthew 2.13-end

'Get up, take the child and his mother, and go ...' (v.20)

The angel had been busy. He warned Joseph to escape to Egypt, encouraged him to return to Israel and then diverted him to Galilee. It was all essential for preserving the little family that carried the hope of the world. God had chosen to reclaim his world in the most down-to-earth manner imaginable – in the life of a child born without favour. However, the sheer fragility of God's methodology required some extra care.

The trouble was that God's way of winning back his people involved a radical vulnerability that put his very mission at risk, and was displayed in its ultimate form on the cross. The scariest thing of all is that God put his Son at the mercy of human beings, and human beings are terrifying. In Matthew's birth narrative, the corruption and distortion at the heart of humanity is expressed most fully in the person of Herod. Herod's brutality was breath-taking; he even had his own sons killed when he saw them as rivals. What did it matter, then, if he killed scores of children in and around Bethlehem? This was just routine barbarity for Herod, and for many others since.

God's chosen approach to saving the world from itself is a constant challenge to us. To take the way of vulnerability; to work from the underside; to refuse power and opt for persuasion; to invite and attract rather than to insist and coerce – these are risky strategies. But they mark out for us a path that has to be utterly characteristic of Christians or we subvert the faith we proclaim. As Jesus later makes plain, we are not called to be served but to serve, and if necessary to give our lives. Are we comfortable with vulnerability and apparent powerlessness?

Reflection by **John Pritchard**

Second Sunday of Christmas

Jeremiah 31.7-14
Psalm 147.13-21
Ephesians 1.3-14
¹John 1.[1-9]10-18

Jeremiah 31.7-14

'... they shall be radiant over the goodness of the Lord' (v.12)

This was originally a message of hope for those in exile in Babylon, and for all who had been driven far from their homes. God promises that those who remain of Israel will return to their homeland, will be gathered from the farthest parts of the earth, will be ransomed and redeemed from their enemies, and will see and rejoice in the goodness of God.

Many exiles did return when the Babylonian empire was defeated, but the Israelites did not truly turn to God, and their long history of repeated failure and repentance was doomed to continue. In this Christmas season, as we move towards the Epiphany, we think of how, through Jesus, this ancient prophecy was opened up to the whole world and reinterpreted in an inward and spiritual sense.

All humanity is in exile in a far country, far from their true home in God. From the four corners of the earth, God will gather people to himself. They will be ransomed with a price, the price of Jesus' life, the life of God in human form, from all the powers that enslave humanity – from hatred, greed and pride. They will be radiant in the knowledge that God is present among them. They will rejoice because they have entered the heavenly Jerusalem, the city of peace and fulfilment in God. And we too shall be there.

Reflection by **Keith Ward**

¹ *For a reflection on John 1.[1-9]10-18, see page 42.*

Jeremiah 31.7-14
Psalm 147.13-21
Ephesians 1.3-14
John 1.[1-9]10-18

Ephesians 1.3-14

*'… who has blessed us in Christ
with every spiritual blessing' (v.3)*

'God rules creation by blessing' claimed the rabbis of Jesus' day. Blessing is that comprehensive praise and thanks that returns all reality to God, and so lets us all be taken up into the spiral of mutual appreciation and delight that is the fulfilment of creation. Truly, it is more blessed to give than to receive.

There is an irony in this, however: as we bless, we are in turn blessed. Paul knows this, and that is why his hymn of praise to the blessings of God in Christ emphasizes the lavish bestowal of God's love. As we are loved, so should we love.

Self-giving is part of God's economy of grace. For God to give anything to anyone, God requires not only a donor, but a tool, a channel, and an agent. True, to become part of it requires sacrifice, but it is much less about abstinence than many may suppose, and much more about the generative power of offering. Giving and offering are part of God's provision of blessing. It is people and things being raised to their true and proper status before God: creation returned to the creator.

I am just about old enough to remember the UK's switch to decimal currency in the early 1970s. I recall the BBC TV programme at the time, *Nationwide*, encouraging us all to get the new money circulating. They had a jingle for the TV programme: 'Give more, you get change'. We are asked to provide what we can – and God will bless that – and do more. Give more, and you'll get change.

Reflection by **Martyn Percy**

The Epiphany

6 January

Principal Feast

Isaiah 60.1-6
Psalm 72.[1-9]10-15
Ephesians 3.1-12
Matthew 2.1-12

Isaiah 60.1-6

'... the Lord will rise upon you,
and his glory will appear over you' (v.2)

These lovely, lyrical verses of Isaiah are full of anticipation, and they fit the Epiphany season well. Whereas in earlier chapters of Isaiah (for example 2.2) the expectation is that the nations will come to Zion to learn about God, now there is no city for them to come to. Instead, all the generations who have been born and bred in exile are now invited to God's new home. So we see the peoples kneeling at the manger, where a baby is building a home for the whole world.

What a depth of longing comes through Isaiah's words. Zion, the once-proud city, has been reduced to rubble, and the rebuilding is slow and hard. In the midst of this 'thick darkness' (v. 2), of depression and hopelessness, the glory of the Lord blazes out. At Epiphany, God shows the world that he has come to make a home for himself among us, a home that cannot be destroyed or conquered. Isaiah's vision is to be fulfilled as all the nations are invited to come home. To see the dawning of God's glory, God invites the poor in the shape of shepherds, the strangers, the wise men, and old Simeon and Anna: these unlikely messengers recognize the gentle glory of God.

Isaiah longed for a time when God would again take up residence with his people and, in Jesus, that is exactly what he does.

Reflection by **Jane Williams**

Isaiah 60.1-6
Psalm 72.[1-9]10-15
Ephesians 3.1-12
Matthew 2.1-12

The Epiphany

6 January
Principal Feast

Ephesians 3.1-12

*'... fellow heirs, members of the same body,
and sharers in the promise' (v.6)*

Looking back on his diocese's strategy for growth, a bishop described a mistake that had been made in its planning. Social engagement, he had thought, would be possible once the Church had grown sufficiently. He came to realize that this was the wrong way round: the Church would grow when it discovered its vocation to serve and transform society.

The author of Ephesians, writing to a Church that is growing from being a local gathering into a far-reaching network, has a very high view of what the Church can do. But being churchy is not part of his strategy. Instead, the Church is to speak the truth to the rulers and authorities of the heavenly places – to what the American biblical scholar, Walter Wink, has called 'all the tangible manifestations which power takes'.

Jesus Christ brought about a new order, which included breaking down walls and barriers between Jews and gentiles. Understanding this revelation led the early Church to grow into a community of belonging, which could reveal through its own example the mystery of God's inclusive love, present from the beginning of time, but revealed anew in Christ.

The Church will not grow now if we invite people to join us so that they may become more like us. The Church will surely grow if, like the imprisoned St Paul, we live in a way that breaks down barriers, models unity, and stands up to the powers that would take us away from God.

Reflection by **Joanne Grenfell**

49

The Epiphany

6 January
Principal Feast

Matthew 2.1-12

'... opening their treasure-chests, they offered him gifts' (v.11)

One of my favourite Christmas cards showed the third wise man sitting in an outdoor cafe with a cool drink before him, clearly not about to head off to follow a star. He's speaking to the other wise men mounted on their camels. 'I don't think I'll come,' he says. 'I'm more of an Old Testament man myself.'

What Matthew shows us is that the wise men are part of the hinge that holds Old and New Testaments together. They come from the east, the land of origins, and they bring the wisdom of the ancient world with them, laying its treasure before the young prince who's about to take centre stage and announce God's new wisdom, his kingdom. Such an auspicious event needed a cosmic sign, and the star fulfilled that role as they wound their weary way westwards, earthly pilgrims on a heavenly mission.

The wise men were 'overwhelmed with joy' when they finally found Jesus (v.10), and they offered the best they had for the family to use. The point of the gifts is not so much their particular reference to Jesus' kingship, divinity and death, but their value as the highest expressions of reverence they could offer. They had nothing better. And therein is the challenge for us. In terms of time, money and effort, do we offer God our best or what we can afford? Do we bring the first fruits of our life or the leftovers? Today, will we let God into the edges of what we do, or the centre? Wise men still search for a king and bring him the best of their lives.

Reflection by **John Pritchard**

Isaiah 42.1-9
Psalm 29
Acts 10.34-43
Matthew 3.13-17

The Baptism of Christ

First Sunday of Epiphany

Isaiah 42.1-9

'... a bruised reed he will not break' (v.3)

The servant of Lord in the past is Israel, descended from Abraham and Jacob. The servant in the present are the exiles, called to serve God's purposes, to sing the Lord's song still in a strange land.

There is another servant, however, described in yet more personal language in at least four of the songs contained in Isaiah 40–55, and the first is here in these verses. This servant is still to come. He is the agent of God's deliverance and God's salvation not for Israel alone but for the whole earth.

From earliest times, Christians have seen in these servant songs a prophecy of God's Messiah, fulfilled in Jesus Christ. He it is who claimed to be the light of the world, who opened the eyes of the blind, who set free those bound by evil and sickness and death (vv.6-7). He it is who is given not just for Israel but to bring justice in the earth.

He it is who comes, indeed, as a servant, according to each of the gospels, not to be served but to serve. He it is who ministers with gentleness and tenderness to those who are poor and hurting and in need.

In the power we exercise as God's servants today, how will we take care of the bruised reed and nurse the dimly burning wick?

Reflection by **Steven Croft**

The Baptism of Christ

First Sunday of Epiphany

Isaiah 42.1-9
Psalm 29
Acts 10.34-43
Matthew 3.13-17

Acts 10.34-43

'I truly understand that God shows no partiality' (v.34)

Totally absorbed, the assembly of gentiles – relatives and close friends of Cornelius the centurion – listens to Peter's retelling of the good news of Jesus Christ. Speaking with the integrity of one who has been with Jesus from the start, has endured the harrowing day of crucifixion and experienced the truth of the resurrection appearances, Peter's presence brings Jesus closer to the gathered hearts.

Have you ever felt the presence of God at a Christian gathering – that loving, intelligent energy pulsing around and within you? Then you will have an idea of what it was like that day – the air charged with the wonder and power of God, the Holy Spirit warming the group so each person's spirit bubbles over in praise and in speech uncluttered by intellectual sophistication (v.46). Following this unmistakable sign of God's delight, baptism is offered, affirming the sovereign movement of the Spirit, binding the new gentile disciples into the widening fellowship of the name of Jesus.

What a lovely example of the Spirit of God moving 'where it chooses' (cf John 3.8). Those listening to Peter didn't have to complete a lengthy course of preparation before God blesses them; there is a simple sacred coming of the Spirit to those whose hearts are longing for God.

Those of us who are sticklers for correct ecclesiastical protocols can lighten up; in this story no one worries that baptism comes after the gift of the Holy Spirit!

Reflection by **Sue Pickering**

Isaiah 42.1-9
Psalm 29
Acts 10.34-43
Matthew 3.13-17

The Baptism of Christ
First Sunday of Epiphany

Matthew 3.13-17

'And a voice from heaven said, "This is my Son, the Beloved, with whom I am well pleased"' (v.17)

It is generally reckoned that the baptism of Jesus marks a pretty important point. It features in all four Gospels, though John simply refers to the descent of the Spirit. It is important because it marks the start of the public ministry of Jesus, a beginning that will eventually lead to another baptism, that of death on a cross. It also marks the character of his ministry: his self-offering is not for his own sake, but on behalf of others.

So we might imagine that, at this start of the ministry, the Spirit, descending from heaven, would grant him a blueprint for the job ahead. After all, there was a huge task to be accomplished. But no. The word he is given is all about who he is. He is a son. He is greatly and dearly loved. The Father takes great delight in him. In other words, it's all about his identity, who-he-is-in-God. That's what kick-starts the ministry.

All service done in the name of Christ flows from this knowledge of being loved by the Father. It's an overflow of love, which we receive for ourselves and allow to flow from us to others. Over and over again, we have to return to the same place – receiving that word from God: 'You are my son, my daughter. You are dearly and deeply loved. I take great delight in you.'

Reflection by **Sue Hope**

Second Sunday of Epiphany

Isaiah 49.1-7
Psalm 40.1-12
I Corinthians 1.1-9
John 1.29-42

Isaiah 49.1-7

'I will give you as a light' (v.6)

The servant in this passage is first of all described as like a weapon: a weapon of God. The servant is 'like a sharp sword', hidden dangerously in the shadow of God's hand, or again like 'a polished arrow' stored in God's quiver until its moment comes (v.2).

The servant has had this destiny – to be a weapon of God – right from the womb. The womb is another image of a place of secrecy and preparation, like the hand and the quiver. In all three cases, the servant lies dormant, waiting to be released upon an unsuspecting world.

The breathtaking turn the passage then takes is to transmute this weapon – the servant – into something wholly unexpected: light (v.6). Drawn from behind the hand, slid from the quiver, emerging from the womb, God's weapon is not going to draw blood. It is going to shine.

If it still makes sense to talk of his being a weapon at all, then the servant's target is the gloom and desolation in which so many people are imprisoned. When this weapon strikes home, what will its effect be? 'Kings shall see' (v.7); and those in darkness will be made visible. When this weapon strikes home, the 'wound' it gives is the wound of sight. How may we, as God's servants today, be instruments of light in God's hands, and what darknesses may we illuminate with the help of his grace?

Reflection by **Ben Quash**

Isaiah 49.1-7
Psalm 40.1-12
1 Corinthians 1.1-9
John 1.29-42

1 Corinthians 1.1-9

*'... to those who are sanctified in Christ Jesus,
called to be saints' (v.2)*

Church factions are nothing new, and Paul starts this letter by tackling the divisions and misunderstandings that have arisen among Christians in Corinth. He begins with a passionate reminder that all believers, 'in every place', share the calling to be 'saints' or 'the sanctified' – a general term used at this time for all church members (cf. Philippians 4.22; Ephesians 1.1). We can take heart from the fact that those early conflicts did not quench the spread of the gospel, nor have denominational boundaries stopped people living and dying for Christ ever since. God's grace is greater than all our schisms and limitations.

What do we have in common? This is Paul's central question as he first encourages and then chides the Corinthians (vv.10 ff.). The answer is Christ, who cannot be divided, and whose presence in the hearts of each other we ignore at our peril. A key concept here is 'fellowship' or *koinonia* (v.9), a word that has nothing to do with cosy, inward-looking faith, but rather challenges us to share in the very life of God's Son, and to remember that even the Christians whom we find most difficult are fellow disciples, loved by Jesus as we are.

Reflection by **Angela Ashwin**

Second Sunday of Epiphany

Isaiah 49.1-7
Psalm 40.1-12
1 Corinthians 1.1-9
John 1.29-42

John 1.29-42

'I saw the Spirit descending from heaven like a dove' (v.32)

This passage, unlike the accounts in the other Gospels, does not state that Jesus was baptized by John. But it records the Baptist's vision of the Spirit descending and resting on Jesus 'like a dove'. In the story of the Great Flood, Noah sent out a dove three times, and the third time, when it did not return, Noah knew that the earth was cleansed and renewed, ready for a new beginning for human life and a new covenant of all living creatures with God. The dove is a symbol of new life; in Jesus, human life is made anew, as he is filled with the Spirit of wisdom and understanding, and in his person human life is united unbreakably to the divine life.

This is not just an event long ago in history. For Jesus, filled with the Spirit, baptizes with the Spirit. Baptism with water symbolizes the washing away of sin, the death of the old self. Baptism with the spirit, with the wind and fire of God's love, infuses the life of God into the lives of men and women. It is the birth of the new self.

The Spirit that rested on Jesus is passed on through him to all who ask, as we become – like him and because of him – spiritually born of God.

Reflection by **Keith Ward**

Isaiah 9.1-4
Psalm 27.1,4-12*
1 Corinthians 1.10-18
Matthew 4.12-23

Third Sunday of Epiphany

Isaiah 9.1-4

'... on them light has shined' (v.2)

Darkness and light: one of the great themes that runs through the book of Isaiah. Darkness means defeat, war, captivity, ignorance and sin, blindness. Against it is set the light of revelation, of sight, rescue and redemption, and new beginnings.

Isaiah speaks here of before and after. Before there has been anguish and defeat. God has withdrawn and allowed his people to be in darkness. But then everything changes. Something new is happening. God is present and active. Light dispels the darkness. The joy it brings is like a great victory or a fantastic harvest. The people are freed from the threats of servitude and death.

Little wonder that we read this passage in Epiphany, when we celebrate the move from before to after, from BC to AD; when God does something completely new; when the darkness of sin and ignorance begins to be dispelled by the coming of the light of the world; when that light begins to spread beyond the lands mentioned by Isaiah, beyond the borders of God's ancient lands and out into the rest of the world.

Darkness remains, in the world and in our hearts, but the light that dawned when before became after can never be entirely extinguished. Once the yoke has been broken and the tools of war burned, there can be no going back. As Jesus proclaims, 'The kingdom of heaven has come near'.

Reflection by **Gillian Cooper**

Third Sunday of Epiphany

Isaiah 9.1-4
Psalm 27.1,4-12*
1 Corinthians 1.10-18
Matthew 4.12-23

1 Corinthians 1.10-18

'Has Christ been divided?' (v.13)

The establishment of a Christian community in Corinth was one of Paul's greatest achievements. Corinth was a busy, socially mobile city, proud of its entrepreneurs and new wealth. Since his mission there, Paul had received bad news from 'Chloe's people' (v.11) that the Church he had founded was now riven with factions. Those with high social status had become over-dominant. They were displaying an arrogance that was causing mayhem. To Paul, this was intolerable. Disunity, rivalry and quarrels undermine the very nature of the Church, which is not just a local, visible reality; the Corinthians belong to the same organism as those in every place who call on Christ. At the heart of this letter is a plea for unity, based on fellowship in Christ. The behaviour reported to Paul shows that the Corinthians have not yet truly understood the implications of the gospel.

This letter speaks to us because we, like them, live in a highly competitive society, which rewards the ambitious and often plays on our insecurities. It is easy for the Church to manifest similar characteristics – to over-value the opinionated and confident. In our own context we might ask: what are we doing to maintain the fellowship of Jesus Christ and the equal dignity of the weaker and stronger members? What would we have to offer a fractured Christian community?

Reflection by **Angela Tilby**

Isaiah 9.1-4
Psalm 27.1,4-12*
1 Corinthians 1.10-18
Matthew 4.12-23

Third Sunday of Epiphany

Matthew 4.12-23

'Immediately they left their nets and followed him' (v.20)

Galilee is part of the dream landscape of every Christian, and to go there only reinforces the magical hold it has upon us. The outline of the hills, the moods of the lake, the villages hugging the shoreline, are all as Jesus would have seen them. And Capernaum, that little settlement where Jesus lived, spoke, healed, called – it's still there for us to tread, ponder and pray.

Jesus came with the simplest of messages: 'Repent.' Why? Because the kingdom of heaven has come near (v.17). That's the heart of the heart of the gospel. Turn around, see things differently, and watch the kingdom come. Something about the way Jesus brought that message to life was so convincing to the two pairs of brothers in today's reading that they couldn't resist it. Matthew may have used the word 'immediately' (vv.20,22) to give dramatic emphasis to the young men's action in leaving the day job and setting off to see the world with Jesus. I imagine they may actually have talked for a fair while over a meal and a drink, but the result is the same – they went.

What does it take for us to leave our comfortable pew and set out with Jesus on a real adventure? Adventures of faith can be of the spirit as well as the body, but getting us aroused into whole-life, risk-taking discipleship is one of God's greatest challenges. Raising the dead is a walk in the park in comparison. Those four young men were happy on the beach, but Jesus wanted to give them more by asking them more.

What would be a first step for us to move off the beach?

Reflection by **John Pritchard**

59

Fourth Sunday of Epiphany

I Kings 17.8-16
Psalm 36.5-10
I Corinthians 1.18-end
John 2.1-11

1 Kings 17.8-16

'The jar of meal was not emptied' (v.16)

The adventure of Elijah starts dramatically. At the beginning of 1 Kings 17, we find him for the first of many times in deadly conflict with the king of Israel. Ahab is a weak king, inclined to do anything for a quiet life, including worshipping the gods of his Phoenician wife Jezebel. The stage is set for a running battle between the king and God's chosen prophet.

There is a drought. God causes it, Elijah announces it and goes into hiding. He takes refuge with a widow and her son, but they are struggling with the effects of the drought and have no food to spare. So Elijah performs a miracle with supplies of grain and oil.

It is a practical solution, but also theologically significant. It shows us who Elijah is. Only God's chosen one can create food and drink. Only by the power of God can the laws of nature be bent. Elijah is new to the reader of his story. We have learned that he is the voice of opposition to the earthly ruler of his day. Now we have been given a sign that he is much more than a political or religious leader. He is God's own prophet, the bearer of God's commission to proclaim truth and oppose oppression.

Centuries later another chosen one will give a sign, turning water into wine at a wedding. Truth will be proclaimed again, and salvation won.

Reflection by **Gillian Cooper**

I Kings 17.8-16
Psalm 36.5-10
1 Corinthians 1.18-end
John 2.1-11

Fourth Sunday of Epiphany

1 Corinthians 1.18-end

'... we proclaim Christ crucified' (v.23)

The bitterness of the quarrels going on in Corinth drives Paul back to fundamentals. The cross is the antithesis of success, the end of ambition, the enemy of human pride. Those enmeshed in quarrels have not understood the power of God, which subverts the way a so-called vibrant and successful society actually works. No one who promotes their own agendas to the detriment of unity in the Church has really grasped what God has revealed in the cross.

The 'wisdom' that was current in Corinthian society is empty from the point of view of the gospel. Where so much depended on charm, money and social status, God works by subverting all pretension. No one could be impressed by the cross. It is sheer 'folly', representing to 'the wise' nothing but failure and degradation. But the truth is that the cross reveals both the power and wisdom of God. The Corinthians would come closer to recognizing this if they reflected on their own social origins. Few of them came from privileged backgrounds, or wielded power or influence. Yet God chose them for a purpose: to shame those who rely on such things to manipulate others.

Today, as much as in Paul's time, Church communities are all too human. Perhaps we should consider how far we use our Church commitment to advance our own agendas or to give ourselves a status that we would not otherwise possess?

Reflection by **Angela Tilby**

Fourth Sunday of Epiphany

I Kings 17.8-16
Psalm 36.5-10
I Corinthians 1.18-end
John 2.1-11

John 2.1-11

*'Jesus did this, the first of his signs, in Cana of Galilee,
and revealed his glory' (v.11)*

This story has certain similarities with another incident where Jesus banters with a woman who asks for a miracle, and then appears to change his mind. In Mark 7.24-30, a Syro-Phoenician woman interrupts Jesus' time off and begs him to heal her sick daughter. Here, Mary asks him to rescue an embarrassing situation at a wedding.

In both cases, Jesus is initially cautious, because his actions could cause problems. In the Gentile territories, Jesus could be swamped by people needing healing. As a single human being, he can only work among the Jews, and it will be his followers who minister more widely. However, he makes an exception out of compassion for this woman. Again at Cana, if Jesus fulfils Mary's request, this could be misconstrued as the act of a popular wonder-worker, whereas he will steadfastly refuse to perform signs on demand (Luke 11.29, 23.8-9). In addition, the time for his inevitable clash with the establishment (often exacerbated by his miracles) has not yet come (v.4). But he does risk an act of kindness in the end.

To the Evangelist, this miracle at Cana reveals Jesus' divine glory. The old, rule-bound order of the Jewish institution is being replaced by the generous wine of the gospel, and all our mundane lives can be transformed into something joyous, loving and grace-filled.

Reflection by **Angela Ashwin**

Malachi 3.1-5
Psalm 24.[1-6]7-10
Hebrews 2.14-end
Luke 2.22-40

The Presentation of Christ

in the Temple (Candlemas)
2 February *Principal Feast*

Malachi 3.1-5

'... who can endure the day of his coming?' (v.2)

'Be careful what you wish for', warns Malachi. 'You ask, "Where is the God of justice?" Well, he is coming, and you will not like it. He will burn and scour you. He will see through your hypocrisy and shine light on your dark deeds. No one will be able to stand in his presence.'

The Old Testament prophets speak often about 'The Day of the Lord'. It is a day desired with a thrill of expectation and dreaded with a sick fear. When the God of Israel appears among his people, there will be both salvation and judgement, and no one can be sure what their fate will be.

Who could have foreseen that the Day of the Lord, when it came, would be so different? That God would come not as a terrible, awesome, overwhelming presence, but as a baby in his mother's arms. That the arrival of salvation and judgement could be so earth-shattering and yet so secret. That it would be recognized only by two old people in a quiet corner of the temple while everyone else went about their business unawares.

On one thing, however, Malachi and the other prophets were quite right. There is no predicting the Day of the Lord. God still shows himself to us in strange ways and unexpected places, and we are still promised another coming. Who knows what will happen when God stands once again on the earth?

Reflection by **Gillian Cooper**

The Presentation of Christ

in the Temple (Candlemas)

2 February *Principal Feast*

Malachi 3.1-5
Psalm 24.[1-6]7-10
Hebrews 2.14-end
Luke 2.22-40

Hebrews 2.14-end

*'Since, therefore, the children share flesh and blood,
he himself likewise shared the same things' (v.14)*

These verses are full of sharing. Christ came to share sonship, for instance: the Son of God was incarnate in order to share with us what he has and is. He came so that he and we together might 'have one Father', as an earlier verse explains (v.11). Sharing also runs in the other direction. Not only does God share what he is with us, but God also shares in what we are. Since those whom Christ came to redeem 'share' flesh and blood (it is what we have 'in common'), the Son shared this with us. Becoming flesh and blood, God now shares in what human beings share in common.

Theologians never tire of revisiting this dynamic of sharing, from God to us and from us to God. 'He became what we are, so that we might become what he is', wrote Athanasius (296–373 AD), among others. He took the whole of human nature upon himself, wrote Gregory of Nazianzus (c.329–390 AD), since 'what he did not assume [or *share*], he did not heal'. Clement of Alexandria (150–215 AD) even went so far as to say that God created the human race 'for sharing'. However, this emphasis on sharing at the centre of Christian thought is not necessarily a comfortable idea; it also has ethical implications, as Clement recognized. If those who are wealthy should say 'I have more than I need, why not just enjoy it?' then, in Clement's estimation, they are neglecting sharing, and that, as he puts it, is 'not properly human'.

Reflection by **Andrew Davison**

Malachi 3.1-5
Psalm 24.[1-6]7-10
Hebrews 2.14-end
Luke 2.22-40

The Presentation of Christ

in the Temple (Candlemas)
2 February *Principal Feast*

Luke 2.22-40

'… destined for the falling and the rising of many' (v.34)

Like his cousin John, Jesus is taken to the temple aged eight days for the Jewish birth rites. Two elderly saints, Simeon and Anna, make prophetic pronouncements about this child. He is the one awaited by Israel. He is the one who will bring salvation to the Jewish nation and beyond. Both Simeon and Anna have waited all their lives to see God's promises for Israel fulfilled. They can die happy, knowing that the child they have met and held is the future made secure.

Simeon brings warnings too. While this is a child of peace and light, such things are threatening to those who hold power. Jesus will be opposed. He will bring into the light thoughts and actions that many would prefer to remain hidden. God's plans are for the entire world. Universal salvation is revealed. This is potentially destabilizing to both sacred and secular forces. Many will fall, many will rise, and Jesus will do both in his calling to secure salvation for all.

As we have rehearsed again the nativity story during Christmas and Epiphany, so we have looked at how ordinary people are called to step out in faith and obedience to play their part in God's plan of salvation for the world. What is God calling you to do? Who is God calling you to be? Step out in faith, like the characters in Luke, to fall and rise with Christ.

Reflection by **Catherine Williams**

Proper 1

Sunday between 3 & 9 February inclusive *(if earlier than the Second Sunday before Lent)*

Isaiah 58.1-9a[b-12]
Psalm 112.1-9[10]
1 Corinthians 2.1-12[13-end]
Matthew 5.13-20

Isaiah 58.1-9a[b-12]

'... the fast that I choose' (v.6)

What does God want? The people Isaiah addresses think they know. They have been defeated and in exile, served their time, and been restored to their land. They have learned the lesson taught so painfully to previous generations. They are faithful to God and dutiful in their religious observance. Not for them their ancestors' flirtation with the gods of other nations. God has granted them peace and security, and they are duly grateful.

But there could be so much more. God has gone quiet. The glory days of past miracles are a very distant memory. They abase themselves with fasting, but it makes no difference. God seems unwilling to listen. The people are puzzled and not a little cross. What more can they do, they ask themselves.

God's prophet has an answer for them. What God hears most clearly are not the prayers of the religious but the pleas of the oppressed. Before there can be renewal, there must be justice. God responds to his people on the basis of their treatment of the weakest members of society, the slaves, the hungry, the homeless, the poor.

As we approach Lent, the prophet speaks to us. 'Fasting' is not only about self-denial, important though that is; it involves looking outwards as well as inwards, and going to the aid of those whose lack is not of their own choosing.

Reflection by **Gillian Cooper**

Isaiah 58.1-9a[b-12]
Psalm 112.1-9[10]
1 Corinthians 2.1-12[13-end]
Matthew 5.13-20

1 Corinthians 2.1-12[13-end]

'Those who are spiritual discern all things' (v.15)

To make his point about God's subversive folly, Paul calls on his own experience as the apostle to the Corinthians, claiming that, when he first preached to the Corinthians, he resisted the clever rhetorical games that might have given him greater plausibility. Instead, he followed his crucified Lord, not concealing his limitations. What happened as a result was a miracle, a manifestation of God's power to change the human heart. There is a divine wisdom for those who accept God's way of foolishness, but it is secret, revealed only to those who have grasped the subversive significance of the cross.

The 'rulers of this age' (v.6) – those who claim power not only on earth but also over the supernatural world – can never understand this. Their failure of judgement was manifest by their involvement in Christ's crucifixion. So Paul links those 'wise' members of the community who are causing strife with the ignorant powers of the age who conspired to put Jesus to death. Those who think of themselves as most spiritual are, in fact, unspiritual. But there is a true spirituality that comes from God's Spirit and enables those who receive his gifts to discern the way God truly works.

Paul's astonishing claim that 'we have the mind of Christ' (v.16) is a call to reality that is as shocking to us as it would have been to his original recipients.

Reflection by **Angela Tilby**

Proper 1

Isaiah 58.1-9a[b-12]
Psalm 112.1-9[10]
1 Corinthians 2.1-12[13-end]
Matthew 5.13-20

Matthew 5.13-20

'A city built on a hill cannot be hidden' (v.14)

A few years ago we went on holiday to Tuscany. The Tuscan countryside is punctuated with towns and villages clinging in precarious fashion to hilltops and high places, sparkling in the sun and perpetually half asleep. Almost invariably the towns are gathered around a medieval church keeping watch over its flock by night and by day.

In today's reading, Jesus is encouraging his listeners (and us, Matthew's readers) to believe in ourselves. We believe we have some inkling of the light and truth that the world needs. Jesus wants us to be like a hilltop town that can't be missed or ignored, or like a lamp that only fulfils its purpose when it's up on a stand giving its light generously and unmistakeably. What these images ask us is an uncomfortable question about our Christian visibility: how obvious is it that we are Christians? On Monday morning is the only difference between us and our colleagues and friends that we went to church yesterday?

Christians are in some ways the most normal human beings and in some ways the most unusual. Normal, because Jesus was the only truly normal person, and we're just a little bit like him; unusual, because we don't fit our culture's current expectations in our beliefs, values and behaviours.

So we stand out like a city on a hill or a lamp on a lampstand. So be it. But it takes courage. How much easier it would be if we could simply mingle unobtrusively with the crowd. Yet what would be the cost to our integrity if we did that? Much better to stick out like a healthy thumb.

Reflection by **John Pritchard**

Deuteronomy 30.15-end
or Ecclesiasticus 15.15-end
Psalm 119.1-8
1 Corinthians 3.1-9
Matthew 5.21-37

**Sunday between 10 & 16 February
inclusive** *(if earlier than the Second
Sunday before Lent)*

Deuteronomy 30.15-end

'Choose life ...' (v.19)

Two truths shine out here, both essential to our humanity, both strongly contested in our culture. They may be summed up in two words: *choice* and *witness*.

Our sense of ourselves is shadowed by a false image of the universe as a mechanism, a piece of clockwork slowly unwinding, and by a reductive picture of our bodies and brains as the inevitable unwinding of selfish genes. Our hearts know better, though, and we should not be bullied by a combination of unfinished science and inadequate philosophy. Some theologians have even imagined a clock-making God whose designs leave no room for freedom. But this is not the God we encounter in the Bible and certainly not the one who shines from the face of Christ. On the contrary, everywhere in Scripture God bestows on us the dignity of choice, and waits with bated breath to see if we will choose life and turn to its source in him. The Creation, far from choking freedom, is called on by God as a witness to the reality of choice. For real choices have real consequences.

In Deuteronomy, the land itself witnesses against the exploitation of its people. Now we look across a world we have wasted. We see the sea levels rising in witness against us, and once again God urges us: 'Choose life so that you and your descendants may live' (v.19). Perhaps it's not too late to make the right choice.

Reflection by **Malcolm Guite**

Proper 2

Deuteronomy 30.15-end
or Ecclesiasticus 15.15-end
Psalm 119.1-8
I Corinthians 3.1-9
Matthew 5.21-37

1 Corinthians 3.1-9

'... you are God's field, God's building' (v.9)

The Corinthian Church was fair fizzing with life, but in the midst of all that was good about it, there were problems and divisions, with different groups trying to line themselves up behind different leaders. They may have been using differences of preaching style between Paul and Apollos to generate disquiet or dissatisfaction with the leadership. Paul would have none of it. This was immature behaviour for people who should by now have grown into mature Christians (vv.2b-3).

Underlying the jealousy and the quarrelling may have been anxiety. This was a Church that was growing and changing rapidly. Spiritual gifts and ministries were developing. In any group, those who feel insecure often make a lot of noise just in order to make themselves heard. Everyone wants to define their place and their purpose in it. Power struggles and personality clashes abound.

Paul sets about refocusing the Church. He works to pull down the pedestals on which the Church would set him and Apollos. He recasts himself and his fellow-worker as servants, as gardeners, as labourers (vv.5-9). He knows that, for the Church to find its stability, it must turn its gaze from human agents to God. It must know that *God* is the one who is the author of this creative work. God's work in us can, at times, feel deeply unsettling. The field of our life can be churned up for fresh planting. The building that has been our life may need some deconstruction in order to be rebuilt. Maintaining a steady gaze on God in times of change or turmoil is not easy, but it is, nevertheless, the task for each one of us. Perhaps it is our task for today?

Reflection by **Sue Hope**

Deuteronomy 30.15-end
or Ecclesiasticus 15.15-end
Psalm 119.1-8
1 Corinthians 3.1-9
Matthew 5.21-37

Matthew 5.21-37

'But I say to you ...' (v.22)

The former Chief Rabbi, Jonathan Sacks, says that this little phrase 'but I say to you' is the point that marks Jesus out from all his contemporaries and from all Jewish prophets throughout history. Others would seek to interpret and explain the words of scripture; no one else has ever dared say 'but I'm saying something different'.

As always, Jesus goes deeper. It's not just murder that matters; it's being angry. It's not just adultery; it's looking lustfully. It's not just swearing falsely; it's swearing by anything, because your 'yes' and 'no' ought to be enough. Jesus enhances and enriches the received teaching and takes it to a new level. Jesus wasn't establishing a new set of laws; he was inviting a new way of looking. He was saying: look deeper, look to the root of the issue, look with God's eyes. If we begin to see things the right way up for a change, instead of the topsy-turvy way the world teaches us, we will begin to glimpse the new creation Jesus was so passionate about. And once seen, never forgotten. We'll want to live from that new vantage point. As C. S. Lewis said: 'I believe in Christianity as I believe the sun has risen; not only because I see it, but because by it I see everything else.'

The challenge for us is to take the profusion of wise sayings that Jesus offers in the collection we call the Sermon on the Mount and ask ourselves where we feel the arrow hitting the mark. It's hard to read these astonishing nuggets without being convicted of something. Read through today's passage again and ask God to show you where there's some issue to address. That's where the praying starts.

Reflection by **John Pritchard**

Leviticus 19.1-2,9-18
Psalm 119.33-40
I Corinthians 3.10-11,16-end
Matthew 5.38-end

Sunday between 17 & 23 February inclusive *(if earlier than the Second Sunday before Lent)*

Leviticus 19.1-2,9-18

'You shall be holy' (v.2)

Holiness doesn't always have a good press. We think it's beyond our reach. People who claim to be holy risk being shown up as hypocrites. This passage is towards the beginning of a section of Leviticus known as the 'holiness code' (chapters 17–26). Much of this code is what we might call 'preached law'. It's not so much a legal code as one long encouragement to put God's commandments into practice in daily life. Its purpose is to show that our faith should reach into the small details and hidden corners of our lives.

Many of the commandments found here are not new. The first verses of today's reading contain three of the ten in Exodus 20. But two things are distinctive here. The first is the reasons given. God's people are called not just to do what God says but to reflect God's very nature: 'You shall be holy, for I the Lord your God am holy' (v.2). The refrain that runs through this needs expanding a little. '(You should be like this because) I am the Lord (your God)'. Belonging to the Lord creates responsibilities as well as privileges.

The second distinctive element, which I love, are the practical touches that run through the holiness code. These are the bits that call for imaginative interpretation today: not many of us will glean fields or measure cloth today. How are we to fulfil these commandments?

Reflection by **Steven Croft**

Leviticus 19.1-2,9-18
Psalm 119.33-40
1 Corinthians 3.10-11,16-end
Matthew 5.38-end

1 Corinthians 3.10-11,16-end

'... you belong to Christ, and Christ belongs to God' (v.23)

The leaders of the Corinthian Church regarded themselves as mature, but here Paul cuts them down to size. The health of the Church is shown by growth, not so much of numbers, but rather of virtue. Christian life is an organic reality in which all grow together, a holy temple to the Lord. Unless God is at the centre of things, the community is no more than any other human institution.

The Church is, of course, a human institution as well as a divine reality. Growth is uneven; the truly mature and the immature rub along together. Paul is aware that a number of individuals have contributed to the life of the Church in Corinth; some for good and some for ill. All come under God's judgement. Most at fault are those who have no insight into their own motivation; who assume that the strength of their opinions and their readiness to state them marks them out as leaders. The truth is that only those who are foolish enough to learn wisdom from God understand the upside-down logic of the cross. 'All things are yours' (v.21). The true leaders are not those who make others say 'I belong to Paul' but those whose life says 'Paul belongs to you'. Leadership is a sacred trust.

Are we ready to be called to account for the responsibilities we bear within the Christian community?

Reflection by **Angela Tilby**

Leviticus 19.1-2,9-18
Psalm 119.33-40
1 Corinthians 3.10-11,16-end
Matthew 5.38-end

Proper 3

Matthew 5.38-end

'Love your enemies …' (v.44)

Here he goes again! Jesus is way over the top in the outrageous behaviour he asks of us. If someone hits you smack in the face, invite him to have another go. It's not sufficient just to love your neighbour; love your implacable enemy as well. How realistic is that? Yet these two examples of the life of the kingdom have been more influential in marking out the Christian difference than almost any other aspect of Christian living. 'If you love those who love you, what reward do you have?' (v.46). That kind of loving is obvious. But loving those who are out to harm you – that's something else again.

In the days of apartheid, a big white farmer had been indoctrinated with the belief that one of the main problems was a small black bishop called Desmond Tutu. Making his way once through an airport concourse, he saw this troublesome priest coming towards him. With great delight the big white farmer purposely bumped into the little bishop and knocked him to the floor. There on the ground, dazed, Desmond Tutu looked up at the gloating face of the big white farmer and said, 'Bless you, my son'. The farmer went on his way contented, but over the next few days the words and the demeanour of the little bishop got under his skin. He couldn't shake them off. Eventually it led to a complete change of heart, a radical conversion.

Such is the power of the Christian practice of loving one's enemy. It can't come naturally; it must be the product of a life energized by the love of God. In terms of people who have somehow fallen into the category of your 'enemy' (however you define it), who is there who you might be called to love?

Reflection by **John Pritchard**

Genesis 1.1 – 2.3
Psalm 136
or Psalm 136.1-9,23-26
Romans 8.18-25
Matthew 6.25-end

Second Sunday before Lent

Genesis 1.1 – 2.3

'And God saw that it was good' (1.12,18,25)

The Bible opens with a picture of God and nothingness. As something comes to be where once there was nothing, the first thing the universe knows is the voice of God. Although there is no created thing to hear, yet God speaks. Human beings will learn that words, and all that they will come to symbolize about communication and relationship, are dear to God. The God we see at the beginning of the world communicates not just with human creation but with everything that is made. God's voice, God's breath, God's ideas and imagination, activate all existence, not just ours.

God is an exuberant creator. Chapter 1 teems with life and sound. Before verse 20, the only sound is God speaking into the beautiful space he has made out of nothingness. Then God's creatures begin to reply, with squeaks, squawks, splashes and grunts, and God loves it. Every creature is born with God's blessing, knowing itself to be a source of joy to God.

At each point, as creation progresses from one state to another, God could have stopped. We, with bitter hindsight, long to call out to him, 'Quit while you're ahead, God! Just look at the sky, sea and earth, lit by sun and moon, and enjoy the exquisite landscape. Or just play with the birds, sea monsters and animals you've made. Playing with your lovely pets is much safer than making human beings!' But God is bolder than us. God does make people. He makes them like himself, so that the created world will recognize God's image in them. Although sharing God's creativity is an awesome responsibility, it is first of all a joy, the joy we see as God makes all things.

Reflection by **Jane Williams**

Second Sunday before Lent

Genesis 1.1 – 2.3
Psalm 136 *or*
Psalm 136.1-9,23-26
Romans 8.18-25
Matthew 6.25-end

Romans 8.18-25

'... the whole creation has been groaning in labour pains'
(v.22)

Part of the new life that the Spirit breathes through our commitment to Christ is an absolute commitment to hope. New life brings hope, whether that is a birth of a child, or a new birth in one's own life that may mean a change in direction.

We don't often think of Paul as a maternal apostle, and yet there was in the early Church a clear celebration of Paul as 'mother'. The New Testament scholar Beverly Gaventa, in her book *Our Mother Saint Paul*, discusses Paul's use of maternal imagery to describe his apostolic labours. This imagery enables Paul to present his own life as an apostle as one of ongoing care for his communities, with all the joys and pains that brings. Such a presentation also brings a more rounded picture of leadership in the early Church. Here in Romans, the emphasis is on God giving birth, and Paul acting as the midwife, helping his communities to grow in the attributes that this new life gives them.

To live such a life of hope is to live in patience (v.25). It also means living with the unexpected and the unknown of what exactly will happen next. The midwife assists the birth, not knowing how the new life will unfold. The midwife tends to the mother, offering compassion and care in this time of creation's emergence from the darkness of the womb into the light of day.

Reflection by **Helen-Ann Hartley**

Genesis 1.1 – 2.3
Psalm 136
or Psalm 136.1-9,23-26
Romans 8.18-25
Matthew 6.25-end

Matthew 6.25-end

'… do not worry about … what you will wear' (v.25)

One of the sharpest comments made on our Western obsession with fashion was made in a colour supplement to a weekend newspaper I once saw that had adverts for the latest beautiful garments worn by impossibly elegant women, interleaved with a feature article on extreme poverty and hunger in Africa. The contrast was so glaring it was hard even to look.

Jesus had a warning not just for fashionistas but for those of us who devour the food and cookery features of our magazines as well. Imagine those pages alongside pictures of the latest famine. How must God see our priorities and passions? Yet in today's passage we don't see a God who condemns us but one who simply redirects us to a higher security and who is utterly to be trusted. 'The birds of the air … are you not of more value than they?' (v.26)

As ever, Jesus goes deeper and asks the fundamental questions. Where is our treasure? Because that's where our heart is too. It's obvious, of course, but it takes a sharp question that cuts through the justifications and relativism and asks us to identify our gods, the things we ultimately value, to make it plain. Pondering that question with absolute honesty can be a sobering experience. Not because God wants to spoil the party, but simply because we only get things straight in our heads and our spirits when we answer that question: where is your treasure? Is it our comfort, success, health, place in society? Is it buying things? Is it what people think of us? Is it our family – good in itself but not God? Where is our treasure?

Reflection by **John Pritchard**

Sunday next before Lent

Exodus 24.12-end
Psalm 2 *or* Psalm 99
2 Peter 1.16-end
Matthew 17.1-9

Exodus 24.12-end

'Moses was on the mountain for forty days and forty nights'
(v.18)

Mountains are good places to expand your horizons. As Lent comes over our horizon, we look ahead from this mountain, where Moses kept the first Lent. Like any good Lent, his was a journey away from the familiar, an encounter with the unknown, an experience of clouds and thick darkness. But then came light and fire, the gift of clarity, the tablets of the law, the guiding principles: ten commandments he could bring down from the mountain and share with the people.

So far so good for that first Lent, but we look forward to a better Lent, and a glorious Easter beyond it. Christianity has its 'mountain-top' moments, but it's not a 'mountain-top' religion. In the old covenant, Moses ascends and deals with God on behalf of everyone else: holiness is distant, unapproachable, mediated through hierarchies, rituals, institutions. Not so the new! Christ, the new Moses, does not leave us to find God, but comes down to us and brings God with him. His 40 days and 40 nights are not on a holy mountain but in the wilderness where we are, feeling with us and for us all 'the thousand natural shocks that flesh is heir to' (to quote Hamlet).

He does not bring down a law whose breaking excludes us, but a gospel of grace that seeks, finds and includes the very people who have not kept the law. What we glimpse from the mountain is grace in the valley.

Reflection by **Malcolm Guite**

Exodus 24.12-end
Psalm 2 *or* Psalm 99
2 Peter 1.16-end
Matthew 17.1-9

Sunday next before Lent

2 Peter 1.16-end

'… eyewitnesses of his majesty' (v.16)

Peter reminds us of two of the great strands of truth that established the Christian faith in the first century and which see it re-established in every generation. We need to be as mindful of them today and pass them on to others.

The first is the witness of real events of history in the life of Jesus of Nazareth. The stories in the Gospels, the events we retell year by year, actually took place in a specific place and time. Real witnesses wrote down what they saw and what they heard and bore testimony to the truth. In these verses Peter describes again the transfiguration, the vision of Christ's glory given on the mountain (see Mark 9.2-8).

The second is witness of prophecy, of Scripture, fulfilled in Christ. Jesus' coming is foretold. This fulfilment of prophecy in the details of Jesus' life, death and resurrection confirms him as the Messiah and confirms the truth of our faith. The prophecy of Scripture fulfilled also gives us the interpretation and meaning of his ministry and his saving death.

God has spoken to us and speaks to us by the prophets and also by a Son (Hebrews 1.1-2). In this present darkness, and especially in our own times of darkness and difficulty, these are truths to anchor us, a lamp to guide us, burning bright until the dawn.

Reflection by **Steven Croft**

Sunday next before Lent

Exodus 24.12-end
Psalm 2 *or* Psalm 99
2 Peter 1.16-end
Matthew 17.1-9

Matthew 17.1-9

'Jesus ... led them up a high mountain' (v.1)

It had to be on a mountain, of course. Mountains are where special encounters took place between God and his chosen messengers. Moses had received the law on Mount Sinai; Jesus was fulfilling Moses' task with the new covenant, so it had to be on a mountain. There's another parallel, too – that between this mountain and the dark hill outside Jerusalem. One was a hill of glory, the other a hill of shame. On one, Jesus is flanked by Moses and Elijah; on the other, he's flanked by two thieves. On one, there's a bright cloud; on the other, darkness. On one, Peter is thrilled; on the other, he's vanished.

On the Mount of Transfiguration, Peter is bowled over by the experience and simply doesn't know how to handle it. He suggests lamely that he might build three shelters for Jesus, Moses and Elijah. (Well, what would you do?) It's a vain attempt to do justice to an experience so overwhelming that all normal categories are blown away. We do the same today, building churches and shrines on sites where earth and heaven have overlapped in special ways. We try in vain to capture profound spiritual experience. You can't brick God in. You can't capture the dawn and bottle it. We have to let the Spirit fly. We have to let God be God.

Is there any way in which we might be trying, without realizing it, to hold God back?

Reflection by **John Pritchard**

Joel 2.1-2,12-17 *or* ¹Isaiah 58.1-12
Psalm 51.1-18
2 Corinthians 5.20*b* – 6.10
Matthew 6.1-6,16-21 *or* John 8.1-11

Ash Wednesday

Principal Holy Day

Joel 2.1-2,12-17

'Who knows whether he will not turn and relent ...?' (v.14)

Dark days require desperate measures. Retreat is cut off, resistance is impossible. What is there to do but pray?

We do not know what calamity was facing God's people. Perhaps an invading army, perhaps the plague of locusts described earlier in the book. What is clear is that something catastrophic is coming, and behind it is Yahweh, the all-powerful God of Israel and ruler of the whole world. Only end-of-the-world language is adequate for Joel. He is looking at 'the day of the Lord' (v.1), a time when God appears in all his power and dreadfulness.

But there is another side to God. Joel reminds the people that God is also gracious. If the people turn to God, there is a chance that God may also turn to them. Destruction may not be the end. There is always another possibility; there can be restoration and healing.

Today is about sin and death. We look at ourselves and know how imperfect we are. We remember that we shall return to the dust from which we came. We are of the earth, and unworthy of anything more, but God 'is gracious and merciful, slow to anger, and abounding in steadfast love' (v.13). When we turn to God, and God turns to us, possibilities open up that take us beyond our sin and mortality and into the realms of God's promise of healing and new life.

Reflection by **Gillian Cooper**

¹*For a reflection on* Isaiah 58.1-12, see page 66.

Joel 2.1-2,12-17 *or* Isaiah 58.1-12
Psalm 51.1-18
2 Corinthians 5.20*b* – 6.10
Matthew 6.1-6,16-21 *or* John 8.1-11

2 Corinthians 5.20*b* – 6.10

'... having nothing, and yet possessing everything' (6.10)

During a long train journey with a friend who is a Muslim, the conversation turned to Ramadan, the month during which Muslims fast between sunrise and sunset. She patiently answered my questions, and the comment that struck me was: 'It is those who have least who value Ramadan most, because during the fast, rich people realize what it feels like to be poor.'

I am reminded of this by Paul's counter-cultural advertisement for the lifestyle that most effectively witnesses to the richness of the gospel of Jesus. It needs to include perseverance during all kinds of difficulty (6.4,5), integrity in character and conversation (6.6-8), and contentment even during times of pain and deprivation (6.9,10). Ambassadors to Jesus most effectively demonstrate the worth of being reconciled to God not by being fine and full, but by their faith when they are bruised and empty.

On this first day of Lent I need to make a confession. I have never once in my life had a day at the end of which I was hungry. Not one. Even now, as I type the words of this reflection, there is a cup of tea and a banana to the right of me on my desk. Over one billion people in the world are hoping to survive this day in absolute poverty, but I have no experience of any kind by which I can measure what that feels like. I intend this Lent to be different.

Reflection by **Peter Graystone**

Joel 2.1-2,12-17 *or* Isaiah 58.1-12
Psalm 51.1-18
2 Corinthians 5.20*b* – 6.10
Matthew 6.1-6,16-21 *or* John 8.1-11

Ash Wednesday

Principal Holy Day

Matthew 6.1-6,16-21

'Beware of practising your piety before others' (v.1)

Jesus didn't like showy religion. He came down hard on those who made sure their piety was seen. Among his followers there were to be no trumpets blown when alms were given, no standing at the street corner when praying, no looking dismal when fasting. This was *hypocrisy* – literally, the wearing of a mask. Praying, fasting, giving to charity were all personal transactions between the believer and God.

What was at stake, and what continues to be at stake for us as we enter Lent, is the extraordinary ability we have to turn even innately good actions into opportunities for self-aggrandisment. We might look on our culture's obsession with celebrity with a superior smile, but the roots of our self-absorption go deep. We long to be noticed, respected, appreciated, admired. We need our name on the door. The essence of sin is addiction to self, and whether this is expressed outrageously or with subtlety, it's a universal ailment. It's heart disease, not skin blemish. You see it in the many expressions of 'self' – selfish, self-centred, self-satisfied, self-opinionated, self-important, self-righteous, self-willed, etc. Christians follow a man who laid that self down, who 'emptied himself... humbled himself ... became obedient to the point of death' (Philippians 2.7,8).

Lent gives us the opportunity to examine how far we remain addicted to self and whether we've discovered that this addiction is like drinking salt water; it's never satisfied. The only cure I know is to commit to the One whose service is perfect freedom.

Reflection by **John Pritchard**

Ash Wednesday

Joel 2.1-2,12-17 *or* Isaiah 58.1-12
Psalm 51.1-18
2 Corinthians 5.20*b* – 6.10
Matthew 6.1-6,16-21 *or* **John 8.1-11**

John 8.1-11

*'Let anyone among you who is without sin be the first
to throw a stone at her' (v.7)*

'Teacher, this woman was caught in the very act of committing adultery' (v.4). There is a grim simplicity to the charge. She is hauled before Jesus with the smoking gun of her guilt written across her face, and plainly seen by those who have caught her, and the Law of Moses plainer still: she must be stoned.

Of course, the scribes and the Pharisees aren't really interested in catching this poor woman. It is Jesus they are after. This question, 'Now what do you say?' (v.5), is just the means to catch him out. But like a bird escaping from the snare of the fowler, Jesus turns it back to them: 'Let anyone among you who is without sin be the first to throw a stone at her' (v.7). One by one they drop their stones to the ground and walk away.

Jesus demonstrates here an astonishing moral authority. He does not condone her sin. Far from it; he tells her to go away and sin no more. However, he will not join in the blood lust of their swift judgement, gleefully pointing out the splinter in another's eye and wilfully ignoring the plank in their own. To stand up to the crowd, to bear witness to a harder and more exacting ethic, is a beautiful sign of the new humanity that is born in Christ. As Lent begins, let us put down our stones and take up the cross instead, following Jesus on the path of forgiving love.

Reflection by **Stephen Cottrell**

Genesis 2.15-17; 3.1-7
Psalm 32
Romans 5.12-19
Matthew 4.1-11

First Sunday of Lent

Genesis 2.15-17; 3.1-7

'... but of the tree of the knowledge of good and evil you shall not eat' (2.17)

It is terribly hard to read the first verses in Chapter 3 without preconceptions. So much theology depends on this one chapter, and it has been reworked so many times, in sermons, in literature, in the whole Christian psyche.

We all know, for example, that the serpent is 'evil', don't we, and then wonder how evil can exist before the first sin has been committed? But actually, the story only says that the serpent is 'subtle' (in the King James Version) or 'crafty' (NRSV). The ingenious word-game it plays with the woman could have been mere mischievous showing-off, if the woman had responded differently. She and the man are supposed to share God's care for the other creatures, so when she follows the serpent's advice instead of her own knowledge of God, she is disturbing the proper order of things. The result is that the relations between God, humans and the rest of creation will now be out of joint. The intimacy between God and people will be lost, as will the easy relationship of trust and nurture between people and the non-human creation.

The voice of God, which drew creation out of nothing, is now calling, through eternity, to the people he has made, calling them back to the intimacy they have lost.

Reflection by **Jane Williams**

Genesis 2.15-17; 3.1-7
Psalm 32
Romans 5.12-19
Matthew 4.1-11

Romans 5.12-19

'... one man's trespass ... one man's act of righteousness'
(v.18)

This dense passage has formed part of the argument for the theology of 'original sin'. It seems to say that death and sin found their entrance into the world through the sin of Adam, and that all human beings, ever since, have been enmeshed in the fatal results of Adam's wrong choice, so that our human ability freely to choose between good and evil is now compromised.

There are good and bad theological arguments on this subject, but 'original sin' does seem to have some psychological and social truth to it. People often find themselves almost constrained to do and be less than they wish; and we are all born into webs of damaged and damaging relationships that at least partially dictate our choices.

However, this is not the argument that Paul is presenting here in Romans. He does seem to say, in verse 12, that Adam opens up the possibility of sin to all of us, and we greedily and stupidly use our choices, just as Adam did. Much more importantly, Paul is saying that God in Christ is at work to give us back our freedom. Our human choices lay burdens on all of us, but God's choice sets us free to live with God and each other, and to give and receive relationships as gifts.

Reflection by **Jane Williams**

Genesis 2.15-17; 3.1-7
Psalm 32
Romans 5.12-19
Matthew 4.1-11

Matthew 4.1-11

'Jesus was led ... into the wilderness to be tempted' (v.1)

Most of us have an ambivalent relationship with temptation. If truth be known, we don't want to discourage it completely. We're rather attached to the regular skirmishes with familiar temptations and would be somewhat lost if the battle was entirely won. On the other hand, we're not entirely easy about this compromise, and experience shows that if we focus on the battle, we will very likely lose nine times out of ten. There must be a better way.

What Jesus faced in the wilderness were the temptations that would constantly snap at his heels throughout his ministry – the temptation to focus on earthly needs rather than their heavenly roots, to be spectacular rather than consistent, to take short cuts rather than to put God first in everything. The fact that he was having to deal with these temptations throughout his life is vividly illustrated by the fierce battle he still had with them in Gethsemane.

What Jesus did with these unwelcome visitors is helpful to us too. Rather than get into battle with them, he 'looked over their shoulder' to Scripture with its positive guidance and reassurance. If we battle with our temptations toe to toe, we'll be exhausted, ill-equipped for more positive discipleship, and we'll probably lose anyway. In dealing with a familiar temptation, General Gordon of Khartoum wrote in his diary that he 'hacked Agag to pieces this morning before the Lord'. Most of us are not so determined or successful. But if, like Jesus, we look beyond the presenting issue to a more attractive alternative, we leave the temptation behind in the dust.

Reflection by **John Pritchard**

Second Sunday of Lent

Genesis 12.1-4a
Psalm 121
Romans 4.1-5,13-17
John 3.1-17

Genesis 12.1-4a

'Now the Lord said to Abram ...' (v.1)

It has been a long time since we last heard God speaking to anyone. He spoke to himself early in Chapter 11 when looking at the tower built by the people of Babel, but the last human being he spoke to was Noah in Chapter 9. Considering how much of Genesis 10 and 11 is genealogies, telling us the generations between Noah and Abram, that is a very long time. It was a long time, too, between Cain and Abel and Noah. The daily conversations of the Garden of Eden are long gone. All the same, the God who now speaks to Abram is not a stranger, even if direct speech with him has been in short supply. Abram knows who he is and how to build altars to him.

Just as with Noah, God breaks his silence now to give Abram a strange command with huge consequences attached: 'Go from your country and your kindred and your father's house to the land that I will show you' (v.1). Noah's obedience saved creation, and Abram's is the start of that creation's new relationship with God. So Abram sets off, in search of a land, with no idea how God will deliver, considering that the land already has inhabitants, but setting up altars everywhere he goes, as symbols of his trust.

Spare a thought for the families, dragged along willy-nilly behind their patriarch. Wives and children don't get to hear God's command, but they, too, have to be obedient.

Reflection by **Jane Williams**

Genesis 12.1-4*a*
Psalm 121
Romans 4.1-5,13-17
John 3.1-17

Romans 4.1-5,13-17

*'Abraham believed God, and it was reckoned to him
as righteousness' (v.3)*

For Paul's readers, Abraham was a hero: the man to whom
God revealed himself, the man who left idolatry behind and
followed the true God. Abraham was the archetypal righteous
person. Yet, as Paul points out, Abraham is commended in
Genesis not for his deeds but rather for his faith: 'And he
believed the Lord; and the Lord reckoned it to him as
righteousness' (Genesis 15.6).

For Paul, this demonstrates that righteousness does not come
from the law. Moses received the law; Abraham came before
Moses and therefore before the law. Abraham was righteous
before there was a law to be righteous by, because Abraham
was righteous by faith (v.13).

What part does faith play in this? It would be a mistake to see
faith as some human effort. That would make faith our
'work', fusing faith and works together. It is equally mistaken
to prise faith and actions apart. By faith we accept the gift
God offers, and believing involves all of us – both our minds
and our bodies, our actions as well as our thoughts.

Abraham is commended for his faith, but, as we know from
Genesis, this faith was a practical matter. Abraham bound his
son Isaac and was willing to raise the knife. Before that, he
had packed up and left the city of Ur.

Faith always involves action.

Reflection by **Andrew Davison**

Genesis 12.1-4*a*
Psalm 121
Romans 4.1-5,13-17
John 3.1-17

John 3.1-17

'The wind blows where it chooses ...
So it is with everyone who is born of the Spirit' (v.8)

Today's account of Jesus' meeting with Nicodemus is a dense and complex text, rich in paradox, irony and word play. Both this and the other incidents from John's Gospel we will be reading about over the next few Sundays share this intricate richness, and all would gain from a deeper study and exploration than is possible here.

Nicodemus is a Jewish religious leader who honestly senses that there is more to Jesus than his colleagues have allowed. He desperately wants to understand more, but is hampered by tradition and literalistic ways of thinking. His night-time visit suggests some anxiety about how his colleagues might react to his seeking Jesus out. There is an almost playful quality about the way Jesus leads him on, using familiar images but presenting them in unfamiliar and slightly startling ways, teasing Nicodemus into expanding and deepening his understanding: 'Are you a teacher of Israel, and yet you do not understand these things?' (v.10).

And so we alight on one thread: Jesus' comments on the nature of the Holy Spirit: 'The wind blows where it chooses...' The Greek word *pneuma* means both 'wind' and 'spirit', and a similar conjunction of images is found in Genesis 1.2. In a way, we are all Nicodemus, pulled conflicting ways: on the one hand, towards the supposed security of what is known and familiar, and on the other, towards the exhilarating, life-enhancing 'risk' of following the unpredictable dance of the Spirit.

Reflection by **Barbara Mosse**

Exodus 17.1-7
Psalm 95
Romans 5.1-11
John 4.5-42

Third Sunday of Lent

Exodus 17.1-7

*'Why do you quarrel with me?
Why do you test the Lord?' (v.2)*

In the wilderness, God has been testing his people (Exodus 15.25, 16.4). This is a difficult but critical theme in Scripture: Abraham leading Isaac up the mountain, Job's cries from the depths. Those whom he loves, God tests – and somehow they are blessed through it.

In this chapter, a line is crossed. No longer just 'complaining', the people are 'quarrelling', and, in their quarrelling, they are testing God. The two names of the place spell this out: Massah and Meribah, 'Test' and 'Quarrel' (v.7). To start testing God is to fail in God's testing of us: 'Do not put the Lord your God to the test, as you tested him at Massah' (Deuteronomy 6.16) – a verse Jesus quotes when the devil suggests he launch himself from the pinnacle of the temple (Luke 4.9-12). As soon as we inch towards trying to force God's hand, to manipulate and control him, we have ceased to trust; we deny that he is our Maker and we are the people of his pasture (Psalm 95.6-9).

It is easy to lapse into quarrelling – at home, at work, at church – and easy to feel sure that, like the Israelites with Moses, we are only the unfortunate victims of other people's failures. Is it possible that, down this accommodating slope, we too might cross some dangerous lines?

Reflection by **Jeremy Worthen**

Third Sunday of Lent

Exodus 17.1-7
Psalm 95
Romans 5.1-11
John 4.5-42

Romans 5.1-11

'... endurance produces character, and character produces hope' (v.4)

One of the many lessons that people living in the Western world can learn from our brothers and sisters in developing nations is how human character can become grateful and hopeful even with very little in the way of financial and material provision. If we have everything we want, in terms of consumer possessions, then we can often reach a 'brick wall' of hopelessness and lack of vision for the future. This can, in turn, lead to depression, breakdown of community, dishonesty and mistrust.

Of course, this is absolutely not to say that we are content for developing nations to remain in horrendous poverty and without adequate food, clean water or shelter. But what we might consider is how those who are struggling can lead the rest of the world by example through trust in and awareness of the love of God. The author of the letter to the Romans is encouraging early Christians who were persecuted and who found the path of faith difficult, to persevere and not lose hope. It is part of the calling of the follower of Christ to look forward to a life when suffering has passed away and we can fully bask in the glory of the Risen Christ. Until then, we can only glimpse such glory, which comes through endurance and patience in suffering. That is the example that people who struggle to make ends meet can often teach those who have more than they will ever need.

Reflection by **Christopher Woods**

Exodus 17.1-7
Psalm 95
Romans 5.1-11
John 4.5-42

John 4.5-42

'Sir, give me this water, so that I may never be thirsty ...'
(v.15)

With Jesus, things are never predictable. In our very different time and context, over-familiarity with the incident of the Samaritan woman at the well may blind us to its original shock value. Jesus openly challenges and breaks through two boundaries: that between the chosen people (the Jews) and those rejected (the Samaritans), and between male and female. The woman herself is taken aback by Jesus' request, recognizing his breach of both boundaries: 'How is it that you, a Jew, ask a drink of me, a woman of Samaria?' (v.9). In his approach to the woman, Jesus challenges each one of us in our natural human tendency to assess others, on whatever grounds – race, gender, age, religion, sexual orientation – in terms of inclusion or exclusion. He is inviting those who claim to be disciples to join him in breaking through those boundaries, instead of helping to construct them and keep them in place.

Yet the challenge goes deeper than this. Jesus offers living water, and the woman's immediate response is to rejoice at the idea of a permanent quenching of physical thirst and the redundancy of a boring and repetitive chore (vv.13-15). So often we approach God on the basis of our immediate perceived need, and indeed, Christ himself urges us to do this (Matthew 7.7-11). But he also beckons us deeper – beyond our surface desires to that fountain of living water that alone can sustain and nurture us for all eternity.

Reflection by **Barbara Mosse**

Fourth Sunday of Lent

1 Samuel 16.1-13
Psalm 23
Ephesians 5.8-14
John 9.1-41

1 Samuel 16.1-13

'... they look on the outward appearance, but the Lord looks on the heart' (v.7)

Today more than ever we find satisfaction in the appearance of things. We are often deceived by what we see because we have not scratched beyond the surface to discover the true essence within. A good example is Christmas, when many cover the true nature of the occasion – a celebration of God becoming human – with a glitzy layer of consumerism and a shiny secular façade; even the message is sanitized so that it becomes unrecognizable and the Nativity becomes a perfumed, tidy, fairy tale.

Another example is when we divert our attention from being a worshipping, serving Church and we worship and serve buildings and all the rituals and paraphernalia that go with them. The Church is the wall-less instrument that God uses to transform people and serve humanity, and many of us have lost this, distracted by the Church as an organization that swallows everything else.

As it says in this passage, 'For the Lord does not see as mortals see; they look on the outward appearance, but the Lord looks on the heart' (v.7). This is also what Jesus said when he criticized the religious leaders: 'Woe to you, scribes and Pharisees, hypocrites! For you are like whitewashed tombs, which on the outside look beautiful, but inside they are full of the bones of the dead and of all kinds of filth' (Matthew 23.27). God is calling us to look beyond the surface, to the heart of all things.

Reflection by **Nadim Nassar**

I Samuel 16.1-13
Psalm 23
Ephesians 5.8-14
John 9.1-41

Ephesians 5.8-14

'... now in the Lord you are light' (v.8)

The same Jesus who, speaking of himself, said 'I am the light' says to his followers: 'You are the light in your whole existence, provided you remain faithful to your calling. And since you are that light, you can no longer remain hidden, even if you want to.'

These are words written by Dietrich Bonhoeffer, the German Lutheran pastor who opposed Hitler. Bonhoeffer lived in the darkest of times, and it was his visibility as a beacon to Christ, the one true light, which led to his execution by the Nazis in 1945.

Today's passage is packed with the language of light and darkness. 'Once you were darkness, but now in the Lord you are light. Live as children of light', urges verse 8. Believers are enlightened people: as we are in Christ, so his light is within us. Its fruit is wholly positive and its glare is searing: darkness cannot conceal its fruitless, death-dealing works. The more our lives are given over to Christ, the more incandescent we become. We may not always feel like the greatest of luminaries, but can perhaps take heart from Bonhoeffer's words: it is simply by remaining faithful to our calling that the inevitable will happen. Hiding is impossible when, in Christ, we are the light in our whole existence.

Reflection by **Helen Orchard**

Fourth Sunday of Lent

I Samuel 16.1-13
Psalm 23
Ephesians 5.8-14
John 9.1-41

John 9.1-41

'But now that you say, "We see", your sin remains' (v.41)

It is clear throughout this story that it is not just about a past physical healing but about our spiritual condition. The Pharisees reveal a lot about themselves when they ask 'Surely we are not blind?' (v.40). They have full confidence that their outlook on reality is trustworthy and in line with God's view of things. The Gospels teach us that Jesus did not so much answer people's questions as question their answers. He gently, but relentlessly, challenged people's belief in their first impressions – of themselves, others or God. The thing about first impressions is that they are not first. They come out of our past, influenced by our experiences of hurt and fear. *First Impressions* was going to be the title of the novel that Jane Austen eventually called *Pride and Prejudice*. Our initial reaction to people or situations can be distorted by our pride and our prejudices that we are so often unaware of. Consequently, our relationships can suffer.

Because first impressions are self-revealing, they also have the potential to be tools for self-revision. Jesus tells the Pharisees that their sin is that they think they see properly. They are not open to transformation, to that new vision of absolutely everything that the lens of belief in God gives. Many think that sin is usually an innovation of some kind, but here it is conservative, a desire to stay put in stale perceptions that are heavy with self-justification. It is very easy today to be seduced by quick clarity, the easy answer or the immediate defensive response. John shows us that Jesus subverts such poor judgement by his divine judgement – making the man, and all Christians with him – say in thankful amazement, 'he opened my eyes' (v.30).

Reflection by **Mark Oakley**

Ezekiel 37.1-14
Psalm 130
Romans 8.6-11
John 11.1-45

Ezekiel 37.1-14

'… can these bones live?' (v.3)

From the depths of hopelessness and despair, the human heart cries out: can these dry bones live? How many times have we asked similar questions? However, we can't really understand what Ezekiel's vision of restoration is saying to us today without understanding something of his context.

He is writing from exile. He was deported to Babylonia in the terrible exile of 597 BC, and all his prophetic writings flow from this experience of what he sees as God's punishment on Israel's disobedience. This valley of dry bones is a scene of defeat and devastation: a battlefield after the victors have left. Can these bones live? Well, it is impossible. All is lost. But note what happens next: God doesn't just raise up the bones himself, he commands the prophet to speak to them. God acts through his prophet. As Ezekiel faithfully obeys, so the dry bones live.

Yet they are still without life. Again, God acts through his prophet. Ezekiel summons the four winds so that the newly enfleshed bones may breathe. Here we come to the whole point of the story: Israel itself is dead, its hope gone. Ezekiel must prophesy to the nation; they too can rise and live and return to their land, but, like Ezekiel, they must be obedient to God's commands. Then, as the enfleshed bones received the breath of the four winds, they can receive the spirit and breath of God.

Reflection by **Stephen Cottrell**

Fifth Sunday of Lent

Ezekiel 37.1-14
Psalm 130
Romans 8.6-11
John 11.1-45

Romans 8.6-11

'… you are not in the flesh; you are in the Spirit' (v.9)

Spirit and flesh are everywhere in Paul. Wherever they turn up, they are usually ciphers for good and evil. To live according to the flesh is to live selfishly and in rebellion from God; to live according to the Spirit is to live aligned with God and for his sake. That does not make flesh evil in itself – only when pursued as a misguided ultimate goal. Paul has not succumbed to the gnostic heresy attacked elsewhere in the New Testament, with its miserable teaching that the body and physical things are evil. Physical life can be lived God's way, as Christ demonstrated. That makes it 'spiritual' in Paul's terminology. Later in this chapter, Paul urges us to hope for the redemption of our bodies, not their abolition (8.23). For that matter, spiritual things can be 'fleshy' when they stand against God. (In 2 Corinthians 7.1, Paul writes that the spirit as well as the flesh can be 'defiled'.)

Do not set your mind on the things of the flesh, urges Paul, but on the things of the Spirit. This is not an injunction to ignore flesh and blood, but rather to see it 'spiritually', from God's perspective, as the bearer of Spirit. Far from being an injunction to ignore flesh and blood, it urges us to respond practically, following God's lead: through the Spirit, he came to the relief of flesh and blood, as flesh and blood.

Reflection by **Andrew Davison**

Ezekiel 37.1-14
Psalm 130
Romans 8.6-11
John 11.1-45

John 11.1-45

'... those who walk at night stumble, because the light is not in them' (v.10)

The writings of John are an object lesson in the expressive use of darkness. Caravaggio's masterpiece *Raising of Lazarus* echoes this well. Darkness occupies the whole upper half of his canvas. We see Jesus, in the presence of Martha and Mary, calling the dead man back. Caravaggio shows the exact moment of transition from death to life. Lazarus' outflung arms – reminiscent of the cross – suggest death, while new life is indicated by the light from Christ that warms the stone-cold corpse of his friend, and by the palm of Lazarus' right hand, which opens upwards, flower-like, reciprocally to receive Christ's illumination.

In many ways, this is best understood as a *call* scene. What we see is a call by God to an individual to leave darkness behind and enter the light. In the painting, darkness and the light visibly separate out and intensify. How appropriate that Lazarus' story is told in John's Gospel, a Gospel so deeply pervaded by the great conflict of light and dark, the Gospel that starts off by declaring that Christ is Light. John depicts Jesus' incarnation as a sort of provocation, which prompts the children of light and the children of darkness to reveal themselves with their 'No' or 'Yes' to him. We may think of our own responses to Christ in this framework. How can we open our hands to receive his light?

Reflection by **Ben Quash**

Liturgy of the Palms:
Matthew 21.1-11
Psalm 118.1-2,19-end*

Matthew 21.1-11

'Hosanna to the Son of David!' (v.9)

In *The Man Born to be King*, her play cycle about the life of Jesus, Dorothy Sayers locates us on Palm Sunday outside the gates of Jerusalem, where two different processions are simultaneously converging.

One is the official procession of Pontius Pilate coming up with all the trappings of state power, soldiers and chariots, to keep order at the Passover. The other is the procession of the rabbi Jesus coming down the Mount of Olives with a single donkey (rather than horses and chariots) and a ragged bunch of cheering followers (rather than armed and disciplined legionaries).

With the patronizing superiority of a colonial governor taking an interest in the strange customs of the natives, Pilate stops and gives way as Jesus goes through the gate. He can watch with impunity, for this pathetic Messiah on his donkey on the way to his cross is no threat to the entrenched power of Rome.

Yet, 2,000 years later, Pilate is remembered only in relation to Jesus; Rome's imperial day is long over, but all over the world, millions sing their hosannas to the Son of David, who comes in the name of the Lord. In whose procession shall we walk: the dominating emperor's or the reigning Lord's?

Reflection by **Tom Smail**

Liturgy of the Passion:
Isaiah 50.4-9*a*
Psalm 31.9-16*
Philippians 2.5-11
Matthew 26.14 – end of 27
or Matthew 27.11-54

Isaiah 50.4-9*a*

'I did not turn backwards.
I gave my back to those who struck me' (vv.5–6)

The image of innocent suffering is one of the most powerful images we ever encounter. Few who saw the film *Gandhi* will easily forget the rows of Indians stepping forward one at a time with dignity and courage to be beaten up by British forces. The local people were simply living out Gandhi's philosophy of passive resistance.

Here, the servant of the Lord did not hide his face from insult and spitting (v.6), but set his face like flint, knowing that God would help him, and his adversaries would wear out like a garment (v.9). With Christians in many different countries of the world facing violent hostility today, this is a bold message and takes a lot of trusting. (Sadly, in a few parts of the world, Christians are just as much to blame.)

What it comes down to is a very basic spiritual question: whom do you trust? If we feel bound to trust the power of our own hands, the vengeance of our own anger, then we've lost the game already. But if we're prepared for life to beat us up a bit, believing that God really does know best, and that an eye for an eye and a tooth for a tooth leaves the world blind and toothless, then we're on the royal road to freedom.

Herbert McCabe, the English priest–philosopher, was right: 'If you don't love, you're dead; and if you do, they'll kill you.' But God always has the last word, and it's 'resurrection'. How will that last word help you today?

Reflection by **John Pritchard**

Palm Sunday

Liturgy of the Passion:
Isaiah 50.4-9*a*
Psalm 31.9-16*
Philippians 2.5-11
Matthew 26.14 – end of 27
or Matthew 27.11-54

Philippians 2.5-11

'Let the same mind be in you that was in Christ Jesus' (v.5)

On Palm Sunday, on the brink of the passion, the final episode of Christ's long self-emptying (v.7), it is good to be reminded that this Philippian 'hymn' is an appeal to a divided Church for humility, an appeal for a unity that will come only from mutual *kenosis* – that is, from our own ways of self-emptying.

So much has been said, and will be said, about what is unique to Christ in this hymn to the divine humility, about the way Christ reveals the heart of God's self-giving love. But to contemplate *kenosis* in the mind of Christ is not for Paul a theological speculation but an *active* participation. 'We have the mind of Christ' – it is possible for our mutual love to continue that divine momentum away from self and towards the other.

As we stare across the divide between conservative and liberal, tradition and fresh expression, North and South, East and West, can we find enough encouragement in what we share, enough compassion and sympathy, enough consolation from the love we all acknowledge, to stop clinging to an identity that depends on being against some heretical 'other', and become instead parts of the bridge that love wants to build between us?

Reflection by **Malcolm Guite**

Liturgy of the Passion:
Isaiah 50.4-9*a*
Psalm 31.9-16*
Philippians 2.5-11
Matthew 26.14 – end of 27
or Matthew 27.11-54

Matthew 26.14 – end of 27

'... you will betray me' (26.21)

Judas is clearly identified as the betrayer of Jesus. This is, of course, true. All the Gospels identify him as the one who handed him over to those who sought to kill him.

The problem of calling him 'The betrayer', however, is that we run the risk of assuming that he was the only person who betrayed Jesus in the run up to his crucifixion. Reading through this whole sweep of Matthew's narrative, from the moment of Judas' decision to betray Jesus (26.14-16) through to Jesus' burial (27.66), we meet many other 'betrayers' along the way: from the disciples who could not even stay awake for an hour while Jesus wept and prayed (26.40) and who fled at Jesus' arrest (26.56); to Peter, who despite his protestations to the contrary (26.35), denied Jesus three times (26.69-75); and the crowd who, despite praising Jesus as he entered Jerusalem a few days before, then called for his death (27.22).

Person after person, group after group, turned their backs on Jesus or egged on those seeking his death. In the last hours of his life, Jesus was betrayed by far more than just one person. Matthew even attempted to ameliorate Judas' reputation as 'The betrayer' by recounting his remorse in 27.3-5.

Betrayal comes in many shapes and sizes. Now as then the question, which rings uncomfortably in our ears so many years later, is whether we are betraying him too.

Reflection by **Paula Gooder**

103

Liturgy of the Passion:
Isaiah 50.4-9*a*
Psalm 31.9-16*
Philippians 2.5-11
Matthew 26.14 – end of 27
or **Matthew 27.11-54**

Matthew 27.11-54

'... he cannot save himself' (27.42)

We live in a world terrified of failure and disgrace. Modern media of all forms often seem to be filled with reports of prominent people 'falling from grace' in one way or another. The way in which these Icarus-like catastrophes are reported suggests that the fall nullifies everything that came before and everything that will come afterwards. It sometimes feels as though failure is today's unforgivable sin.

It is intriguing to contemplate how Jesus' crucifixion would be reported in modern media. It might well take the form of something like 'former celebrity Rabbi dies alone and in disgrace'. On one level, Matthew's narrative suggests to us that this is the nadir of Jesus' ministry: Jesus has failed; he tried to bring in the kingdom but lost and now hangs dying on a cross.

This might appear to be the story, but Matthew's telling of Jesus' death reminds us that much more is going on. Jesus may appear to have failed, but the reality is quite the opposite: the tearing of the temple veil, the earthquake and breaking open of tombs, the centurion's acknowledgement that Jesus truly was the Son of God – these all remind us that Jesus' apparent failure was in fact a world-changing, life-transforming victory. Jesus' 'failure' changed the world forever. Where God is, there is always life and always hope. Failure is simply the precursor to new life.

Reflection by **Paula Gooder**

¹Exodus 12.1-4[5-10] 11-14
Psalm 116.1,10-17*
1 Corinthians 11.23-26
John 13.1-17,31b-35

1 Corinthians 11.23-26

'Do this in remembrance of me' (v.24)

In the New Testament, we find the words with which Christ instituted the Eucharist four separate times: three times in the Gospels and here in this epistle. When St Paul comes to pass them on, it is in the middle of a rebuke about divisions in the Christian community and a lack of interest in the poor. It is sobering that we should encounter them here.

Paul has a profound reverence for the Lord's Supper. It is a participation – a 'sharing' – in the body and blood of Christ (1 Corinthians 10.16). He has an equally profound reverence for the Church. It too is the body of Christ.

The Corinthians had been sharing communion with enmity against one another in their hearts. For some, it had become an opportunity for indulgence, with contemptuous disregard for the poor and hungry.

Paul calls this a failure to 'discern the body'. It is a failure of discernment twice over: they do not discern in the sacrament the seriousness it deserves as the body of Christ, nor do they discern the presence of Christ in his people, and especially in the needy.

If our emphasis is usually on the bread as Christ's body, this passage directs us also to the Church. If our emphasis is on Jesus in his people, Paul reminds us that the bread and the cup are a unique participation in Christ.

Reflection by **Andrew Davison**

¹*For a reflection on Exodus 12.1-4[5-10] 11-14, see page 214.*

Exodus 12.1-4[5-10] 11-14
Psalm 116.1,10-17*
1 Corinthians 11.23-26
John 13.1-17,31b-35

John 13.1-17,31b-35

'... he loved them to the end' (v.1)

Jesus' act of loving service to his disciples is scored into the Christian memory. It is acted out in the liturgy of Maundy Thursday, and down the centuries it has inspired many to imitate the Lord's example in daring acts of care and compassion. Yet, as so often with John's Gospel, the passage has layers of meaning that unfold as the story progresses.

Jesus is poised between two realities. He is utterly grounded in his identity as having come from the Father, and out of that identity he expresses the depth of his love for 'his own', by washing them, purifying them for the ordeal which lies ahead. Yet even as he does so, he is aware of their vulnerability. He knows that his betrayer is present. He also meets Peter's embarrassed exclamation (v.6) by assuring him that he does not need extra washing – he already belongs to Christ.

Our Christian service is sometimes motivated more by anxiety than by love. Sometimes we forget that the quality of what we offer depends on what our acts of service actually communicate to others. Are we attempting to justify ourselves? Are we striving so hard to express God's love that we forget to rest in it ourselves? Jesus' example should remind us that we can give only what we have received.

Reflection by **Angela Tilby**

Isaiah 52.13 – 53.12
Psalm 22*
Hebrews 10.16-25 *or*
Hebrews 4.14-16; 5.7-9
John 18.1 – end of 19

Isaiah 52.13 – 53.12

'... as one from whom others hide their faces' (53.3)

At the 1975 gathering of the World Council of Churches, a sculpture called 'The Tortured Christ', by Brazilian artist Guido Rocha, himself the victim of torture, was displayed in the lobby where delegates met for their plenary, but it proved to be so horrific and disturbing that they asked for it to be removed. And so it was put down into a basement room, where only those who were looking would find it.* The conference was meant to highlight torture but, ironically, even the image of such suffering was hidden away in just such a dark basement as forms the scene of so much modern torture.

Isaiah knows that some pain is so gross, some visages so marred, that we turn our own faces away. But God does not turn his face away; rather, he enters into our suffering with such compassionate attention that his own face becomes the face of the tortured. It is unbearable to think how those who are marred and maimed in our conflicts were once babes whom some mother loved. We may flinch and draw back, but no suffering is hidden from God, for as Isaiah reminds us, he came in Christ to bear the grief we cannot bear, and carry the sorrows of those from whom we have averted our eyes.

Reflection by **Malcolm Guite**

Story recounted by Maggi Dawn in The Writing on the Wall
(Hodder & Stoughton 2010)

Good Friday

Isaiah 52.13 – 53.12
Psalm 22*
Hebrews 10.16-25
or Hebrews 4.14-16; 5.7-9
John 18.1 – end of 19

Hebrews 10.16-25

*'Let us hold fast to the confession of our hope
without wavering' (v.23)*

The fruit of Good Friday is the forgiveness of sins and the assurance of forgiveness. The writer to the Hebrews urges us to have confidence to follow Jesus into God's presence, sure that we have direct access to God. This boldness is not a feeling or an intellectual certainty. It is 'holding fast' to the hope that we have been given because 'he who has promised is faithful' (v.23).

Great though this confidence is, it is not to make us complacent. Confidence is corporate. We belong to the community of believers, and we should not neglect the habit of coming together in prayer and praise. This is the context in which we are able to build each other up, 'provoking one another to love and good deeds' (v.24). The common life of the Church is where we are formed as Christians and learn Christ-like habits of gentleness and virtue. Going to church is not simply a matter of choice. It is an expression of the confidence we have in Christ, a confidence to be seen and counted as Christians. Hope and faith and love increase when they are shared.

Reflection by **Angela Tilby**

Isaiah 52.13 – 53.12
Psalm 22*
Hebrews 10.16-25
or **Hebrews 4.14-16; 5.7-9**
John 18.1 – end of 19

Hebrews 4.14-16; 5.7-9

'... he learned obedience through what he suffered' (5.8)

Good Friday confronts us with a Saviour who suffers. The cross is the climax of that suffering, but we should never think of Jesus as being immune to the tests and trials of human life. We can bear our crosses because he was faithful in bearing his; his sufferings are part of his offering to God. He deals gently with those who are struggling because he is aware of his own weakness. He has been through the same trials and temptations as we have, and yet, unlike us, he has not fallen short. All this should give us the ultimate confidence to trust him as we approach God with our particular needs.

Yet we misunderstand our great high priest if we assume his obedience was effortless. Even as the Son of God, he needed the discipline of prayer. He was not spared the dilemmas and ambiguities that test us every day. His human life, like ours, was a pilgrimage towards God's perfection. It is because he has persevered to the end that he manifests the eternal priesthood attributed in Hebrews 5.6 to Melchizedek.

The fourth-century theologian Gregory of Nazianzus insisted on the reality of Christ's humanity with the statement, 'That which he has not assumed he has not healed'. Our salvation depends not only on Christ's divine Sonship, but on the authenticity of his human struggle.

Reflection by **Angela Tilby**

Isaiah 52.13 – 53.12
Psalm 22*
Hebrews 10.16-25 *or*
Hebrews 4.14-16; 5.7-9
John 18.1 – end of 19

Good Friday

John 18.1 – end of 19

'What is truth?' (18.38)

One of the striking features of John's trial narratives is the lengthy conversation between Jesus and Pilate. In this account, John makes clear that the Jews were unable to enter Pilate's headquarters lest they render themselves impure in the run-up to Passover (18.28). As a result, Pilate was forced to go backwards and forwards between the Jews and Jesus. This gives this long conversation some structure and shaping. There are three events that take place 'inside': in the first, Pilate talked with Jesus about truth (18.33-38); in the second, Jesus was beaten by the guards (19.1-3); in the third, Pilate talked with Jesus about power (19.9-11).

The account brings out the emphasis that Pilate had a role that he could not fully inhabit. As the source of justice in the land, he should have well known what truth was. Without the ability to see and recognize truth, justice is impossible. As the Roman ruler, he should have been all powerful, but his running to and fro between the Jews and Jesus, and his fear of the crowd, revealed that his power was very shallow indeed.

John's Gospel often reveals what is *really* going on in the world, as opposed to what *appears* to be going on. Here we see, revealed, the true nature of power and truth and where these really lie. Jesus, even at his weakest, lowest moment, remained the source of all power and truth.

Reflection by **Paula Gooder**

Easter Vigil

A minimum of three Old Testament readings should be chosen.
The reading from Exodus 14 should always be used.

[1]Genesis 1.1 – 2.4*a*	Psalm 136.1-9,23-end
Genesis 7.1-5,11-18; 8.6-18; 9.8-13	Psalm 46
[2]Genesis 22.1-18	Psalm 16
Exodus 14.10-end; 15.20,21	*Canticle:* **Exodus 15.1*b*-13,17,18**
Isaiah 55.1-11	*Canticle:* Isaiah 12.2-end
Baruch 3.9-15,32 – 4.4	
or Proverbs 8.1-8,19-21; 9.4*b*-6	Psalm 19
[3]Ezekiel 36.24-28	Psalms 42, 43
[4]Ezekiel 37.1-14	Psalm 143
[5]Zephaniah 3.14-end	Psalm 98

Romans 6.3-11   **Psalm 114**
Matthew 28.1-10

[1]*For a reflection on Genesis 1.1 – 2.3, see page 75.*
[2]*For a reflection on Genesis 22.1-18, see page 174.*
[3]*For a reflection on Ezekiel 36.24-28, see page 146.*
[4]*For a reflection on Ezekiel 37.1-14, see page 97.*
[5]*For a reflection on Zephaniah 3.14-end, see page 126.*

See page 111 for a list of the Easter Vigil readings

Genesis 7.1-5,11-18; 8.6-18; 9.8-13

'... the covenant between me and the earth' (9.13)

All the old covenants foretell and are fulfilled in the new. St Paul shows us how the covenant with Abraham is fulfilled in Christ, and St Matthew does the same for the covenant with Moses. But what of this, the oldest covenant of all, God's covenant not with one people but with the whole earth? Surely this covenant with 'every living creature', 'for all future generations' (9.12) is also fulfilled and renewed in Christ, for in him all things were made, and in him all things hold together.

The ark itself is a sign of his cross. In the wood of the ark all the seeds of life were saved and held aloft, so too Christ, lifted high on the cross, lifts us and his creation with him. No wonder the first Christians understood the Church itself as a kind of ark in which Christ gathered and nurtured the seeds of his new creation.

If that is so, have we in our generation been less generous and just than Noah? Have we left room only for a few correct believers, only for one 'kind', one species, one understanding? If God's covenant is with the whole creation, then we should be expressing his love for that whole creation, seeking with him to cherish and preserve its every type and variety. Our world needs biodiversity, but true spiritual flourishing calls the church to cherish diversity too.

Reflection by **Malcolm Guite**

*See page 111 for a list of
the Easter Vigil readings*

Easter Vigil

Exodus 14.10-end; 15.20,21

'Sing to the Lord, for he has triumphed gloriously' (15.21)

The letter kills, but the Spirit gives life. Nowhere is that more true than in this seminal and life-giving story, whose 'letter' is so crowded with images of death. Read literally, and only literally, that last picture of the Egyptians dead on the seashore and a song to glorify the triumph of one race over another and to gloat over the dead is dark and repellant. But we do not stay with the dead letter; Christ's Easter triumph breathes new life and meaning into every story, especially this one. Exodus tells the story of rescue and redemption, of freedom from tyranny, but a local rescue, a small redemption, brief freedom soon squandered and one fallen tyrant soon replaced by another. The real triumph and the real glory were still to come.

Easter tells the story of rescue from the deepest slavery, the universal slavery to sin. It celebrates the overthrow of the last and greatest tyrant and fear-monger, the tyranny of death itself. Moses stood on dry land and held out his arm from a distance, but Christ, our new Moses, goes down with us into the deep waters of death and raises us to life in triumph – all of us, Egypt as well as Israel. If the Easter gospel is true, then one day those Egyptians dead on the shore will be invited to dance with their sister Miriam in heaven.

Reflection by **Malcolm Guite**

Easter Vigil

*See page I I I for a list of
the Easter Vigil readings*

Exodus 15.1*b*-13,17,18

'I will sing to the Lord, for he has triumphed gloriously' (v.1)

'How can I keep from singing?' It's the refrain of a Quaker hymn, and in this passage joy overflows into song. What an amazing thing God has done in delivering his people! How can Moses and Miriam and everyone else keep from singing?

Yet this song does more than express emotion. It celebrates how God has acted at the Red Sea by making it one act within a whole drama. The overcoming of watery chaos reminds us of how it all began with creation (see Isaiah 51.9-10). For those who have just escaped from Egypt, the other side of the Jordan and the home to be established there can already be glimpsed and affirmed: Israel flourishing in God's abode, his holy place (v.17). Egypt and Pharaoh are not named after the opening verses, as the song finds in this unique event the pattern of God's deliverance of us from danger and death time and time again. It is a pattern illuminated for ever by the encounter of Easter morning.

In other words, what we are reading is liturgical song. It's so precious to be able to use the psalms and canticles of Scripture in our worship today. But how often do we actually sing them – and, as we do so, let joy overflow through us to our God?

Reflection by **Jeremy Worthen**

See page 111 for a list of the Easter Vigil readings

Isaiah 55.1-11

'Ho, everyone who thirsts, come to the waters' (v.1)

I've yet to meet anyone who greets people with the word 'Ho', but I understand the sentiment. It's a call for attention, rather like a town crier's 'Oyez!'. What is on offer here is no less than abundant life, symbolized by water, wine, milk and bread. 'Delight yourselves in rich food' is the invitation (v.2). You may not understand the ways and means of God (v.8), because they are gloriously higher than human expectation, yet they're on offer for the whole community, now.

It's an offer I wish our culture would recognize. I once went on a seven-day expedition across the Sinai and we were warned that we must drink large quantities of water. One of the signs that we were becoming dehydrated would be that we would become grumpy. That got me thinking. We live in a grumpy society where anger easily boils over and litigation is never far away. Could it be because we're spiritually dehydrated? We're short of the living water that Isaiah and later Jesus would offer, and which takes us into the realm of the new creation where 'the trees of the field shall clap their hands ... instead of the brier shall come up the myrtle' (Isaiah 55.12,13). Paradise regained.

One of the challenges for us is to drink so fully of that living water that people recognize something that provokes, interests and attracts them – so much so that they ask what it is that we're drinking. Tomorrow gives us the answer.

Reflection by **John Pritchard**

See page 111 for a list of
the Easter Vigil readings

Isaiah 12.2-6

'Shout aloud and sing for joy' (v.6)

To draw water with joy from the wells of salvation and to give thanks to God, singing praises and shouting aloud of the greatness of the holiness of God, is indeed the highest form of human worship. As the saying goes, 'God listens to me when I pray, but God loves me when I sing.' This is to be the calling and destiny of the people. This will come from a deep appreciation of God's saving grace and liberating comfort. This is to name the worth-ship of God: to celebrate the great value that God is to us and within us, because we have been ransomed, healed, restored and forgiven. As the Jesuit theologian Teilhard de Chardin once said: 'Worship is ... to lose oneself in the unfathomable, to plunge into the inexhaustible, to find peace in the incorruptible ... to give of one's deepest to that whose depth has no end.'

The message of hope in the act of worship described is not for a special clique or a single city. It is a proclamation of God's name in all the earth. Those who sing do so for the whole world, and so we are reminded that worship in a particular congregation is actually centred in God's concern for everyone and every nation. This worth-ship of God finally enriches our own worth as part of the great worth of all that lives and breathes.

Reflection by **David Moxon**

*See page 111 for a list of
the Easter Vigil readings*

Proverbs 8.1-8,19-21; 9.4*b*-6

'... from my lips will come what is right' (8.6)

I'm interested how often, when I'm praying for myself or for someone else, I find I'm praying for wisdom. It seems that instinctively I know that one of the deepest needs all of us have is that Godly common sense and insight that enables us to 'get it right'. But that isn't quite what the writer means by wisdom in today's reading.

Here, wisdom is personified and takes her stand in a public place to teach what she knows. She is confident that her words are true and righteous, with nothing twisted or crooked in them' (vv.7-8), probably in contrast to the words of the prostitute who stood in a similar place in Proverbs 7 and tried to seduce passers by. She has riches and honour to share, and her fruit is better than gold (v.19). She's not exactly backward in coming forward!

That's the confidence that comes from walking close to God, as we learn right at the start of the book (Proverbs 1.7). In a society that is more and more bewildered and lacking fixed points by which to navigate, such confidence looks extremely attractive. We long for society to re-own the ancient wisdom that pre-dated the self-centred consumerist compulsions we seem to live by that have such tragic consequences.

Didn't Jesus say something about specks in someone else's eye and logs in our own?

Reflection by **John Pritchard**

Easter Vigil

*See page 111 for a list of
the Easter Vigil readings*

Romans 6.3-11

'... dead to sin and alive to God in Christ Jesus' (v.11)

If you have ever witnessed an adult baptism by total immersion, you will know that wonderful moment when the nervous-looking candidate is plunged underwater. They hold their breath, and sometimes their nose, and for a moment they are submerged – almost lifeless – until the minister pulls them up out of the water – and they gasp for breath – like a newborn baby. Amid the spluttering and water, eyes open as if for the first time, and joy fills the face of the one who radiates with new life.

Most of us have not lived lives of extremes, as Paul did. Maybe for some of us our faith journey seems to us to be so unspectacular that to talk of being dead and alive seems rather extreme. But Paul invites us into a liberating story where our baptism is not something that happened many years ago, but can be a new experience every day as we wash ourselves in the waters of the new life that Jesus has given us as much a share of as he did to Paul. This prayer from *Common Worship* sums up the liberating joy which Paul longs for us all to bathe in:

*We bless you for your new creation, brought to birth by water
and the Spirit, and for your grace bestowed upon us your
children, washing away our sins.
May your holy and life-giving Spirit move upon these waters.
Restore through them the beauty of your creation, and bring
those who are baptized to new birth in the family of your Church.
Drown sin in the waters of judgement, anoint your children
with power from on high, and make them one with Christ
in the freedom of your kingdom. For all might, majesty,
dominion and power are yours, now and for ever.*

Reflection by **Tim Sledge**

*See page 111 for a list of
the Easter Vigil readings*

Easter Vigil

Matthew 28.1-10
'Do not be afraid ...' (vv.5,10)

Have you noticed how many times in the Bible people are told not to be afraid? It is said so often that it almost becomes a refrain. What is really interesting in this passage is that the guards are absolutely terrified, so much so that they fall down apparently senseless, but they are not the ones who are told not to fear. Instead it is the women. This fact is emphasized in the Greek text (though not our English translations) by the fact the angel says 'Do not you be afraid', the implication of which is that it is fine for the guards to be afraid, but not for the women.

The reason for this is because God, as well as being all-loving, is also all-holy. God is so far beyond our imaginings that when people encounter him – or even just his angels – the appropriate response is fear. In my view, we often read wrongly these encouragements not to be afraid. They are not saying that there is no need to be afraid, but that God invites you to step beyond your fear into a new relationship. If we lose all aspects of awe and wonder, then we are in danger of not treating God as God. God generously and lovingly invites us not to fear, but he is still a great and wonderful God.

On this Easter morning, the appropriate response to this God is fear and wonder, followed by worship and then by service.

Reflection by **Paula Gooder**

Easter Day

[1] Acts 10.34-43 *or* **Jeremiah 31.1-6**
Psalm 118.1-2,14-24*
Colossians 3.1-4 *or* [1] Acts 10.34-43
John 20.1-18 *or* Matthew 28.1-10

Jeremiah 31.1-6

'I have loved you with an everlasting love' (v.3)

The language of everlasting love is something we may more easily associate with pop songs and rom-coms than religion. It evokes scenes of misty-eyed swooning passion and rash declarations in the early stages of a love affair. However, the everlasting love that Yahweh declares for Israel is of a much more gritty nature, though it is no less passionate. It is a love that does not burn down to embers over the course of time, but always blazes brightly. The purging that is punishment from God is simply one way in which the flame of his love radiates.

The real test of everlasting love is shown through a faithfulness that, after such purging, enables the relationship to start anew. It is the pattern of death and resurrection that is hard-wired into Christian life. We see this in the threefold promise of verses 4-5, each couplet of which begins with 'Again'. Urban, social and rural life will be restored and, in verse 6, so will the spiritual centre when sentinels call 'Come, let us go up to Zion' in an allusion to temple worship.

Starting afresh requires letting go of what has gone before in a kind of holy forgetting of what was there before the cleansing fire. It is only in this way that Israel who 'played the whore' (Jeremiah 3.1) can be like a virgin again (v.4). What is it that we need to forget in order for love to begin again?

Reflection by **Helen Orchard**

[1] *For a reflection on Acts 10.34-43, see page 52.*

[1]Acts 10.34-43 *or* Jeremiah 31.1-6
Psalm 118.1-2,14-24*
Colossians 3.1-4 *or* [1]Acts 10.34-43
John 20.1-18 *or* Matthew 28.1-10

Colossians 3.1-4

'... the things that are above' (v.1)

Pay attention to the things that are above, Paul urges the Colossians, twice in this very short passage. Clearly they are finding it hard to get their priorities right. The excitement about the good news of Jesus Christ has evidently worn off rather quickly, as they have become absorbed in bickering about lifestyle regulations within the new faith community, and satisfying their human desires. Paul offers them a very different perspective.

Don't grub around in the dirt, Paul says. Don't spend your time looking sideways, comparing yourselves with others, finding fault. Instead, stand side by side with your Christian brothers and sisters, looking up. What do you see? Look beyond the buildings, beyond the trees, up into the air. Look beyond the moon and the stars, beyond our galaxy, look past it all and into the infinity of space. Look as far as you can and imagine the immeasurable distances beyond, and remember that it is impossible to look beyond God.

That is where we belong, says Paul. We are children of infinity. Our lives are not contained within the world we know, but are out there, 'hidden with Christ in God' (v.3). Because on Easter Day the world changes. Death has been destroyed. The division between earth and heaven has been torn down. Our physical limitations have been rendered irrelevant, and we know ourselves immortal. What could matter more than that?

Reflection by **Gillian Cooper**

[1]*For a reflection on Acts 10.34-43, see page 52.*

Easter Day

Acts 10.34-43 *or* Jeremiah 31.1-6
Psalm 118.1-2,14-24*
Colossians 3.1-4 *or* Acts 10.34-43
John 20.1-18 *or* [1] Matthew 28.1-10

John 20.1-18

'... she turned round and saw Jesus' (v.14)

During World War II, a painting of the risen Christ with Mary Magdalene, *Noli me Tangere*, by the sixteenth-century artist Titian, was London's most treasured picture. For a month in 1942 it was, by public demand, the sole painting on display in the National Gallery when thousands had been removed to Welsh slate mines for safekeeping. It was cherished because, as the bombs fell, Londoners found reassurance in this story that love is so strong that it can survive death.

The resurrection appearances of Jesus have the ring of truth about them because they are so downbeat. Hollywood film directors scripting this turning point in the whole of Western civilization would devise a scene in which superhuman hands toppled the tombstone while the enemies of Jesus staggered back aghast. John's account could not possibly be more different. Resurrection came with the whisper of a name and a message of good news.

Jesus' first appearance after his resurrection was to Mary Magdalene. She was a woman who had lost her way through life and then found calm and purpose when she followed Jesus. She was a forgiven sinner. She was a person who, on that Sunday morning, was demoralized and in distress. And she was someone whose evidence had every likelihood of being dismissed in the male-dominated culture of the day.

You couldn't make it up!

Reflection by **Peter Graystone**

[1] For a reflection on Matthew 28.1-10, see page 119.

¹Exodus 14.10-end;15.20,21
Acts 2.14a,22-32
Psalm 16
1 Peter 1.3-9
John 20.19-end

Second Sunday of Easter

Acts 2.14a,22-32

'This Jesus God raised up, and of that all of us are witnesses'
(v.32)

Standing in the street at just after nine in the morning, surrounded by people from many nations who have gathered in Jerusalem for the feast, Peter preaches the first sermon in Christian history. Although countless millions of sermons have been preached since, has any Christian preacher ever had anything else worth saying? For the scandalous heart of the Christian gospel is not some human philosophy, no matter how edifying or wise, but a blunt and basic proclamation that this Jesus who was crucified has been raised to life.

What is offered? What is said? Nothing other than that this motley band of Palestinian fishermen and assorted odd-bods are witnesses to God's breaking into history. Furthermore, this has been God's plan from the beginning. All the Jewish Scriptures actually point to this decisive event where God makes peace with the world through the shed blood of Christ and creates a new humanity. The gift of the Spirit is the sign that this rescue mission is complete, and that a new age of a new availability to God has commenced.

Nothing will ever be the same again. Let all Israel know – and soon, as we shall see, the entire world – this Jesus whom you crucified; God has made him both Lord and Messiah.

Reflection by **Stephen Cottrell**

¹*For a reflection on Exodus 14.10-end;15.20,21, see page 113.*
If the reading from Exodus is used, the reading from Acts must be used
as the second reading.

Second Sunday of Easter

Exodus 14.10-end;15.20,21
Acts 2.14a,22-32
Psalm 16
I Peter 1.3-9
John 20.19-end

1 Peter 1.3-9

*'By his great mercy he has given us a new birth
into a living hope' (v.3)*

Christians live a double life. We live in this world (in Ipswich or Gateshead or Taunton) and in the new world of God's re-creation where his writ runs fully and joyfully – 'an inheritance that is imperishable, undefiled, and unfading' (v.4). It's not easy having dual citizenship because we have our loyalties in both (possibly competing) places, but the unifying factor is our identity in Christ; we have been chosen and destined by God.

Does that mean some haven't been chosen and destined? No; it means some haven't realized what a privilege and opportunity they have. When I see people reported in the media, falling over themselves to deny such an implausible thing as belief in God, I simply grieve. I don't think it worries God too much whether people believe in him or not. God isn't proud, and he has the last word, after all. But I do think he grieves that people are denying themselves the freedom, depth and abundance for which he created them. Why live in three dimensions when you could have half a dozen?

But Peter's ebullient opening to his letter is actually meant to put his readers' current experience into a bigger context. They're up against it. They're suffering for their faith. So let's get the big picture straight, he says. So too for us; whatever we're up against, may we never forget the joy of Christ risen. Would you please read that last sentence again?

Reflection by **John Pritchard**

Exodus 14.10-end;15.20,21
Acts 2.14a,22-32
Psalm 16
1 Peter 1.3-9
John 20.19-end

John 20.19-end

'Jesus ... stood among them and said "Peace be with you"'
(v.19)

One of the reasons John's account of the resurrection is so persuasive is that it effectively sides with the doubters and leaves the reader with lingering hesitancy. Indeed, it is only when Jesus begins to explain how the past has been fulfilled in the present – and how the present has now fulfilled the past – that we begin to gain a sense of how 'peace be with you' might be more than a mere greeting.

Resurrections challenge our worldviews. The task of the disciples is not to guard an empty tomb; it is to follow the risen Jesus, and to try and understand something of how he appears to us afresh, even at the meal table. Easter is about finding and encountering the risen Jesus in the very present. 'Peace be with you', then, is not just a state of mind; it is the core of being for the Church.

So, a story of stark absence – Good Friday – is now one of intense presence. The reality of Jesus is now bigger than reality itself. Jesus is no longer a figure of the past. Nor does he merely live through the memories of the disciples. When Jesus tells Mary Magdalene 'do not cling to me', or to the disciples 'touch me', he is really saying something quite simple. You cannot hold on to the Jesus you once knew. You cannot have the past back. You cannot possess Jesus any longer. You can touch, but you cannot hold. But be assured, he will hold you.

Reflection by **Martyn Percy**

Zephaniah 3.14-end
Acts 2.14*a*,36-41
Psalm 116.1-3,10-17*
1 Peter 1.17-23
Luke 24.13-35

Zephaniah 3.14-end

'Rejoice and exult with all your heart' (v.14)

Hope is one of the great theological virtues of the Christian tradition: something we are meant to practise each day like faith and love. The prophets challenge us to see the world as it really is: greed, emptiness and vanity in ourselves as well as in others. Yet they also unfold for us a picture of eternal reality and of God's goodness and purpose.

Hope is the reason Zephaniah's terrible prophecy of judgement and destruction ends in song. We have seen the stark corruption of his own city and ours. Yet there is an even deeper vision of eternal reality, which is about the coming of the king of Israel, the Lord.

Like all the prophets, Zephaniah sees the coming of the King through a glass darkly. Even so, it is instructive to read his song of praise with Jesus in our minds. We can celebrate that God himself came into our midst, that Jesus came to save the lame and gather the outcast.

If we hold a picture of God's kingdom in our minds but lose sight of the reality of the world, we become romantics. If we hold a truthful picture of the world yet lose sight of God's kingdom, we become cynics. We must hold fast to both horizons and Zephaniah's way of hope.

Reflection by **Steven Croft**

Zephaniah 3.14-end
Acts 2.14a,36-41
Psalm 116.1-3,10-17*
1 Peter 1.17-23
Luke 24.13-35

Third Sunday of Easter

Acts 2.14a,36-41

'Repent, and be baptized ... and you will receive the gift of the Holy Spirit' (v.38)

The Holy Spirit, as Jesus said, is like the wind that blows where it will – and we need to be always open to the Holy Spirit; we cannot place conditions on the work of the Holy Spirit, nor can we erect barriers against it.

As Peter asked the people to repent and be baptized, we should today pause and examine our hearts, which is the essence of repentance, and reflect upon whether we live up to our vows of baptism. Being the light, the salt and the leaven in the world, as Jesus asked us to be, requires continuous self-examination so that we can change our ways. Jesus is our compass.

People of all nations, all colours, all genders, all backgrounds, all cultures, all abilities have experienced the power of the Holy Spirit, who empowers people to celebrate their differences. The Holy Spirit is our hope to find our identity and the way to belong to the household of God and rejoice in all our gifts. The call of Peter included all, and this invitation is for us today to go out and show the world the power of the same Holy Spirit. After nearly 2,000 years, we keep breaking bread together and lifting the cup together, witnessing to the presence of the risen Lord in us and amongst us. This is the way to be true disciples of Jesus Christ and true citizens of his kingdom.

Reflection by **Nadim Nassar**

Third Sunday of Easter

Zephaniah 3.14-end
Acts 2.14a,36-41
Psalm 116.1-3,10-17*
1 Peter 1.17-23
Luke 24.13-35

1 Peter 1.17-23

'... love one another deeply from the heart' (v.22)

Redemption, sacrifice, purification. These words at the heart of this passage all come from a world unfamiliar to us – the world of ancient worship. Jews and pagans both recognized that God could not be approached lightly. We humans approach God as soiled, damaged goods. Approaching God requires sacrifice, or the giving up of something precious to overcome the breach in our relationship with God. The offering of sacrifice brought purity, cleansing and access to God. The writer reminds these Christians that their new life of joy and hope was won for them with the gift from God of the most precious sacrifice of all – the blood of Christ shed on Calvary.

On that basis, the writer appeals for this sacrifice to be echoed in a life characterized by holiness (vv.15-16) and love (v.22). These two qualities mirror the nature of the God whose Son was given up for them – a God who has no truck with evil and whose heart bursts with love for his creation. To enjoy fully the access to God brought through the cross means learning to shun the evil that destroys life (1 Peter 2.11) and to love from the heart.

What evils are you called to avoid, and whom are you asked to love today?

Reflection by **Graham Tomlin**

Zephaniah 3.14-end
Acts 2.14a,36-41
Psalm 116.1-3,10-17*
1 Peter 1.17-23
Luke 24.13-35

Luke 24.13-35

'Oh, how foolish you are ...' (v.25)

Do you feel the mutual exasperation in this story? When the disciples meet the risen Jesus, they cannot believe that he does not know the news. Indeed, they are so surprised that they have to stop walking to be able to tell him. But the risen Jesus is even more direct back. 'Aaagh' might be a good translation of 'Oh!' (v.25). He then describes them as being 'without understanding', 'obtuse', 'dull', 'slow'. 'Dumb' might be a good colloquial translation. He is not mincing his words.

I am grateful that we have glimpses of the exasperation of Jesus, including the risen Jesus. As a theological educator and a parish priest, I experience lots of exasperation ... as indeed do my students and parishioners too at times! Sometimes we are just slow to 'get it'. And while I do not excuse either my own bad temper or pomposity, a little plain speaking together might help the Church to be a more honest institution, as well as a more effective one ...

But Jesus does not leave it there. Loving patience is the under-girding value and he works with these dopey disciples till they begin to 'get it' and then there is that unforgettable moment of recognition and reconciliation.

Plain talking and deep loving don't have to be opposites. 'Speaking the truth in love' can be a cover for verbal abuse. Or it can be a moment of mutual love in Christ.

Reflection by **Alan Bartlett**

Fourth Sunday of Easter

Genesis 7
Acts 2.42-end
Psalm 23
1 Peter 2.19-end
John 10.1-10

Genesis 7

'He blotted out every living thing that was on the face of the ground' (v.23)

Irresistibly, our imaginations people the ark. We tell stories about Noah and his family, their squabbles, their joys and struggles. We imagine the animals, in their foetid and overcrowded conditions, forced to live closely together and to adjust to each other. In the Garden of Eden, they were used to doing this, but they, like human beings, have learned different ways since those days.

However, the Genesis account is focused *outside* the ark, not inside. The authors of Genesis do not concentrate on the tiny, frail boat, tossing on the water, with its valiant and comic cargo. Instead, they see the waters of chaos overwhelming the creation, rushing back into their original possession of all that is. God made space for creation by giving the mighty water boundaries, which it obediently and meekly respected. It was the human creation that transgressed the limits God laid out, and now they see what happens when creation breaks out of its proper course. Everything God made in Genesis 1 is interdependent, designed to function as a whole. That is its strength. When it forgets that, how very fragile it is. Only God exists in complete freedom and autonomy. The waters of chaos do not care about their drowned cargo. In that, they represent us, when we forget what we are.

Reflection by **Jane Williams**

Genesis 7
Acts 2.42-end
Psalm 23
1 Peter 2.19-end
John 10.1-10

Acts 2.42-47

'They devoted themselves ...' (v.42)

This is what the Church looks like. Isn't it? Or is it choral evensong? Luke certainly intends us to see this as a description of the ideal church: mass conversion marked by public repentance and baptism; devotion to learning the faith, prayer and eucharist; miracles; communal living. Indeed, during periods of renewal, the Church does often look like this. This was true of the radical sects in seventeenth-century England. It was also, in a different way, true of early Franciscanism. It has been true of some parts of the modern Church. Should the Church always be striving for this degree of enthusiasm and commitment?

Some of us may well be cautious about the claims to the miraculous and wary of the style of leadership that can be characteristic of this mode of Church. This level of spiritual temperature can foster self-deception and hypocrisy. It also seems not to be sustainable. This energy burns itself out. There is a deep and deeply Christian wisdom in the slow rhythms of the Anglican Church; patient growth in communal holiness.

Perhaps, though – especially in a period when we can see with our own eyes the consequences of two generations when the the Church has often failed to recruit new members, and when the old ways of being Church are under immense strain – a bit of Lucan passion might not go amiss?

Reflection by **Alan Bartlett**

Fourth Sunday of Easter

Genesis 7
Acts 2.42-end
Psalm 23
1 Peter 2.19-end
John 10.1-10

1 Peter 2.19-25

'Christ also suffered' (v.21)

Our Lectionary omits the first half of this chapter – or rather holds it back until next Sunday – but it is worth looking briefly at verses 4 to 10 for the rich images contained in 1 Peter's high doctrine of the Church. Despite their heavenly inheritance, however, here on earth Christians are 'aliens and exiles' (v.11) who are subject to worldly powers and spiritual attacks.

Freedom (vv.16,24) is a big Christian word – and a paradoxical notion for those who claim to be servants (literally 'slaves') of God. But, as Bob Dylan sings, 'You're gonna have to serve somebody', because we all have an instinct to give allegiance and to follow.

In the Bible, freedom is apparently compatible with slavery (vv.18-20). Perhaps this is because the freedom intended here is essentially a freedom for others, a freedom to serve others, and not the independent mastery of one's own destiny. (How could it be that, as freedom is essentially a gift of God – a thing of grace, not a human achievement?)

Was Jesus free? Like the abused slave, subject or even citizen, he too suffered unjustly. But he bore that suffering to and on the cross. And there he absorbed it – and with it all our human rebellion against our one true Master.

Only a truly free person submits to be bound in order that others may be released.

Reflection by **Jeff Astley**

Genesis 7
Acts 2.42-end
Psalm 23
1 Peter 2.19-end
John 10.1-10

Fourth Sunday of Easter

John 10.1-10

'I came that they may have life, and have it abundantly' (v.10)

The image of Jesus as a gate has not captured the imagination as much as others have for some obvious, maybe artistic, reasons. However, in past centuries it would have been different. To Greek readers of this Gospel, Jesus referring to himself as a door would have resonated with their understanding, found in literature from Homer onwards, that a heaven above the earth was entered through such a gate. In the Jewish scriptures we also find many references to the heavenly gates such as in Psalm 118:

> 'Open to me the gates of righteousness,
> that I may enter through them
> and give thanks to the Lord.
> This is the gate of the Lord;
> the righteous shall enter through it.' (Psalm 118.19-20)

Many of us today feel as if we live on a threshold of faith, tentative about commitment because we are too full of questions or unease about what we may be getting ourselves into. In this passage, Jesus implies that, far from being a constricting route to a place where we have to surrender our integrity, to follow him means to 'come in and go out and find pasture' (v.9). He opens up the way to a place of safety and rest, a sheepfold, where in all our confused hustle and bustle, it is the presence of the shepherd that reassures and makes life worthy of our trust. He has not come to close down the complexity of living but to enrich it and make it abundant.

Reflection by **Mark Oakley**

Fifth Sunday of Easter

Genesis 8.1-19
Acts 7.55-end
Psalm 31.1-5,15-16*
1 Peter 2.2-10
John 14.1-14

Genesis 8.1-19

'But God remembered Noah ...' (v.1)

There has been a lot of forgetting in the story so far. Human beings forgot that they were made to be with God and share his care of creation. They forgot that they were not independent and god-like beings, but creatures. The waters forgot the boundaries that God had set for them, and thundered back over creation. The living things, drowning helplessly in the indifferent, violent strength of the waters, forgot everything in the deep darkness of death. It is as though the universe had forgotten that there had ever been a creation, now that there is only formless void and empty waters again. The tiny bobbing craft, carrying all that remains of creation, is utterly forgotten by the elements.

But God remembers. God's 'remembering' is one of the ways in which the Bible describes God's faithfulness, while emphasizing that God is faithful because he chooses to be, not because we have rights over him. God 'remembers' his promises to Abraham and Isaac; he 'remembers' his covenant with David; and now, he 'remembers' the ark and its contents, and replays his first creative acts, restraining the waters and making room for the hospitable ground again.

When we 'remember' Jesus, in the Eucharist, we are trusting ourselves to God's remembering, which brings new life out of the grave.

Reflection by **Jane Williams**

Genesis 8.1-19
Acts 7.55-end
Psalm 31.1-5,15-16*
1 Peter 2.2-10
John 14.1-14

Fifth Sunday of Easter

Acts 7.55-end

*'While they were stoning Stephen, he prayed,
"Lord Jesus, receive my spirit."' (v.59)*

The martyrdom of Stephen is one of the defining moments in the history of the early Church. It is a great act of apostolic witness. Stephen doesn't choose death, but he does not flinch from witnessing to the life-changing truth of Jesus Christ that leads to his death. His witness so enrages the religious council that, filled with fury, they drag him into the street and stone him.

Luke carefully tells this story to show how the witness, Stephen, is united with the Saviour, Jesus. He dies uplifted by a vision of Jesus in glory. Right to the end he continues to bear witness to the lordship of Christ. Like Jesus, he pleads forgiveness of those whose blindness compels them towards this hideous violence. 'Lord, do not hold this sin against them,' are his final words (v.60).

All this shows that the witness of the Church is the witness of Christ, and that, even in the smallest acts of witness or service, Christ is present with us through the Holy Spirit.

Stephen's clothes are laid at the feet of a young man called Saul. He approved of the killing (Acts 8.1). There is great lamentation for Stephen, but his witness has not ended. Saul's witnessing of this shocking and horrible death is part of what changes him; for it is to this persecutor of the Church that the baton of its witness is about to be passed.

Reflection by **Stephen Cottrell**

Fifth Sunday of Easter

Genesis 8.1-19
Acts 7.55-end
Psalm 31.1-5,15-16*
1 Peter 2.2-10
John 14.1-14

1 Peter 2.2-10

'... let yourselves be built into a spiritual house' (v.5)

Within the Church, we are often encouraged not to focus too much on buildings. 'The Church is more than bricks and mortar', we say; 'it is the people who are important, not the building.' True enough, but in this passage the two conflate: the people are the building – a house made up of different 'living stones', built by God.

I often imagine such a structure looking rather like a dry stone wall. If you have ever examined such a wall, you will appreciate what a complex and fascinating creation it is. Dry stone walls are constructed without mortar and are held up purely by the interlocking of the stones. The builder uses every size and shape of stone, rock and chock to make the wall, placing each one carefully so that it fits snugly against the others and gives the structure stability.

This is the sort of edifice we should allow ourselves be built into. It is the master builder who knows exactly where to put each stone for best effect to make the house strong and secure.

If we sometimes feel we have ended up next to a living stone with a rather sharp edge, it is as well to reflect that we may have a similarly shaped one that fits rather neatly against it.

Reflection by **Helen Orchard**

Genesis 8.1-19
Acts 7.55-end
Psalm 31.1-5,15-16*
1 Peter 2.2-10
John 14.1-14

Fifth Sunday of Easter

John 14.1-14

'Lord, we do not know where you are going.
How can we know the way?' (v.5)

He may be known as 'doubting Thomas', but perhaps 'honest Thomas' or 'courageous Thomas', or even 'tenacious Thomas' would be nearer the mark!

I thank God for Saint Thomas, the one disciple who had the courage to say what everyone else was thinking but didn't dare say. He had the courage to ask the awkward questions that drew from Jesus one of the most beautiful and profoundly comforting of all his sayings. 'We don't know where you're going, how can we know the way?' asked Thomas, and because he had the courage to confess his ignorance, we were given these words of life: 'I am the way, and the truth, and the life' (v.6).

And the Thomas in me has more to ask of this passage every time I return to it. Philip may be satisfied to have seen the Father in seeing Jesus, but I wasn't there – how can I see either Jesus or the Father now? I believe in Jesus, not having seen, but still I ask how. That last promise of 'greater works' begs as many questions as it answers. Saint Thomas puts his finger on the nub of things, and so must I, touching the wounds of one whose wounds are healing mine.

Reflection by **Malcolm Guite**

Sixth Sunday of Easter

Genesis 8.20 – 9.17
Acts 17.22-31
Psalm 66.7-end
1 Peter 3.13-end
John 14.15-21

Genesis 8.20 – 9.17

'I am establishing my covenant with you and your descendants ... and with every living creature' (9.9-10)

A covenant was a legally binding agreement between two parties, before witnesses and with penalties imposed if either side broke the promise. So it is an odd word for God to use here. Noah is not promising anything, nor is he forfeiting anything. God, on the other hand, is promising to restrain his own divine powers and bind himself to his creatures. He is forfeiting his right to unmake what he has made. So God deliberately allows himself and his creation to be vulnerable to these human beings. He binds his own hands, while leaving Noah and his descendants free. They still bear the image of God, and they are still free to multiply and take over God's world (9.6-7), but God is no longer free to unloose the waters of chaos again. He has made a solemn covenant.

Although there is real continuity between the world before and after the Flood, things have changed for ever. The boundaries between God and people, and people and the rest of creation have shifted significantly. God's covenant with Noah is automatically a covenant with all other living creatures, not just human beings, because the image of God in humanity still binds them together with the animals that God brought to meet Adam in Genesis 2.

Human beings may not always recognize this connection, but the rest of creation knows it, often to its cost.

Reflection by **Jane Williams**

138

Genesis 8.20 – 9.17
Acts 17.22-31
Psalm 66.7-end
1 Peter 3.13-end
John 14.15-21

Sixth Sunday of Easter

Acts 17.22-31

'... he is not far from each one of us' (v.27)

In Athens, Paul did something he hadn't done before. Of course, he went to the synagogue and talked with local Jews about the Hebrew Scriptures (our Old Testament). But then he went to the marketplace and spoke to anyone who happened to be there. There was no point in discussing the Scriptures as his way of introducing Jesus. The Greeks would not have understood what he was talking about. So instead he began to chat about their contemporary culture – poets, statues, popular ideas. They joined the conversation, sarcastically at first, but then with interest. The reason they engaged is that Paul didn't tell them that everything they yearned after was worthless. Instead, he told them to go on yearning because Jesus offered the fulfilment of those hopes.

It makes me wonder how Paul would begin a conversation today with someone who has never been to church. I'm sure he would not ask, 'Have you heard of The Acts of the Apostles?' Instead he might ask, 'Have you heard of *Game of Thrones*?' (It is, after all, the world's most pirated and watched TV drama.) I can imagine him continuing, 'You know how the characters speak of the gods of death? Well, I've made a life-changing discovery that there is a God of Life.'

Have you seen anything on television that you are eager to chat about? Go ahead! See whether God makes himself known in the conversation.

Reflection by **Peter Graystone**

Sixth Sunday of Easter

Genesis 8.20 – 9.17
Acts 17.22-31
Psalm 66.7-end
1 Peter 3.13-end
John 14.15-21

1 Peter 3.13-22

'... yet do it with gentleness and reverence' (v.16)

To what extent are 'gentleness and reverence' features of contemporary evangelism? Despite the clear command of 1 Peter, some evangelistic enterprises are anything but gentle. The wild-eyed style of the hellfire preacher may be viewed as comic and outdated, but the same content is often present today wherever the central message of the gospel is portrayed as an emotional threat: 'turn or burn'. No wonder then that the World Council of Churches called on Christians to ensure that their evangelism be Christlike rather than domineering in its style and content, promoting peace not division.

For the original audience of this epistle, the advice of this passage was wise and practical. Do good, fear not, and be ready to give 'an account of the hope that is in you' (v.15), with gentleness and reverence. The way they conducted their lives within a hostile environment was important. Making the best possible impression on outsiders would avoid persecution and draw in converts: there was no question of bullish evangelism.

These days, the environments we live in in the West are rarely violently hostile to Christianity, but the guidance remains pertinent. An attractive exhibition and reasoned defence of the faith, shared respectfully with genuine concern for others, is far more effective than any amount of crusading.

Reflection by **Jeff Astley**

Genesis 8.20 – 9.17
Acts 17.22-31
Psalm 66.7-end
1 Peter 3.13-end
John 14.15-21

John 14.15-21

'I will not leave you orphaned' (v.18)

Jesus continues to prepare his disciples for his passion, building them up in the expectation that, though he must leave them, he is not abandoning them. He will ask the Father to send the Advocate, the Spirit, to continue to teach them and remind them of what he has already shown them. The promise of the Spirit makes explicit what was hinted at in the first part of this chapter, read last Sunday: the mutual love within the Godhead has a threefold shape. True life springs from love, given, received and communicated.

One of the spiritual tragedies of our time is the loss of personal relationship in daily life that has come through our increasingly automated world. We are in danger of becoming spiritually autistic, isolated and empty, aware only of our own needs and incapable of recognizing the reality of other people. Christ shows us that our neediness cannot be met by grasping at what we imagine will satisfy us. Ultimately, we need to recognize our emptiness and turn away from ourselves to the love that already embraces us. At the point at which Jesus faces utter exclusion and rejection, he assures us that the divine persons make their home with those who believe. 'On that day you will know that I am in my Father, and you in me, and I in you' (v.20).

We have our own passion to bear and may experience loneliness, trouble and abandonment, but Christ leaves us his promise that all will be well.

Reflection by **Angela Tilby**

Ascension Day

Principal Feast

Acts 1.1-11 *or* Daniel 7.9-14
Psalm 47 *or* Psalm 93
Ephesians 1.15-end *or* Acts 1.1-11
Luke 24.44-end

Acts 1.1-11

'... you will be my witnesses ... to the ends of the earth' (v.8)

Although this book is called 'Acts of the Apostles', I reckon 'Gospel of the Holy Spirit' might be a better name. This sequel to Luke's Gospel (whose final verses form the Gospel reading for today) is going to be a Spirit-filled story of a Spirit-led movement of change.

Both books are addressed to someone called Theophilus. We're not sure who this is – perhaps a Roman official investigating the Christian movement – but his name means 'beloved of God'. In which case, let us imagine it is us! God's beloved, invited to participate in his story.

We start at the Ascension. The bewildered disciples stare into the sky, wondering where Jesus has gone. This is a hinge event for Luke. His Gospel ends, and this book begins, with this strange story of arrival and departure. Jesus' mission is complete. He departs from the earth and takes humanity into heaven. The mission of his Church begins. The apostles await the arrival of the Spirit, which is the new presence of Jesus no longer constrained by space and time. It is about absence and presence. Jesus is absent to them in the flesh, but will soon be present to them in a new and dynamic way.

The disciples are about to be woken with a start. They think it is all over. It is only just beginning.

Reflection by **Stephen Cottrell**

Acts 1.1-11 *or* **Daniel 7.9-14**
Psalm 47 *or* Psalm 93
Ephesians 1.15-end *or* Acts 1.1-11
Luke 24.44-end

Ascension Day

Daniel 7.9-14

'To him was given dominion and glory and kingship' (v.14)

Daniel draws back the curtain of heaven and helps us to see eternal realities even in the midst of suffering, persecution and difficulty. Today's reading follows a vision of four beasts: the changing empires of the world (Daniel 7.1-8). Behind the changing drama of this game of thrones lies another, more enduring eternal kingship, in three parts.

The first concerns the Ancient One, the creator of heaven and earth (vv.9-10). His kingship is eternal and endures in majesty whatever is happening on earth. The second celebrates God's victory over all earthly powers and empires (vv.11-12). The third Christians see as a prophecy of the Messiah, God's coming king (vv.13-14). Today we celebrate in the Ascension that Christ has been given a kingship that shall never be destroyed, for all eternity.

The chapter is written to strengthen God's people in times of great persecution. Behind the most terrible of human events lies another much deeper reality, which we can lose sight of in our suffering or the press of daily life. The most powerful kingdom is transitory, yet there is a kingdom founded by God that will never be destroyed. Every human kingdom is a shadow and a pale reflection of God's kingdom, which is both present and still to come in all its fullness.

Reflection by **Steven Croft**

Acts 1.1-11 *or* Daniel 7.9-14
Psalm 47 *or* Psalm 93
Ephesians 1.15-end *or* Acts 1.1-11
Luke 24.44-end

Ephesians 1.15-end

'... the hope to which he has called you' (v.18)

Pauls' prayer for the Ephesian Church is rooted in what he has already heard of them: of their love for God, and for one another. Ephesus, like any other city, would have been a hub of cultural and ethnic diversity, and the Church, no doubt, mirrored that. Yet even though it is early days for the Christian Church, it is already apparent that this body is not tribal or sectarian. Slave, free, male, female, Jew and gentile – all are welcome. Paul knows that in Christ, there are abundant riches of God's grace – to be shared with all.

So, the Church transcends race, class, gender and other differences. The unity of the Church does not consist of people thinking alike, but in people acting together. Diversity does not mean division. It is, rather, essential for what unity is fully meant to be. The hope to which we are called – to receive and share God's rich blessings and grace in Christ – is all the Church is called to be.

So the very gift that God gives us to share is something we cannot possess. It possesses us and, in so doing, invites us to offer – what we have seen and heard; tasted and felt; understood and embodied – with our neighbours and with the world. The blessing of Christ enlarges our lives, leading to justice, mercy and fidelity, and generosity in personal relations and political structures alike. Paul's vision of the gospel is one that seeks to be at home in the world. And yet the moment we receive it, it reshapes our world more radically than we could have imagined.

Reflection by **Martyn Percy**

Acts 1.1-11 *or* Daniel 7.9-14
Psalm 47 *or* Psalm 93
Ephesians 1.15-end *or* Acts 1.1-11
Luke 24.44-end

Luke 24.44-53

'... he withdrew from them' (v.51)

The crucifixion can be endlessly painted and sculpted and every image shows another facet of the mystery, but the Ascension is impossible to portray. As soon as we suggest heaven as having some co-ordinate in space and time, and show Jesus 'going up', we go wrong. Worst of all are those risible representations of a pair of feet sticking out beneath a cloud. The 'height' of heaven is spiritual, not literal; the cloud that receives him is the cloud of unknowing the presence and Glory of God that was also with Moses on the mountain.

There is a further paradox, one that Luke captures here. Though in one sense ' he withdrew from them', in another he came close, and they continue to worship him in the temple with great joy. He withdraws in one way to become utterly available in another; he brings one thing to an end to make a new beginning. They wait, and we with them, to be clothed with power from on high. I tried to suggest something of this in these lines from the sonnet I wrote for the Ascension:

'We saw him go and yet we were not parted,
He took us with him to the heart of things,
The heart that broke for all the broken-hearted
Is whole and heaven-centered now...'

Reflection by **Malcolm Guite**

Seventh Sunday of Easter
Sunday after Ascension Day

Ezekiel 36.24-28
Acts 1.6-14
Psalm 68.1-10,32-35*
1 Peter 4.12-14; 5.6-11
John 17.1-11

Ezekiel 36.24-28

'... a new spirit I will put within you' (v.26)

The first day of Lent now seems a long time ago ... Do the reflections of Lent remain in sharp focus? Are its resolutions enshrined in daily practice, or has the old life resurrected? Is chocolate once again in the ascendancy?

Considering these questions, we might feel as frustrated as Paul: 'I do not do the good I want, but the evil I do not want is what I do' (Romans 7.19). Like him, we might feel that we cannot quite subdue our more flamboyant appetites, that our end-of-term report is destined always to read 'must try harder'.

We are called to try harder, to return to this cycle of self-examination and self-discipline, not just in Lent but Sunday by Sunday, day by day, as we aim to shape our lives after the pattern of Jesus Christ. We are not left to do this work alone, however. In fact, holiness is not mainly the fruit of our own efforts but is a gift of God who sprinkles us with clean water (v.25), gives us a new heart and puts a new spirit within us (v.26). Our own dogged pursuit of the way of holiness is in thankful response to God who has already set us on this path and counted us as holy.

In Southwark Cathedral, a plaque to William Winkworth, 'late chaplain of this parish' concludes that 'he fell asleep in Jesus, a debtor to grace'. We are all 'debtors to grace'.

Reflection by **Mary Gregory**

Ezekiel 36.24-28
Acts 1.6-14
Psalm 68.1-10,32-35*
1 Peter 4.12-14; 5.6-11
John 17.1-11

Seventh Sunday of Easter

Acts 1.6-14

*'But you will receive power when the Holy Spirit
has come upon you' (v.8)*

St Luke, the doctor and writer, starts recording in this book
not the acts of the apostles but the act of the Holy Spirit. Luke
is passionate and enthusiastic about the presence and the role
of the Holy Spirit in the Church. He writes the account of the
ascension, but his focus is on the work of the Holy Spirit,
which is the continuity of the presence of Christ in the world.
Jesus is not with us in the body, but he is always with us
through the Holy Spirit.

This is an account of hope and power. The ascension is not a
sad occasion when the world 'lost Christ'. Even today, it is a
time to celebrate the era of the work of the Holy Spirit in us.
Through our baptism and the Eucharist, we go out into the
world as the disciples of Christ, the risen and the ascended
Lord, empowered just like the first disciples with the Holy
Spirit. Through that same power of that same Spirit, we
continue Christ's mission to be the light, the salt and the
leaven in the world.

By living our faith well, people do not see us – they see Christ
in us! This is how we shine and how we become true agents
of the Holy Spirit.

Reflection by **Nadim Nassar**

Seventh Sunday of Easter

Ezekiel 36.24-28
Acts 1.6-14
Psalm 68.1-10,32-35*
1 Peter 4.12-14; 5.6-11
John 17.1-11

1 Peter 4.12-14; 5.6-11

'Like a roaring lion ... looking for someone to devour' (5.8)

When we experience the discomforts of being people of faith, we in the West will do well not to think we're being persecuted. Persecution is of a quite different order. Nevertheless, it can make us think hard about the origin of evil. Peter likens the devil to a ravenous lion bent on the destruction of anything edible – mostly us. It's a vivid picture, which we tame nicely in the soothing ritual of compline, but Peter is at his clearest. His readers are having a hard time, but the real foe isn't the intermediate persecutors but the lion behind them, the devil. That's why he has insisted throughout the letter that we should treat non-Christians with respect, obey the authorities, behave with humility and patience, and so on. Name the real enemy and 'resist him, steadfast in your faith' (5.9), but remain gracious and Christ-like with everyone.

Modern readers will inevitably ask themselves what they make of talk of the devil. C. S. Lewis was keen to make the point that we should avoid both extremes – the extreme of dismissing the idea of the devil because we can't believe in a ridiculous little chap with horns and red tights, and the other extreme of being fascinated with the idea of a devil and seeing him at work under every stone. For most of us, the personification of the devil doesn't matter so much as the need to take evil seriously, and resist it, steadfast in our faith. Perhaps even more importantly, instead of asking where this misfortune came from, we could ask the much more telling question: what does this occurrence enable me to do that I couldn't have done before?

Reflection by **John Pritchard**

Ezekiel 36.24-28
Acts 1.6-14
Psalm 68.1-10,32-35*
1 Peter 4.12-14; 5.6-11
John 17.1-11

Seventh Sunday of Easter

John 17.1-11

'Father, glorify me ...' (v.5)

In Saint Paul's second letter to the Corinthians, Paul talks about the glory of God revealed in the face of Jesus Christ (2 Corinthians 4.6): 'For it is the God who said, "Let light shine out of darkness", who has shone in our hearts to give the light of the knowledge of the glory of God in the face of Jesus Christ.' It is one of the boldest statements we have in scripture. Our faces smile, frown, weep, laugh, wink, puzzle, grimace, grin – and much, much more. Our faces give us the most distinctive thing about our identity. So the idea that the glory of God is revealed in just one face – that of Jesus – is remarkable. But we know, of course, that our faces change, too, as we reflect that glory and look at Christ.

It takes a lifetime of discipleship to find that our faces can 'shine' with wisdom and love – but they can. And the key to this lies in understanding 'glory'. When we glorify God, we start to see the world as God sees it: with full and deep love. God loved the world enough to send his son to abide in it, so that we might abide in him eternally.

Faces that do shine with the glory of God are seen for what they are; reflections or images of God. One of C.S. Lewis' most mature Christian reflections is *Till We Have Faces*. His theme is that of transfiguration. Our faces can 'reflect' the glory of God revealed in the face of Jesus Christ. When this correspondence occurs, we see the world differently and we can look in love, just as God gazes upon his creation.

Reflection by **Martyn Percy**

149

Day of Pentecost
(Whit Sunday)

Acts 2.1-21 *or* Numbers 11.24-30
Psalm 104.26-36,37*b**
1 Corinthians 12.3*b*-13 *or* **Acts 2.1-21**
John 20.19-23 *or* John 7.37-39

Acts 2.1-21

'Amazed and astonished ...' (v.7)

When the world stops being amazed by what we offer to it, by what we do and by what we say as Christians, that is a sure sign that we need to reconsider our baptism of fire. When Luke wanted to describe the Holy Spirit descending on the disciples, the best way he found was to depict it as 'tongues, as of fire' (v.3), because he was conscious that fire represents both power and warmth. As Christians, we have continued to receive this gift of the Spirit of the Lord in order to carry on our mission to amaze the world by reflecting the love of God in Jesus Christ and living in it with the power of the resurrection.

Sometimes, we lose this ability to amaze the world when we get too busy with our little selves, shifting the focus away from the risen Lord, exactly like Peter when he shifted his gaze from the Lord to the storm and he began to sink. If we want to continue as the force for love and for the transformation of the world and if we want to keep receiving the gift of the Spirit, then we must make sure that our focus is on the Lord himself. Only then can we continue to receive the very same gift of the same Holy Spirit that worked in the disciples to amaze the world at Pentecost.

Reflection by **Nadim Nassar**

Acts 2.1-21 *or* **Numbers 11.24-30**
Psalm 104.26-36,37*b**
1 Corinthians 12.3*b*-13 *or* Acts 2.1-21
John 20.19-23 *or* John 7.37-39

Day of Pentecost

(Whit Sunday)

Numbers 11.24-30

'Would that all the Lord's people were prophets' (v.29)

If you were choosing the leader for a new, radical movement, you would not choose Moses. Such a leader, you consider, must be unimpeachable, decisive, articulate and resilient, and Moses simply does not meet the criteria. He is a killer. He is beset by self-doubt. He is horrified at the thought of public speaking. He gets so worn out that he fantasizes about the deep sleep of death.

Moses might never be your choice of leader, but he is God's. Untrammelled by a human understanding of meritocracy, God calls whomsoever he will, equipping them through his Spirit, who is like the wind that 'blows where it chooses' (John 3.8).

The scandal of God's approach is felt by Joshua who, dismayed by Eldad and Medad's sudden ability to prophesy, implores Moses to stop them. They are not amongst the 70 elders, Joshua implies, nor are they in the inner sanctum of the Tent of Meeting and yet the Spirit has rested on them. This is not how things should be done! Who do they think they are? Or, rather, who does God think they are?

By way of contrast, Moses welcomes the unbounded dance of the Spirit who shares his burdens with others. Like Moses, can you celebrate God's radical, gracious gift of the Spirit to others, however undeserving they seem? And are you open to the surprising possibility that God may have so blessed you, however unworthy you feel?

Reflection by **Mary Gregory**

Acts 2.1-21 *or* Numbers 11.24-30
Psalm 104.26-36,37b*
1 Corinthians 12.3b-13 *or* Acts 2.1-21
John 20.19-23 *or* John 7.37-39

1 Corinthians 12.3b-13

'... in the one Spirit we were all baptized into one body'
(v.13)

Years ago, I attended a fellowship for young adults hosted by a wealthy parish that also had a programme feeding homeless people. One evening on my way to the fellowship, I saw outside the church a homeless friend who, like me, was a young adult. I told him about the fellowship meeting and started introducing him around inside. But one of the priests told my friend that he should leave and come back for the morning 'outreach' food. Fortunately, better sense prevailed, and my friend Charles had dinner with the rest of the young adult fellowship in the parish hall.

A lot of congregations have 'outreach' programmes for poor people and 'fellowship' programmes for 'members', the latter sharing greater wealth and status. It's an exceptionally unhelpful distinction. As Paul writes here, God's Spirit showers gifts on all people. God gives each of God's children gifts that we need to be Christ's Body, the temple in which the Holy Spirit dwells. For all that that wealthy parish knew, Charles had the gifts to be an excellent Sunday-school teacher or parish-board member. Wise Christians rejoice whenever they can engage God's mission to bring abundant, fruitful life to all – not because fewer of 'those poor people' will miss out what we enjoy, but because all of God's children benefit from each person's gifts used fully.

Reflection by **Sarah Dylan Breuer**

Year A • Pentecost

Acts 2.1-21 *or* Numbers 11.24-30
Psalm 104.26-36,37*b**
1 Corinthians 12.3*b*-13 *or* Acts 2.1-21
John 20.19-23 *or* John 7.37-39

Day of Pentecost
(Whit Sunday)

John 20.19-23

'As the Father has sent me, so I send you' (v.21)

Possibly, this verse should be called the great commission. Following the resurrection, we are sent, as the Father sent his Son. We are to participate intimately in God's activity, in the Trinity's very nature. But what does this imply?

In today's passage, Jesus says 'Peace be with you' (vv.19,21) twice, an exhortation he repeats for a third time a week later, this time with Thomas present (v.26). Peace, *shalom*, is the nature of the triune God. This is not peace in a political or economic sense; the disciples will go on to face persecution. The peace of the Father and Son is the peace of forgiveness and wholeness. It is also a peace that we offer to others by being their servant, as Christ was the servant of many. We are sent, as was Christ, metaphorically and literally to empty ourselves and wash feet. The peace we proclaim is likely to become increasingly vital in our society, which is facing economic and structural transition.

Re-creation is also present in today's passage. The Holy Spirit is given to the disciples by Jesus breathing over them. This recalls the wind, breath or Spirit of God moving over the face of the waters at the beginning of creation. Life came forth then, just as new life is now experienced in the risen Christ.

Go and do likewise.

Reflection by **Paul Kennedy**

Day of Pentecost
(Whit Sunday)

Acts 2.1-21 *or* Numbers 11.24-30
Psalm 104.26-36,37b*
1 Corinthians 12.3b-13 *or* Acts 2.1-21
John 20.19-23 *or* **John 7.37-39**

John 7.37-39

'Let anyone who is thirsty come to me' (v.37)

I can only remember one occasion in my life when I've been really thirsty. Even that was only for a few hours, but when I was able to slake my aching thirst, it was a fantastic relief. My whole being was irrigated and refreshed. Well, if you've ever been just a little bit thirsty, and known that longing for cool, fresh water, then you'll have an inkling of the power of these words. Jesus offers himself as one who can quench thirst: 'If you believe in me,' says Jesus, 'drink.' It is an astonishing invitation.

But it goes further. Alluding to the Holy Spirit, Jesus says that if we drink from him, then gushing streams of living water will not just flow into our lives, they will flow out of them as well. We too will become a source of blessing. Jesus will give himself to others through his giving of himself to us.

Everyone then carries on arguing about whether he is the Messiah or not, and stressing about the fact that he wasn't born in the right place (vv. 40ff.). After all, Messiahs are supposed to have the right postcode. But Jesus has not just moved the goalposts, he has redrawn the whole map. He is now speaking and acting as if he is God's Messiah, and offering gifts that only God can give.

Reflection by **Stephen Cottrell**

Isaiah 40.12-17,27-end
Psalm 8
2 Corinthians 13.11-end
Matthew 28.16-20

Isaiah 40.12-17,27-end

'... they shall mount up with wings like eagles' (v.31)

Exhaustion distorts perspective. All manner of things can drain our vitality: illness, bereavement and stress, sheer hard work sustained over a number of months, a number of different demands coming all at once with no chance to draw breath and recover.

Whatever the cause, we should recognize that tiredness will affect us spiritually as well as physically. When our inner batteries are drained, we begin to live less joyfully, less adventurously in our discipleship. Step by step, we make the easier choices and take the less demanding road. We become more vulnerable to temptation and harder to rouse. As the old collect for the last Sunday before Advent has it: 'Stir up O Lord the wills of your faithful people'.

The Christian life is demanding and requires strength and resilience. The purpose of these final verses in Chapter 40 is to pass on a message of comfort and gentleness to those who are weary. We need to hear them in that way, but these are words that require action as well. To advance, when we are tired, there is always a need to retreat.

The promise is sure: '... those who wait for the Lord shall renew their strength' (v.31). When you are tired, get off the treadmill of overactivity. Press the pause button. Take time to wait on God. Spread your wings like an eagle and wait for the warm thermal currents to lift you up.

Reflection by **Steven Croft**

Isaiah 40.12-17,27-end
Psalm 8
2 Corinthians 13.11-end
Matthew 28.16-20

2 Corinthians 13.11-end

'Put things in order' (v.11)

Paul wrote several letters to the Christians in Corinth, a Church he loved and worried about in equal measure. Two of these letters survive. The first opens with anguish about divisions. Just twenty years after Jesus' resurrection there were already disagreements about what it meant to be his follower (1 Corinthians 1.10-13). The second closes with the words we have read today – a much gentler reminder to 'agree with one another' and 'live in peace' (v.11).

I sometimes wonder what Paul would have made of today's worldwide Church, staggering in size but deeply divided. Is it simply inevitable that such a large number of people will argue themselves into groups believing different things?

Paul suggests that God has offered us three things to heal and unite us – his grace, his love and his fellowship (v.13). Undeserved, unrestrained and endlessly welcoming.

How will these help us? Because they are the qualities of the Trinity that is our God. The Creator God, the Saviour Jesus and the Holy Spirit are eternally three but eternally one. They have distinct identities, but absolutely no divisions. They are our model for how a Church can keep its unity without losing its diversity.

The first step in putting things in order in any Church is to stand alongside those with whom we have principled disagreements and together look outwards to the kaleidoscopic but undivided beauty of the Trinity.

Reflection by **Peter Graystone**

Isaiah 40.12-17,27-end
Psalm 8
2 Corinthians 13.11-end
Matthew 28.16-20

Matthew 28.16-20

*'When they saw him, they worshipped him;
but some doubted' (v.17)*

How much do you need to know in order to be a Christian? And how much do you need to know to get involved in ministry? For many people, Christian faith is an intellectual exercise. We work out what we believe and don't believe. We explore ideas, come to conclusions, and wait for that moment when we are confident and know what we are talking about before we finally jump in and get involved.

The ending of Matthew's Gospel challenges this approach. When the disciples first saw Jesus, they worshipped, but some doubted. It doesn't say that some worshipped and some doubted, but that they all worshipped and some doubted. Although not all were confident yet of what they thought about this risen Jesus, they worshipped nevertheless. In the same kind of way, Jesus sends the disciples out to make disciples of all nations – baptizing and teaching (not, as we might expect, teaching and then baptizing).

This seems to be reminding us that Christian faith is a work in progress: we worship while we doubt. We baptize and we teach, but we do not make people sit an exam before they are deemed worthy for baptism. Christian faith does not demand that we have all the answers, nor are constantly certain about every single matter of doctrine, but invites us to jump in, to follow and to worship – and to work as much out later as we can.

Reflection by **Paula Gooder**

Proper 4

Sunday between
29 May & 4 June inclusive
(if after Trinity Sunday)

Continuous:
Genesis 6.9-22; 7.24; 8.14-19
Psalm 46
Romans 1.16,17; 3.22b-28[29-31]
Matthew 7.21-end

Genesis 6.9-22; 7.24; 8.14-19

'And God said to Noah, "I have determined to make an end of all flesh"' (6.13)

Today's Old Testament reading is a potted version of the story of Noah's ark, from across three chapters of Genesis. At the heart of this is a great paradox. On the one hand, we are told that God is so angry that he proposes to destroy the world. On the other hand, we see God acting with great care to preserve what he has made. God's instructions to Noah are precise and detailed – designed to ensure that what emerges after the flood is continuous with what went before. Odd behaviour from a destructive deity?

Yet this paradox is one of the identifying characteristics of the God of the Bible. 'Hatred' and 'anger' are the only human words we can find to express God's attitude to sin. But while human hatred and anger are always destructive, God's hatred and anger renew. When Israel is decimated and exiled, what emerges is a people as numerous as the stars in the sky. When Jesus is crucified, his resurrection provides life for the world. When Christians are baptized, destroying our old lives in the flood water, we are reborn into the new life of Christ.

None of this is without pain, but it is the extraordinary fruit of the creative anger of God.

Reflection by **Jane Williams**

Related:
Deuteronomy 11.18-21,26-28
Psalm 31.1-5,19-24*
Romans 1.16,17; 3.22*b*-28[29-31]
Matthew 7.21-end

Deuteronomy 11.18-21,26-28

'You shall put these words ... in your heart and soul' (v.18)

One of the most powerful elements of the teaching in this part of Deuteronomy is the command to make the words of God central to the lives of his people. The people of God were instructed to place the words of God at the centre of who they were by binding it to their foreheads and hands; teaching it to their children and writing it on their doorposts. This is something that is carefully lived out in Jewish practice, through the wearing of *tefillin* on their foreheads and arms (small black boxes containing parchment upon which are inscribed verses of Torah) and the affixing of a *mezuzah* to every doorpost in the house (a *mezuzah* contains the words of the *Shema*, 'Hear O Israel ...', the opening of the central statement of Jewish belief about and devotion to God). The command to teach the words to their children is also carefully observed at Torah school.

The command to put the words of God in their heart and soul is observed very carefully indeed within Jewish tradition. This challenges those in the Christian tradition to think again about whether we place God's words sufficiently at the centre of who we are. Admittedly we have a very different relationship with God's Word – looking to it more for inspiration than command – but the question remains. Are God's words placed deep within our hearts and souls, and what might we need to do to make them more central to our lives?

Reflection by **Paula Gooder**

Proper 4	*Continuous:*	*Related:*
	Genesis 6.9-22; 7.24;	Deuteronomy
	8.14-19	11.18-21,26-28
	Psalm 46	Psalm 31.1-5,19-24*

Romans 1.16,17; 3.22b-28[29-31]
Matthew 7.21-end

Romans 1.16,17; 3.22b-28[29-31]

*'For there is no distinction, since all have sinned
and fall short of the glory of God' (3.22b-3)*

It is all too easy for us to categorize salvation and make it hierarchical. Somehow or other, it often seems a natural inclination to say either that I am less of a Christian person than *X*, or that *Y* is more of a Christian than *Z*. The uncomfortable truth is that this is a senseless pattern of thought for the follower of Christ. The life of Christ and the pattern of God's action in his birth, life, death and resurrection mean that our relationship with God is no different from that of Her Majesty the Queen or a person who attends a neighbouring parish church or who lives on the other side of the village or town. The only distinction, to which the author of Romans alludes, is between those who have faith and those who do not. In fact, the author is at pains to make clear that the God whom we claim to be our own is not our own private household God, but also the God of those who live outside our cultural, economic or social circle.

It is sometimes difficult to prevent the popular belief that good acts of witness and work result in God's limitless love. What is clear from today's reading is that faith is the key to release God's gift of love. Faith is clinging to the belief that even in the darkest depths, God is there, somewhere. Even though we can't always even recognize God, God's higher power is within us all, ready to be unlocked.

Reflection by **Christopher Woods**

Continuous:
Genesis 6.9-22; 7.24;
8.14-19
Psalm 46

Related:
Deuteronomy
11.18-21,26-28
Psalm 31.1-5,19-24*

Romans 1.16,17; 3.22b-28[29-31]
Matthew 7.21-end

Matthew 7.21-end

'... who hears these words of mine and acts on them' (v.24)

To the Western reader, the parable of the wise and foolish builders is obvious in the extreme. Who in their right mind would choose to build their house on a sandy beach instead of on the rocky cliffs above it? (This is often how the story is depicted in children's Bibles.) This parable makes much more sense in a Middle Eastern context.

In the sweltering Middle Eastern summer, the ground is baked hard. The significance of this is that during the summer time sand and rock could look very similar, the sand baked to the same density as the rock. The problems come in the autumn when there are regular flash floods. If the ground is packed hard, the water runs off it and, as it does, wears away that which is sand, leaving the firm rock secure. A house built on sand might look like it is built on firm foundations, only to be washed away when the storm comes.

This adds extra depth to Jesus' parable. Few people are stupid enough to build on shifting sand, but many are tempted to build on foundations that look firm only to discover later that they are eroded by the storms of life. What Jesus says here is that his words provide firm, tried and tested foundations – foundations that last and will not be eroded by even the fiercest storm of life.

Reflection by **Paula Gooder**

Proper 5

**Sunday between
5 & 11 June inclusive**
(if after Trinity Sunday)

Continuous:
Genesis 12.1-9
Psalm 33.1-12
Romans 4.13-end
Matthew 9.9-13,18-26

Genesis 12.1-9

'I will bless you ... so that you will be a blessing' (v.2)

In Genesis 11, after the tower of Babel episode, the Lord scattered the people over the face of all the earth (Genesis 11.9). The people had feared being spread abroad – would they be lost? In Genesis 12, we have the resounding answer: 'no', because in far-off Ur of the Chaldeans, God calls a family. But it is a family with no future: Sarai has no child. Terah sets out but stops en route. Things are at a standstill. Then God speaks and Abram listens. In the Bible, if people don't act on what they hear, they have not listened properly. Abram acts, and the story moves from creation myths to human saga with more rounded characters with whom we can identify as they try to be faithful to God.

Despite his lack of heirs, all the families of the earth will be blessed in Abram. Nothing is impossible with God, and promise is at the heart of God's ways with the world. If we despair because we can't see how God can work in our situation, we can be encouraged by the way God used Abram's unpromising family situation to bless not just him but the whole earth. So Abram moves, putting a human face on nomadic life and challenging the prevailing idea that gods were powerful only in their own territory. All the earth is God's.

How are you listening for God? Pray today for God to renew you in your weakness and make you a blessing to others.

Reflection by **Rosalind Brown**

Related:
Hosea 5.15 – 6.6
Psalm 50.7-15
Romans 4.13-end
Matthew 9.9-13,18-26

Proper 5

Hosea 5.15 – 6.6

'For I desire steadfast love and not sacrifice' (6.6)

Here, as in much of Hosea, we are in the territory of troubling imagery – a God who is presented as both perpetrator and liberator (6.1). Hosea talks almost as if God inflicts disasters on his people to teach them a lesson; this is the language of fear and manipulation rather than love and liberty.

The prophets who wrote 200 or so years later give a more measured account of God's wrath as expressing not so much the reactive jealous rage of a slighted husband, but rather a carefully calibrated punishment that reflects God's holiness, justice and 'otherness', meted out in perfect fairness to the different nations (e.g. Isaiah 51.17,22; Jeremiah 25.15). These later writings also explore the notion that suffering may not be neatly linked to human wrongdoing. Finally, in the 'servant songs' of Isaiah 42–53, a deep insight is expressed: God can sometimes be found in the midst of suffering, not apart from it.

This idea is developed in the New Testament (Luke 24.26; Acts 8.32-35), and appears to have played a significant part in Jesus' self-understanding. But he also took the earlier message of Hosea to his heart. Like Hosea, Jesus treats the judgement of God very seriously, but he doesn't talk of anger or wrath; instead he spells out what it would actually mean for people to return to the Lord (6.1). It's about an inner change of the moral compass, not a slavish adherence to religious practice, and Jesus quotes Hosea 6.6 twice as his authority on this point (Matthew 9.13; 12.7).

Reflection by **Joanna Collicutt**

Proper 5

Continuous:
Genesis 12.1-9
Psalm 33.1-12

Related:
Hosea 5.15 – 6.6
Psalm 50.7-15

Romans 4.13-end
Matthew 9.9-13,18-26

Romans 4.13-end

'God ... gives life to the dead and calls into existence the things that do not exist' (v.17)

Paul looks for images to describe the grace of God. It is like raising the dead, he says; it is like the creation of the world.

God's grace is more than we could have imagined – is it also more than we can believe? God gives us what we do not deserve – is that too good to be true? Paul bolsters our faith by pointing to creation and the resurrection of Christ.

God is the great giver, and his first and primordial gift is creation. Through and through, creation is a matter of grace. God did not create us because we deserved to be created. Before God made the world, there was no one to deserve anything.

If we want reassurance that God is gracious, we need therefore only turn to creation. Salvation burst upon the world ever anew with all the novelty of the big bang. It brings us up short, just like Paul's other example – the resurrection of Christ – overwhelmed the first apostles. That happy ending to the Easter story was for them a 'sudden and miraculous grace', to use a wonderful phrase from J. R. R. Tolkien. God's grace is sure, and yet it should never cease to amaze us.

Reflection by **Andrew Davison**

Matthew 9.9-13,18-26

Continuous:
Genesis 12.1-9
Psalm 33.1-12

Related:
Hosea 5.15 – 6.6
Psalm 50.7-15

Proper 5

Romans 4.13-end
Matthew 9.9-13,18-26

Matthew 9.9-13,18-26

'Take heart, daughter; your faith has made you well' (v.22)

This phrase used by Jesus is, ironically, one that is almost spell-like in its quality, rather like the favourite Swahili words *'Hakuna matata'* or 'every thing is going to be all right'. We like to be assured that everything is going to be well and that worries will fade away sooner rather than later. We are often dogged by worry and preoccupation with matters such as money, relationships, employment, health or similar. Jesus recognizes the deep worry in the woman who is bleeding (and therefore an outcast of society) but also the determination for something good to happen. She does not lose hope, but rather perseveres until she finds a way through her difficulties.

When she manages to make contact with Jesus, it is almost as if he himself has nothing to do with making her well, as he declares that her faith is the enzyme that bring to an end her ailments. It is clear then that Jesus is not in the business of casting quick spells to make people's problems disappear, even if his words have a haunting quality to them when read aloud liturgically. Rather, Jesus wants us to make some effort at helping ourselves, working out some method of improvement for difficulties that we face in our lives. But if we display that measure of faith, the promise is that we shall, by the grace of God, be made well and full of life again.

Reflection by **Christopher Woods**

Proper 6

**Sunday between
12 & 18 June inclusive**
(if after Trinity Sunday)

Continuous:
Genesis 18.1-15 [21.1-7]
Psalm 116.1,10-17*
Romans 5.1-8
Matthew 9.35 – 10.8 [9-23]

Genesis 18.1-15 [21.1-7]

'Is anything too wonderful for the Lord?' (18.14)

Rublev's famous icon of the Trinity starts from this visit of the three mysterious strangers to Abraham. While this is certainly reading Christian theology back into Genesis, there is undoubtedly something very odd about the syntax in this chapter when it talks about the three visitors. Verse 1 says that 'the Lord' appeared to Abraham, but that when he looked up, what he saw was 'three men standing near him' (18.1). He addresses them as 'My lord', in the singular and, later on, when Sarah laughs, it is again 'the Lord' (18.13) who queries her scorn. No wonder Rublev picked this up as an allusion to the God who is both three and one.

However, it is not just the peculiar alternations from singular to plural; there is also a theological impetus here. Abraham believes that he is the one offering hospitality to the visitors, but in fact, he is encountering the generosity of God. He and Sarah have reached the end of their hopes of having a child of their own, but God has not reached the end of what is possible for God.

Here is the God who brought creation out of nothing, life out of death, healing and transformation for all who gather at the hospitable table spread by the cross and resurrection. Don't laugh when this God offers the impossible.

Reflection by **Jane Williams**

Related:
Exodus 19.2-8*a*
Psalm 100
Romans 5.1-8
Matthew 9.35 – 10.8 [9-23]

Proper 6

Exodus 19.2-8*a*

*'If you ... keep my covenant,
you shall be my treasured possession' (v.5)*

I was very nervous when I proposed marriage to my wife. What if she should say 'no'? And yet, I had to take that step for anything to happen. Only if we make ourselves vulnerable in our relationships and open ourselves to rejection and hurt can love flourish and grow.

Having shown his power and his love by bringing the people of Israel out of Egypt, God now makes himself vulnerable to them by offering them a covenant. 'Will you be my people?' he asks, touchingly. It is all the more affecting by virtue of the fearsome way in which he makes himself known following their acceptance, with thunder, lightning, trumpet blasts, fire and smoke (vv. 16-19).

The contrast between God the lover asking for the hand of his beloved in today's reading and the mystery and terrifying power of the same God we see in the rest of the chapter could not be more striking. He could have simply imposed himself, but despite his awesome power, God will never impose: he loves and respects those whom he has created too much.

Here is the astonishing wonder, that the God who flung stars into space asks for your hand and mine in covenant love.

Reflection by **John Inge**

Proper 6

Continuous:
Genesis 18.1-15 [21.1-7]
Psalm 116.1,10-17*

Related:
Exodus 19.2-8a
Psalm 100

Romans 5.1-8
Matthew 9.35 – 10.8 [9-23]

Romans 5.1-8

*'God proves his love for us in that while we still
were sinners Christ died for us' (v.8)*

Paul's task in the first few chapters of the Epistle to the Romans has been to strip away every reason for human self-confidence before God: confidence in our own works, in our own goodness, in the power of the law to make us just. Then came his message about the grace of God, and a right standing before him that rests on Christ and is his gift. With that in place, Paul now returns to the topic of confidence. He now offers his readers a different sort of confidence before God and before the world. It is as sturdy as their prior self-confidence was flimsy.

Our confidence rests on what God has given us. Since it rests on God and not on ourselves, our confidence can be as secure as the grace of God is lavish.

Where we once had a confidence based on works, we now have a confidence based on faith. That brings us back to the role faith plays. Our confidence is not confidence in the strength of our own faith but confidence in the strength of the one in whom our faith is placed. We may have a confidence based on faith – but it is not confidence in our own faith; it is confidence in the faithfulness of God.

Reflection by **Andrew Davison**

Continuous:
Genesis 18.1-15 [21.1-7]
Psalm 116.1,10-17*
      Romans 5.1-8

Related:
Exodus 19.2-8*a*
Psalm 100

Proper 6

Matthew 9.35 – 10.8 [9-23]

Matthew 9.35 – 10.8 [9-23]

'These twelve Jesus sent out ...' (10.5)

This passage is packed with the principles of Christian mission. There's the starting place of prayer (9.38), and of call and equipping (10.1). There's the clarity of focus: the disciples know to whom they are sent (10.5,6). The mission is to be conducted both in word and in deed (10.7,8). And it's freely given – no fees!

Matthew suggests, through the coupling of the names, that they are sent out two by two – Luke's account of the sending of the 72 endorses this practice (Luke 10.1). As well as the practical companionship this provides, it also serves as a demonstration of the Spirit's presence in the Body of Christ. 'For where two or three are gathered in my name, I am there among them' (Matthew 18.20). Those whom they meet taste something of the reality of *koinonia*, 'participation in the Spirit'. They are invited in to something. The goal of the mission is not a cerebral assent to dogma but participation in a new life.

But this mini-community is not to be a ghetto. When they arrive in a village, they are to find a way of locking their little community onto someone else's (10.11). That gives the possibility of real communication, what postmodernists call 'flow'. It also means that the missioners are dependent upon those to whom they are sent. There is mutuality, a common sharing. No missionary compounds here!

Reflection by **Sue Hope**

Proper 7

Sunday between
19 & 25 June inclusive
(if after Trinity Sunday)

Continuous:
Genesis 21.8-21
Psalm 86.1-10,16-17*
Romans 6.1b-11
Matthew 10.24-39

Genesis 21.8-21

'Do not be afraid' (v.17)

Red letter day. For a few brief verses, Sarah has been happy (Genesis 21.1-8). It doesn't last, of course; happiness doesn't seem to be a natural condition for Sarah. Although she now has all she thought she wanted, and is assured that her son is upheld by God's promise, yet she cannot bear to share anything, not even happiness, with another. Apparently, she still doesn't trust God; she still feels she has to take things into her own hands, however disastrously it went the last time she did that.

It is, in a way, consoling to see this massively dysfunctional family at the heart of God's action. Abraham is a hero of faith, but he still allows his wife to drive him to an action he knows to be wrong. Neither he nor Sarah seems to think at all about what Isaac will feel as his brother and playfellow is taken away. God does not need perfect people with whom to work. Our very imperfections emphasize the simple truth that we are wholly dependent upon God, justified by God's faithfulness, not by our own actions.

As Abraham and Sarah squabble over how to make the faithful God keep his promises, Hagar plumbs the depths of that faithfulness. Her son grows up in the wilderness, given all that he needs by the hand of God, sheltered from human cruelty and faithlessness.

Reflection by **Jane Williams**

Related:
Jeremiah 20.7-13

Psalm 69.8-11[12-17]18-20*
Romans 6.1b-11
Matthew 10.24-39

Jeremiah 20.7-13

'I have become a laughing-stock all day long' (v.7)

These powerful verses offer us a passage of intense poignancy. In earliers chapters of Jeremiah, we read of the prophet's courage and resilient determination; nothing then can quite prepare us for the shock of this haunting passage. This is a soul in the very depths of despair: 'You have duped me, Lord, and I have been your dupe ...'

God is nowhere to be found. He is appallingly absent. It is a cry of dereliction from the depths of Jeremiah's being. For a moment, we are left to wonder what will become of this once audacious but now broken man.

His courage wells up. He recalls that trying not to speak of the things of God was impossible; it was like a fire burning in his heart. And, as soon as he remembers this inner reality, he calls out, 'But the Lord is with me like a dread warrior' (v.11), and soon he is singing out the praises of God (only to succumb almost immediately to spiritual anguish in the following verses: 'Cursed be the day on which I was born!', v.14).

There are some biblical passages where the very core of our humanity is exposed, our noblest and our most fragile self has nowhere left to hide. We are alone.

Words stop. All we can do is to wait in that place where certainty and uncertainty are one, and in our desolation call upon God for mercy.

Reflection by **Christopher Herbert**

Proper 7

Continuous: *Related:*
Genesis 21.8-21   Jeremiah 20.7-13
Psalm 86.1-10,16-17*   Psalm 69.8-11[12-17]18-20*
Romans 6.1*b*-11
Matthew 10.24-39

Romans 6.1*b*-11

'... dead to sin and alive to God in Christ Jesus' (v.11)

If you have ever witnessed an adult baptism by total immersion, you will know that wonderful moment when the nervous-looking candidate is plunged underwater. They hold their breath, and sometimes their nose, and for a moment they are submerged – almost lifeless – until the minister pulls them up out of the water – and they gasp for breath – like a newborn baby. Amid the spluttering and water, eyes open as if for the first time, and joy fills the face of the one who radiates with new life.

Most of us have not lived lives of extremes, as Paul did. Maybe for some of us our faith journey seems to us to be so unspectacular that to talk of being dead and alive seems rather extreme. But Paul invites us into a liberating story where our baptism is not something that happened many years ago, but can be a new experience every day as we wash ourselves in the waters of the new life that Jesus has given us as much a share of as he did to Paul. This prayer from *Common Worship* sums up the liberating joy which Paul longs for us all to bathe in:

We bless you for your new creation, brought to birth by water
and the Spirit, and for your grace bestowed upon us your
children, washing away our sins.
May your holy and life-giving Spirit move upon these waters.
Restore through them the beauty of your creation, and bring
those who are baptized to new birth in the family of your Church.
Drown sin in the waters of judgement, anoint your children
with power from on high, and make them one with Christ
in the freedom of your kingdom. For all might, majesty,
dominion and power are yours, now and for ever.

Reflection by **Tim Sledge**

Continuous:
Genesis 21.8-21
Psalm 86.1-10,16-17*

Related:
Jeremiah 20.7-13
Psalm 69.8-11[12-17]18-20*

Proper 7

Romans 6.1b-11
Matthew 10.24-39

Matthew 10.24-39

'... what you hear whispered, proclaim from the housetops'
(v.27)

It is easy to slip into assuming that what happens to others can't happen to us. It is fascinating to watch the media, in the days following tragedies, searching frantically for explanations of why something happened. If they find one, we breathe a collective sigh of relief. If we can point to an explanation of why something happened, it becomes easier to believe it won't happen to us.

In Matthew 10.24-28, Jesus makes very clear that the disciples should not for a moment imagine that they will escape the abuse that he has received. He came full of compassion for those around him; he healed them; listened to them; proclaimed the good news of the kingdom and ultimately died for them – and they called him the devil ('Beelzebul' in verse 25 was a name used for the devil).

The disciples, Jesus declares, when faced with the same challenge will fare no better. If this is what happened to Jesus, the disciples can expect it to happen to them to. By extension, if it happens to the disciples, we can expect to be treated in the same way too.

The importance of this is that we should not allow fear of what could happen – what people might say or do – to constrict us. If they are going to act like this anyway, we might as well proclaim our good news from the rooftops and at the top of our lungs!

Reflection by **Paula Gooder**

**Sunday between
26 June & 2 July inclusive**

Continuous:
Genesis 22.1-14
Psalm 13
Romans 6.12-end
Matthew 10.40-end

Genesis 22.1-14

'God himself will provide the lamb' (v.8)

The narrative of the sacrifice of Isaac is often called a 'type' of the atonement. Here we see a father, prepared to offer up his son, without question, although everything he is and hopes for depends upon this son, and everything he knows or feels about God is bound up with the child.

There are echoes here that are profoundly helpful in our understanding of the way of the cross, particularly if we see Jesus not only as God, but also as both Abraham and Isaac. Jesus goes to the cross in obedience, although all he was sent to be and to do is at stake, although it makes no apparent sense, although he longs to have misunderstood what is required. However, because Jesus is also God, he is himself the sacrifice that God provides, he is both priest and victim, both the one who obeys and the one who commands. There is no gap between what the Son wills and what the Father wills here, no merciless Father and broken Son, only the costly and faithful action of God.

What of this episode's place in Abraham's own story? Does Abraham get ready to sacrifice Isaac, believing that, because of the way he has treated Hagar and Ishmael, he deserves to lose this son, too? If so, he meets what we meet when we approach the cross: the God who provides from his own mercy all that we need to be forgiven and restored.

Reflection by **Jane Williams**

Related:
Jeremiah 28.5-9
Psalm 89.1-4,15-18*
Romans 6.12-end
Matthew 10.40-end

Jeremiah 28.5-9

'As for the prophet who prophesies peace ...' (v.9)

The meaning of Hananiah's name – 'Yahweh is gracious' – perhaps gives an indication of the kind of prophetic utterances he is going to be making. He is a prophet of peace who stands in contrast to Jeremiah, the prophet of doom. The two men represent contrasting futures for Judah in the short term. Hananiah predicts salvation within two years with everyone back home and Babylon broken. Jeremiah maintains his message of judgement, placing himself in the line of prophets who bring hard truths to the people. Oh that it would all be over quickly ... but that is not going to be the case. After all, what has changed? What about the covenant and its requirements, which have been flouted? Hananiah wishes to bring a message of hope and reassurance – Yahweh is gracious – but his timing is all wrong. That is not God's truth for the people at this moment, as the passage of time will show.

It is easy to say the things that people want to hear, especially when it is likely to cheer them up. If they like the message, they will like the messenger. But the Christian prophetic tradition is about discerning and speaking God's word, regardless of how it will be received. Only the truth, be it challenging or comforting, has the power to bring about the transformation that God requires.

Reflection by **Helen Orchard**

Proper 8

Continuous:
Genesis 22.1-14
Psalm 13

Related:
Jeremiah 28.5-9
Psalm 89.1-4,15-18*

Romans 6.12-end
Matthew 10.40-end

Romans 6.12-end

'... the free gift of God is eternal life in Christ Jesus our Lord' (v.23)

Many people regard the word 'sin' as 'churchy'. While it is certainly an important word for Christians (because it is through the forgiveness of sin that humans are clothed with the mantle of Christ-likeness), it is not a particularly accessible term for those who are not regular churchgoers.

At the most fundamental, sin can be explained as the breaking of a community's moral code. This kind of moral code is important for the healthy flow of communication, respect and progress towards a goal. That is why most businesses and corporate organizations will spend time investing in ethical codes of conduct, so that everyone who belongs to the community has a common standard of 'morality' to follow. In the contemporary sense, 'sin' could be understood as breaking the rules of workplace ethics, or breaching the code of conduct. Often in the workplace, to 'come clean', or to admit a fault, will allow some compassion from senior managers and so avoid sanction. However, a repeated offence, or one without any remorse, is likely to result in dismissal.

With God, however, it is different. Sin is more than just the breaking of a code of morality; it is the removal of trust and can be the cause of great hurt. Forgiveness is a renewable and unrestricted gift. Sin is forgiven each time remorse is shown. That is why sin is often seen as a churchy or religious word. Because the freedom from sin is something that no corporate organization can offer – only God.

Reflection by **Christopher Woods**

Continuous:
Genesis 22.1-14
Psalm 13

Related:
Jeremiah 28.5-9
Psalm 89.1-4,15-18*

Proper 8

Romans 6.12-end
Matthew 10.40-end

Matthew 10.40-end

'... truly I tell you, none of these will lose their reward' (v.42)

It is not attractive to contemplate reward in the framework of religious faith. Much of that difficulty comes from how we look at rewards – it is normally a 'prize' or a financial benefit for having achieved a task that has demanded much effort, normally in the world of showbusiness or as the result of someone's attractive or popular personality. In many ways this is – accurately – a most unattractive definition of reward.

Fortunately this is precisely not the kind of meaning that is meant by Jesus when 'reward' is the translation of the Greek. In this context, reward is fundamentally the fulfilling of the promise of God, the keeping of his covenant with his people and the manifestation of his mercy and kindness. It is hard at first to equate 'reward' with a recognition of how wide God's mercy really is.

As today's reading suggests, minimal hospitality, generosity and compassion on our part is enough for God to keep his faithful promise to us. God never breaks a promise or destroys the covenant that he has made with us through the person of Christ, and so we should be affirmed in the knowledge that even the little that we do to help others see the faintest of glimpses of God in the thick dark patches is more than a sign of his in-breaking kingdom of love and peace.

Reflection by **Christopher Woods**

Proper 9

**Sunday between
3 & 9 July inclusive**

Continuous:
Genesis 24.34-38,42-49,58-67
Psalm 45.10-17
or Canticle: Song of Solomon 2.8-13
Romans 7.15-25*a*
Matthew 11.16-19,25-30

Genesis 24.34-38,42-49,58-67

*'... you shall go to my father's house, to my kindred,
and get a wife for my son' (v.40)*

Behind the events of the story lies the faith of Abraham, forged in his call to leave his kindred, rekindled in the conception of Isaac in old age, refined in the encounter on Mount Moriah. Abraham's long journey is one of close friendship with God, one in which his whole household and his descendants share. Faith and friendship come together in the final great crisis of Abraham's life: finding a wife for Isaac and the securing of the next generation of God's people.

This faith and this friendship are enough to overcome practical difficulties and scepticism. They create the right conditions for synchronicity: the coming together of events in remarkable ways, in which God's people discern God's guidance and blessing. The synchronicity here is so remarkable and such an important part of the founding of God's people that the storytellers of Genesis recount the whole tale twice – first in the verses before today's reading and then again to Laban and his family.

All the way through the stories of the patriarchs, the identity and faith of the mother as well as the father is emphasized. Here Rebecca is shown to be a suitable wife for Isaac through her hospitality and graciousness to a stranger, through her faith, through her courage and trust, and finally through her giving of herself to Isaac.

Reflection by **Steven Croft**

Zechariah 9.9-12
Psalm 145.8-15
Romans 7.15-25a
Matthew 11.16-19,25-30

Proper 9

Zechariah 9.9-12

'Lo, your king comes to you; triumphant and victorious is he'
(v.9)

For Christians, the centre of today's passage is the prophecy of the victorious king coming into the holy city. This passage has coloured the Gospel accounts of Palm Sunday when Jesus entered Jerusalem on a donkey before his passion. The 'colt, the foal of a donkey' is not a second beast as Matthew's Gospel seems to understand it (Matthew 21.7) but a poetic phrase which could be rendered as: 'He's on a donkey, yes the foal of a donkey!'.

This victorious king is reminiscent of royal figures in the Psalms, godly rulers who emerge after trials and defeat to rule God's people in humility (Psalm 2.6-7; 110). The humiliation of the Son of God occurs after his victorious entry, not before, but it leads to the final victory of life over death. In its context the prophet promises that God's appointed ruler will be the bringer of peace, not only to Israel but also to the nations that have oppressed and made war against her.

The hint in both the original prophecy and the Christian interpretation of it is that God's greatest victory is not vengeance, but mercy. He comes to us as he came to the newly restored Jerusalem in the humility that rebukes our pride and sin. The challenge to us is to be humble enough to join him on the road to peace.

Reflection by **Angela Tilby**

Proper 9

Continuous:
Genesis 24.34-38,42-49,58-67
Psalm 45.10-17 *or Canticle:*
Song of Solomon 2.8-13
Romans 7.15-25*a*
Matthew 11.16-19,25-30

Related:
Zechariah 9.9-12
Psalm 145.8-15

Romans 7.15-25*a*

'For I do not do the good I want, but the evil I do not want is what I do' (v.19)

Sin is a strange kind of separation from ourselves. We find goodness compelling and yet we choose to act otherwise. We want to do what is right, and do not do it. Since at least the time of Socrates, human beings have recognized that evil is a sort of madness. To do what we do not want to do is insanity.

God rescues us from this malady in Jesus Christ. Viewed from the perspective of eternity, this is a done deal. Viewed from within time, there is still a transformation to undergo for each one of us. The tradition has spoken of this as an 'education of desire'. We have still to learn to see, understand and desire clearly and rightly. This is part of our return to God, who is the truest object of our desire.

St Augustine describes it as coming home to ourselves: God was with us in all our foolishness; it was we who strayed from ourselves. God's 'service is perfect freedom' because he truly wishes our best good. In contrast, serving ourselves can be slavery, since we often stray from our own best interests. God's will is not divided, although ours can be. Return to God and you return to yourself.

Reflection by **Andrew Davison**

Continuous:
Genesis 24.34-38,42-49,58-67
Psalm 45.10-17 *or Canticle:*
Song of Solomon 2.8-13

Related:
Zechariah 9.9-12
Psalm 145.8-15

Proper 9

Romans 7.15-25*a*
Matthew 11.16-19,25-30

Matthew 11.16-19,25-30

'We played the flute for you, and you did not dance' (v.17)

It is tempting to subtitle verses 16-19: 'some people are never happy'. In this passage Jesus pinpoints with characteristically uncomfortable accuracy a human tendency that we must all recognize: that tendency to grumble and groan on the sidelines rather than to join in with joy and delight.

Jesus' comment about his generation being like children in a market-place calling to each other (v.16) is thought by many scholars to be an allusion to the vision of hope in Zechariah 8.4-5, which presents a vision of the old and young alike being in the market square, the old with a staff to mark respect and the children playing together. In Matthew the children aren't playing; they are simply sitting there grumbling.

In other words, the day of rejoicing has come. John came to point the way to the glorious new future. Jesus, the Messiah, is here, but his generation, rather than getting up and celebrating, sat around complaining that others wouldn't do as they were told – wouldn't dance when the music played nor mourn when they wailed. Their reproach didn't end there: John was criticized for eating and drinking too little and Jesus for eating and drinking too much (vv.18-19).

It is all too easy to miss the good news of the kingdom, not because it is missing but because we are too busy carping and complaining to see it. Such attitudes are not restricted to Jesus' generation.

Reflection by **Paula Gooder**

Proper 10

**Sunday between
10 & 16 July inclusive**

Continuous:
Genesis 25.19-end
Psalm 119.105-112
Romans 8.1-11
Matthew 13.1-9,18-23

Genesis 25.19-end

'The children struggled together within her' (v.22)

Abraham blessed his son Isaac, but that blessing does not mean that life is a bed of roses for the family who are to grow into the people of God. Despite Abraham's blessing and despite the faith they share, the way ahead is difficult. The pains, thorns and thistles described in the fallen world of Genesis 3 affect even those who are blessed by God. Progress for God's people is difficult and takes place over generations not days.

Rebecca and Isaac are together for 20 years before Rebecca conceives. Perseverance and prayer are needed. The pregnancy and birth of the twins, Esau and Jacob, are difficult, with conflict and rivalry even in the womb. Rebecca despairs of life itself. The two brothers are radically different by nature, temperament and instinct. The family itself is divided with the mother siding with one son and the father with another. The birthright and blessing come to Jacob, father of the twelve tribes of Israel, but only through cunning and deceit.

In our Christian life today, it is important from time to time to remember that this fallen world is full of thistles, thorns and pain, even now. The progress of God's kingdom is often slow. For Rebecca, for the early Christians and for us, it is through many tribulations that we must enter the kingdom of God (Acts 14.22).

Reflection by **Steven Croft**

Related:
Isaiah 55.10-13
Psalm 65.[1-7]8-13*
Romans 8.1-11
Matthew 13.1-9,18-23

Isaiah 55.10-13

'... an everlasting sign that shall not be cut off' (v.13)

'I came that they may have life, and have it abundantly' (John 10.10). John's Gospel is pregnant with the possibility of abundant life, and, almost from the outset of his Gospel, new disciples are inducted into the secrets of the kingdom that will bring a life of abundance that can barely be dreamed of. It is implied in the miracle at Cana, revealed to the woman at the well, and preached to Nicodemus.

Yet this is no new gospel. It is one that reaches back to the iconic and halcyon imagery to be found in the Old Testament, such as we find in Isaiah. The abundance of nature will testify to the glory of God; a created and redeemed world will speak of the glory of God revealed in the world around us. For an arable people who constantly lived between the extremes of fertility and famine, and between the wilderness of the desert and the abundance of the Promised Land, such imagery would speak powerfully. Yet here Isaiah goes one step further. The cypress will replace the thorn, and myrtle the brier (v.13).

This is why the covenant with God is so vital to Isaiah's audience – and to us today. Obedience and faithfulness will always yield a reward of plenty. The word of God will accomplish its task; it will never return to God empty. Our task, therefore, is to forsake our ways for his – to seek the Lord while he may be found, and call upon him while he is near. This is our vocation. Through being both called and found, we are then able to be sent out in joy and led back in peace.

Reflection by **Martyn Percy**

Proper 10

Continuous:
Genesis 25.19-end
Psalm 119.105-112

Related:
Isaiah 55.10-13
Psalm 65.[1-7]8-13*

Romans 8.1-11
Matthew 13.1-9,18-23

Romans 8.1-11

'… you are not in the flesh; you are in the Spirit' (v.9)

Spirit and flesh are everywhere in Paul. Wherever they turn up, they are usually ciphers for good and evil. To live according to the flesh is to live selfishly and in rebellion from God; to live according to the Spirit is to live aligned with God and for his sake. That does not make flesh evil in itself – only when pursued as a misguided ultimate goal.

Paul has not succumbed to the gnostic heresy attacked elsewhere in the New Testament, with its miserable teaching that the body and physical things are evil. Physical life can be lived God's way, as Christ demonstrated. That makes it 'spiritual' in Paul's terminology. This is exactly what we will read in next Sunday's continuation of Romans 8, when Paul urges us to hope for the redemption of our bodies, not their abolition. For that matter, spiritual things can be 'fleshy' when they stand against God. (In 2 Corinthians 7.1, Paul writes that the spirit as well as the flesh can be 'defiled'.)

Do not set your mind on the things of the flesh, urges Paul, but on the things of the Spirit. This is not an injunction to ignore flesh and blood, but rather to see it 'spiritually', from God's perspective, as the bearer of Spirit. Far from being an injunction to ignore flesh and blood, it urges us to respond practically, following God's lead: though all Spirit, he came to the relief of flesh and blood, as flesh and blood.

Reflection by **Andrew Davison**

Continuous:
Genesis 25.19-end
Psalm 119.105-112

Related:
Isaiah 55.10-13
Psalm 65.[1-7]8-13*

Romans 8.1-11
Matthew 13.1-9,18-23

Matthew 13.1-9,18-23

'A sower went out to sow' (v.3)

The parable of the sower is in part a challenge to the crowds to provoke them to thought and help them ponder what it means to follow Christ. There are clues here about the commitment and perseverance required to be a disciple and about the fruit that is evidence of a transformed life.

But the parable is also instruction to the disciples. For every disciple will share in sowing the seed of the word of God. For that reason, every disciple needs some understanding of what happens when the word is sown.

Not every seed bears fruit. Some is snatched away. Note another walk-on part for the evil one. Some takes root, but never matures. New believers must be prepared for the times of trial that will come. Some seed begins to grow, but riches and the lure of wealth choke the new life. New believers must be well taught and pastored as the seed grows. And some bears fruit in abundance.

The one who sows the seed must be prepared for all of this. It is foolish to sow the seed and not be alert to the care of the crop as that seed begins to grow. There is life and creativity in the word, the message that is sown.

Where are you sowing the word of life today, this month and this year? Are you sowing in abundance?

Reflection by **Steven Croft**

Proper 11

**Sunday between
17 & 23 July inclusive**

Continuous:
Genesis 28.10-19a
Psalm 139.1-11,23,24*
Romans 8.12-25
Matthew 13.24-30,36-43

Genesis 28.10-19a

'All the families of the earth shall be blessed in you' (v.14)

The deep bitterness and long rivalry in the family home of Isaac drive both Jacob and Esau away in the end. Jacob is sent back to Paddan-aram, following in the footsteps of Abraham's faithful servant and bearing his father's blessing.

Here, at this low point in the story, Jacob the deceiver encounters the living God in his dream at Bethel. Jacob sees in his dream that a deeper spiritual reality lies beneath the physical world we inhabit. Like many who have encountered God since, Jacob is alone, at a low point in his life, and on a journey. In a profound moment of encounter and reality, the faith of his fathers becomes his own faith. The call to his fathers becomes his own call.

The Lord's promise to Jacob echoes the promise to Abraham (compare Genesis 12.3 with 28.14). We see here clearly the missionary purpose of the God of Abraham: in calling one family and nation, the Lord is seeking to bless every family and nation.

God's promise to Jacob, like his promise to Abraham, demands a response of faith. Jacob's faith is shown in his establishing a pillar and an offering and a renaming of the place, later to become a great shrine for the northern kingdom.

What promises does God make to us today and how do we respond?

Reflection by **Steven Croft**

Related:
Wisdom of Solomon 12.13,16-19
or **Isaiah 44.6-8**
Psalm 86.11-17
Romans 8.12-25
Matthew 13.24-30,36-43

Isaiah 44.6-8

'There is no other rock; I know not one' (v.8)

What was an idol? When all's said and done, it was a lump of metal with an extremely clever marketing plan.

Come to that, so is a diamond ring.

These verses in Isaiah are in the middle of a devastating satire on the uselessness of idols. A craftsman labours to create an idol, decorates it and treasures it. Then he prays to it and feels strangely warm. (Well of course he does – he's been next to a furnace all day, 44.16-17.) Will that idol help when he is desperate in grief or scared about the future? Not one jot.

Come to that, neither will a diamond ring.

In contrast, Isaiah puts a series of questions in the mouth of God. They are questions about all the things idols and jewellery can never help with.

This is the God who needed no craftsman to make him because he was before time and will be after time (v.6). This is the God into whose hands we can confidently entrust our future, because he knows it already (v.7). This is the God on whom we can depend in our times of greatest anxiety, because he is changeless (v.8).

Under the onslaught of marketing for things that sparkle and bleep and speed and entertain, it's worth asking whether any of these things can be of use to us when we face the most important questions of life and death. I know not one.

Reflection by **Peter Graystone**

Proper 11	*Continuous:*	*Related:*
	Genesis 28.10-19*a*	Wisdom of Solomon 12.13, 16-19 *or* Isaiah 44.6-8
	Psalm 139.1-11,23,24*	Psalm 86.11-17

Romans 8.12-25

Matthew 13.24-30,36-43

Romans 8.12-25

'When we cry, "Abba! Father!" it is ... [the] Spirit bearing witness ... that we are ... joint heirs with Christ' (vv.15-17)

Today we read another of Paul's favourite linkages: between freedom and being children of God (and therefore Christ's brothers and sisters). Adoption is a central image of salvation for Paul. It deserves an honoured place alongside his language of justification, something warm and engaging alongside that other, more abstract, less emotionally charged, legal image.

Paul is rarely more explicitly Trinitarian than he is in this passage. When we call out to God as *Father*, then the *Spirit* is testifying to us that we are 'joint heirs' (and therefore, brothers and sisters) of *Christ*. All this happens when we pray.

One of the most significant developments in theological thinking about the Trinity in the past decade or two has been to take this point seriously. Christians in the Early Church, or today for that matter, do not come to faith in God as One-in-Three simply through abstract thought about divinity, or even through careful scholarship of texts. Also vital is the Christian experience of prayer, with its Trinitarian shape. We confess Father, Son and Holy Spirit not only because of the Bible, St Athanasius, or the Nicene Creed, but also because of the day-by-day privilege and experience of praying to the Father, through the Son and in the power of the Holy Spirit.

There is one to whom we pray, and one who prays in us, and one who has opened the way for us to pray, and these Three are One.

Reflection by **Andrew Davison**

Continuous:
Genesis 28.10-19*a*

Psalm 139.1-11,23,24*

Related:
Wisdom of Solomon 12.13,
16-19 *or* Isaiah 44.6-8
Psalm 86.11-17
Romans 8.12-25
Matthew 13.24-30,36-43

Proper 11

Matthew 13.24-30,36-43

'... an enemy came and sowed weeds among the wheat'
(v.25)

Have you ever read the Sunday newspaper and been so disturbed by all the mess you've seen there that you've wished God would step in and sort things out once and for all? It's entirely understandable. It's what the slaves in today's parable want to happen. 'Let's just pull up all the weeds.'

However, God plays a longer game. For one thing, premature judgement removes any chance of redemption. In any case, this isn't a world you can 'fix' – it's a field to work in until harvest time, the end of time, the judgement time. Moreover, said Jesus, uproot the weeds and you'll uproot the wheat as well. Ah! That's a tricky point. The distinction between good and bad is rather more complex than we'd like. It seems to run through the middle of each of us – our own lives are a confusing mixture of wheat and weeds.

Wouldn't it be better to leave the outcome to God? Wouldn't it be better to carry on sowing good deeds day by day? Wouldn't it be better not to judge others, nor volunteer to tear up their weeds? (I fear I might not come out of such 'reciprocal weeding' too well.) If God can be patient with a world in such open rebellion against God's love, perhaps I can manage to be a smidgen more patient too.

Reflection by **John Pritchard**

Proper 12

**Sunday between
24 & 30 July inclusive**

Continuous:
Genesis 29.15-28
Psalm 105.1-11,45b* *or* Psalm 128
Romans 8.26-end
Matthew 13.31-33,44-52

Genesis 29.15-28

'Why then have you deceived me?' (v.25)

There is a strong theme in Scripture of the sins of one generation being passed on to the next. It's a theme that resonates with modern understandings of psychology. Jacob the trickster now reaps what he has sown. The one who has deceived his father and brother now encounters greedy uncle Laban, who recognizes profit and free labour when he sees it.

Jacob himself is painted now as reformed and sincere. His love for Rachel is genuine, and the seven years he serves for her seem but a few days. Yet Laban substitutes his elder daughter Leah for Rachel just as his sister Rebecca had substituted Jacob for Esau. Jacob is deceived but receives the gift of Rachel also. Not surprisingly, he loves one of his wives more than the other (Genesis 29.30).

So the intense rivalry is passed from one generation to another. Laban sets up the situation where his own daughters, Leah and Rachel are in competition for the affections of a single husband. This, in turn, creates the rivalry and jealousy between the twelve sons of Jacob that will result in further evil in the next generation and which, in turn, will only be overcome by Joseph's extraordinary wisdom and willingness to forgive.

A moment to reflect today, then, on the deep patterns in our own families and what we are called to do to change them in our own generation.

Reflection by **Steven Croft**

Related:
1 Kings 3.5-12
Psalm 119.129-136
Romans 8.26-end
Matthew 13.31-33,44-52

Proper 12

1 Kings 3.5-12

'Give your servant therefore an understanding mind' (v.9)

Solomon got away to a fast start. He married sensibly (securing peace on his southern border); he made good appointments; and he started building the temple that his father had never quite managed. He had a bit of a dip by sacrificing to local deities (1 Kings 3.3), but he got top marks when the Lord offered him whatever he wanted and he asked for wisdom – 'an understanding mind ... able to discern between good and evil' (v.9) – rather than wealth or long life. He then goes on to demonstrate that wisdom in the strange case of the two prostitutes and the disputed maternity of the surviving child (1 Kings 3.16-28).

What Solomon realized is that wisdom is priceless. It helped, of course, that because he'd answered the question well, God then gave him as much wealth as he could cope with. Nevertheless, he knew that he couldn't hope to hold down his job without the gift of wisdom. If only we could all make a similar choice and realize that 'all that glisters is not gold'! Greater wealth simply doesn't give greater happiness: it's proven both by research and by hard personal experience.

Real gold lies in recognizing that every day we will be faced with both good and evil – and having the wisdom to know the difference.

Reflection by **John Pritchard**

Proper 12

Continuous:
Genesis 29.15-28
Psalm 105.1-11,45b*
or Psalm 128

Related:
1 Kings 3.5-12
Psalm 119.129-136

Romans 8.26-end
Matthew 13.31-33,44-52

Romans 8.26-end

'… we are more than conquerors through him who loved us'
(v.37)

Some of Paul's most poetic writing comes in the form of lists. There is one earlier in this Letter, in Romans 5: 'suffering produces endurance, and endurance produces character, and character produces hope, and hope does not disappoint us' (Romans 5.3-5). That theme of triumph in the face of adversity often catches Paul at his most lyrical, as in 2 Corinthians 6.4-10: 'calamities, beatings … riots, labours … honour and dishonour … punished, and yet not killed … having nothing, and yet possessing everything'. It is also the theme of the list in our passage today. Nothing can separate us from the love of God in Christ Jesus our Lord: not 'hardship, or distress, or persecution, or famine, or nakedness, or peril, or sword' (v.35).

Like the other lists, it mentions both triumph and adversity, and teaches that the first is won in the face of the second. None of the things he lists can separate us from God, and indeed it is often in these things 'hardship … distress … or peril' that we meet him, since this is how God came to meet us.

God 'did not withhold his own Son' (v.32), nor withhold hardship from him, nor distress or peril. He did not withhold him then, and he does not withhold fellowship with him now, especially not to those who tread Christ's way of the cross.

Reflection by **Andrew Davison**

Continuous:
Genesis 29.15-28
Psalm 105.1-11,45b*
or Psalm 128

Related:
1 Kings 3.5-12
Psalm 119.129-136

Romans 8.26-end
Matthew 13.31-33,44-52

Matthew 13.31-33,44-52

'... one pearl of great value' (v.46)

The parables of the hidden treasure and the pearl of great price are a matching set. Together they describe the mystery that some people stumble on the kingdom almost by accident when they are looking for something else. Others search diligently all their lives and in the end find what they are looking for. But when you find the kingdom – the reign of God on earth of justice, peace and presence – whether by accident or design, the response is exactly the same. You know this is what you have been searching for all your life. You know this is worth everything. And so you go and sell everything you have and buy the field or the pearl.

Sometimes people read these parables as if they are about sacrifice. The emphasis is placed on the words 'sells all that he has' (v.44). We focus on what we might be called to give up to discover the kingdom and follow God's call. But that's not the point at all. The parables are about value not sacrifice. Is the man digging the field richer at the beginning or at the end of the story? Is the merchant better off after he sells everything or before?

When Paul writes of the surpassing value of knowing Christ Jesus my Lord, he is not exaggerating (Philippians 3.8). Knowing God in Jesus Christ and discovering the kingdom is the greatest treasure this world affords and lasts into the next. How does the value of the kingdom affect our values in this world?

Reflection by **Steven Croft**

Proper 13

Sunday between
31 July & **6 August inclusive**

Continuous:
Genesis 32.22-31
Psalm 17.1-7,16*
Romans 9.1-5
Matthew 14.13-21

Genesis 32.22-31

'And there he blessed him' (v.29)

During his exile Jacob has learnt self-discipline. Now he learns fear. He is coming to the territory controlled by Esau and realizes that he will either have to fight or make peace with the brother he has cheated. He has no resources to fight; making peace is the only option. So he sends extravagant presents to Esau, hoping that his brother will refrain from revenge. Alone at night 'a man wrestles with him until daybreak' (v.24). Jacob's inner struggle is worked out in the encounter with the mysterious stranger. Jacob wrestles alone with his past and his future; with his treachery and with the promise of God; with his sin against his brother and with the mercy that God offers him.

The fight has a double conclusion: Jacob wins the struggle, but he is injured. He is given a new name, Israel, signifying his destiny, but in spite of trying he cannot force a name out of his opponent.

This passage yields profound insight into our relationship with God. It shows us that God takes us on as we are, but does not leave us unchanged. God struggles with the flaws of our nature; we struggle with the contradictions of our experience. God want us to be healed, but we need to be humbled. The blessing that Jacob receives is the blessing of integrity. Mysterious though it is, it is our wounds that make us whole.

Reflection by **Angela Tilby**

Related:
Isaiah 55.1-5
Psalm 145.8-9,15-22*
Romans 9.1-5
Matthew 14.13-21

Proper 13

Isaiah 55.1-5

'Why do you spend your money for that which is not bread?'
(v.2)

Often on the news – especially in increasingly long run-up to Christmas – you see the faces of the drained and laden, trudging home from shopping centres somehow disappointed by their retail therapy, the sad and cynical faces of the wealthy West, puzzled at how happiness has passed them by. But sometimes, on the same news, in a clip from some poor part of the earth, you see gaggles of giggling and radiantly smiling children, happy with nothing but the torn shirts on their backs and a home-made football.

How bitterly we have learned what it is to spend our money 'for that which is not bread' and our labour 'for that which does not satisfy' (v.2). Could it be that the secret of happiness for many of the world's poorest people is that they have come already to drink from the waters of this prophecy? That the generous and generative Word Isaiah speaks of here is already unfolding and feeding them?

Perhaps only when we put down the shopping, let go of the burden, and receive instead the gift of this Word as a seed in our hearts, will we, who have come in with such sadness, at last go out with joy (Isaiah 55.12).

Reflection by **Malcolm Guite**

Proper 13

Continuous:
Genesis 32.22-31
Psalm 17.1-7,16*

Related:
Isaiah 55.1-5
Psalm 145.8-9,15-22*

Romans 9.1-5
Matthew 14.13-21

Romans 9.1-5

'I have great sorrow and unceasing anguish in my heart'
(v.2)

Those words of emotion represent the underlying feelings for the next three chapters of Romans. Paul, a Jew, must wrestle with the deep pain and anguish of what faith in Jesus Christ means for his forebears in faith. He begins by outlining the foundations of his people: they are Israel, children of God, who have seen God's glory, received his laws and have dedicated themselves to worship and service. From them come the great ancestors in faith and Jesus Christ himself.

We would do well to note the positive way in which the word 'flesh' is used; it is the very fabric of what binds Paul inextricably with his Jewish heritage. Paul never loses sight of that, but it causes him to search deeply for its implications on his new life in Christ.

It is hard for us to recognize the depth of Paul's despair, or at least to understand the difficulty that Paul would have experienced. However, there are ways in which living out our faith might have implications for our relationships with friends and family. Often this requires a reframing of ourselves in order to recognize the new thing that God is doing in and through us. So it is with Paul, whose voice we can hear clearly as if he were speaking these words with passion – Paul, whose whole life had been turned upside down because of his faith in the risen Lord.

Reflection by **Helen-Ann Hartley**

Continuous:
Genesis 32.22-31
Psalm 17.1-7,16*

Related:
Isaiah 55.1-5
Psalm 145.8-9,15-22*

Romans 9.1-5
Matthew 14.13-21

Proper 13

Matthew 14.13-21

'... he withdrew ... to a deserted place by himself' (v.13)

The crowds seem bigger, the ministry more public, the miracles even greater. The feeding of the 5,000 recalls the ministry of Moses and manna in the wilderness. Next Sunday's description of Jesus walking on water recalls the great nature miracles of the Old Testament.

How does Jesus respond to this larger, more public canvas? It is no accident that as the crowds grow, Matthew tells us deliberately that Jesus takes time to be by himself. In the opening verse, the withdrawal is in response to the news of the death of John the Baptist. We might speculate that Jesus is taking time to grieve and to take stock about what John's death means for his own ministry. After the feeding of the 5,000, we are specifically told that Jesus dismisses the crowds and goes up the mountain by himself to pray.

The lesson is a valuable one. The more public the ministry, the more this needs to be balanced by times of withdrawal and solitude. The more on display we are, the more we need to tend our private world. This is in part about paying attention to our emotions, our inner self. It is in part about paying attention to God's direction and call and values in the midst of tumultuous events around us and within us.

Reflection by **Steven Croft**

Proper 14

**Sunday between
7 & 13 August inclusive**

Continuous:
Genesis 37.1-4,12-28
Psalm 105.1-6,16-22,45*b**
Romans 10.5-15
Matthew 14.22-33

Genesis 37.1-4,12-28

'This is the story of the family ...' (v.2)

Some people think the Bible is full of stained-glass saints when it is actually full of dysfunctional families, and none more so than Jacob's. If old Jacob finally saw the desperate sibling rivalry in his children, which he had such a part in fostering, he might have reflected ruefully that it hadn't been much better between him and his brother Esau!

We might be tempted at this point to despair, to see only the dark ways in which in our woundedness we wound one another, to see the wrongs and hurts of one generation always, and inevitably, visited on the next. But we would be wrong.

The Joseph cycle is ultimately a story of redemption, mercy, and reconciliation. Even in this episode, the one who is thrown into a pit is drawn out of it. In the end even his slavery will redeem and renew the very family that sold him into it.

Furthermore, this family story is set, just like our own, within the arc of a much bigger story, in which a beloved son is cast by his brothers right into the pit of Hell, and, like Joseph, Jesus makes his very suffering the means of rescuing, reconciling and blessing the family that God has given him.

Reflection by **Malcolm Guite**

Related:
1 Kings 19.9-18
Psalm 85.8-13
Romans 10.5-15
Matthew 14.22-33

Proper 14

1 Kings 19.9-18

'… a sound of sheer silence ' (v.12)

The modern Church seems to be being offered two clichés. Either that faith has to be minutely and definitely expressed, so that there is no room for doubt or error. Or that faith is too uncertain to be defined and so cannot be – except that it is obviously true that it is too uncertain to be defined … The story of Elijah takes us to the heart of how it is to be human in the face of God.

Elijah does not doubt the existence of God. He appears to be doubting his own effectiveness in God's service and perhaps even God's commitment to him. He is utterly spent – defeated even. He is so worn out, he just wants to die.

God does not come to him with a 'statement of faith'. Nor does God overwhelm him. God just comes to him. The encounter is indescribable – NRSV says 'a sound of sheer silence' – but Elijah knows it is God who has come to him. This is not noisy faith or thin faith. Rather, it is an authentic encounter with God in this world, but one that is beyond words.

And what is the first thing that God does? Not a telling off. Not a theological statement. No. God provides colleagues. Which, of course, is what worn-out and depressed Elijah needs most of all. Authentic encounter with God will be indescribable, but it will have tangible consequences.

Reflection by **Alan Bartlett**

Proper 14

Continuous:
Genesis 37.1-4,12-28
Psalm 105.1-6,16-22,45*b**

Related:
1 Kings 19.9-18
Psalm 85.8-13

Romans 10.5-15
Matthew 14.22-33

Romans 10.5-15

'... confess with your lips ... and believe in your heart' (v.9)

At the end of Paul's continued wrestling with the difficulties the law presents, is his assertion that all that is needed is confession of faith and belief in the heart (v.9). In fact, the connection is made *inwards* then *outwards*: lips to heart, and heart to mouth. There is something very physical about faith that we often miss if we are too focused on the word. The ability to profess our faith is made through the physical action of speaking, and we cannot but be moved within by what we proclaim.

Paul's point then, as he goes on to say in verses 12-13, is that we are all the same and we all have the ability to profess faith. Thus salvation is for everyone, Jew and gentile, and Paul remains passionately optimistic that precisely that will come about. What matters is not the law, but Christ. Again, part of the fabric of Paul's argument is the theme of the freedom that faith in Jesus brings. While we may now take that assertion for granted, Paul's reflections here present a radical argument.

Reading these words is an invitation to us to reconsider the ways in which we might take our faith for granted. As we confess our faith, how does that confession work its way out in the physicality of our life and the way in which we lead it?

Reflection by **Helen-Ann Hartley**

Continuous:
Genesis 37.1-4,12-28
Psalm 105.1-6,16-22,45*b**

Related:
1 Kings 19.9-18
Psalm 85.8-13

Romans 10.5-15
Matthew 14.22-33

Proper 14

Matthew 14.22-33

'... he came walking towards them on the lake' (v.25)

Being around Jesus was never boring. (Why do many people today think it must be?) After a hard day's teaching and feeding 5,000 people on the everlasting bits and pieces of a picnic, he now walks across the nearby lake (finding Peter a willing but unreliable student) to Gennesaret, where a crowd of people touch his cloak and get healed.

In today's verses from Chapter 14, we're faced with the second of two miracles of nature that will always divide Christian opinion. Fortunately, eternal salvation doesn't depend on it. Perhaps we might just claim the insight of Austin Farrer that, if Jesus did indeed walk on water, it wasn't because of an arbitrary power over nature, but because love demanded it.

We don't know what the limits of Almighty love really are. However, we can also see Matthew demonstrating that Jesus embodies divine creativity because he has creative mastery over nature, in the form of the wild, chaotic lake.

As we watch Jesus, we learn more about him and more about ourselves. Do we resist this portrait of Jesus or do we embrace it? Are we embarrassed by it or encouraged by it? How comfortable are we with this Jesus? Above all, is there any chance that we would get out of our boat and walk towards Jesus? Because, metaphorically at least, that's what we're called to do every day.

Reflection by **John Pritchard**

Proper 15

**Sunday between
14 & 20 August inclusive**

Continuous:
Genesis 45.1-15
Psalm 133
Romans 11.1-2*a*, 29-32
Matthew 15.[10-20]21-28

Genesis 45.1-15

'And he kissed all his brothers and wept upon them' (v.15)

We are witness to one of the most remarkable acts of reconciliation recorded in the Bible. This is a reconciliation that finally overcomes long-standing family distancing, falsehood, betrayal, envy and trickery. For the sake of reconciliation in this tragedy, Joseph steps outside the dignity, pride and security of his royal office and enters into the emotional complexity of his own family. Royal power will not heal the dysfunctions of his family, but empathy and vulnerability will. Joseph doesn't want guilt from his brothers – he wants the restoration of the brotherhood itself.

His inspiration and guide is God, who he believes has been working invisibly and unnoticed in everything that has happened in the family drama. This *shalom* of God can now be revealed. What God does is not dependent on the brothers' remorse. Joseph shares good news in terms of grace, partly because he himself has known grace in his own story. God has given abundant life through Joseph, rather than death by Joseph, and the brothers' own journey becomes the means for restoring this family to fullness of life again.

God works within a situation, however sinful it has become, and constantly pours out the possibility of justice and grace. Even though the brothers have an evil goal, this is outmanoeuvred by the larger sway of God's providence and good purpose – bringing life rather than death. Such are the ways of God in the world.

Reflection by **David Moxon**

Related:
Isaiah 56.1,6-8
Psalm 67
Romans 11.1-2*a*,29-32
Matthew 15.[10-20]21-28

Isaiah 56.1,6-8

*'...for my house shall be called a house of prayer
for all peoples' (v.7)*

In the chapters leading up to this one, Isaiah has been helping forsaken Zion to call on her deep memory, to remember those special stories embedded in her faith and culture, the tales of Sarah, the badges of her racial and religious identity. But now, just as Israel recovers her joy, he tells her this: this joyful news, patterned as it is in your memory, is not just for you, but for all the nations, all the races. You, who were outcast, must welcome other outcasts too, especially the ones you yourself cast out – the foreigners and the eunuchs, the ones whose race, whose bodies, whose genders or identities could never fit your rules.

Israel, the outcast, had made her outcasts too, but here is the astonishing paradox, the liberality of God's love: the God of Israel nevertheless 'gathers the outcasts of Israel' (v.8). The one to be born in Bethlehem, the one who fulfils, page by page, all these prophecies of Isaiah, came to break down just those barriers of race and religion that pride had set across the temple gates. For the promised one came to the temple, as he comes to our churches now, with a scourge in his hand and these words on his lips: 'my house shall be called a house of prayer for all peoples' (v.7).

Reflection by **Malcolm Guite**

Proper 15	*Continuous:*	*Related:*
	Genesis 45.1-15	Isaiah 56.1,6-8
	Psalm 133	Psalm 67

Romans 11.1-2*a*, 29-32
Matthew 15.[10-20]21-28

Romans 11.1-2*a*, 29-32

*'... by the mercy shown to you,
they too may now receive mercy' (v.31)*

Talk of mercy is never far away in Paul's writing. Justice is also one of his primary concerns, not least in the idea of *justification*. It might well seem that these two ideas – justice and mercy – are in tension, as if they pull in opposite directions. If that is the case, then Paul has quite a task on his hands squaring one with the other. We might say that God – who is *supremely* just and supremely merciful – has an even bigger task.

We will certainly face this sort of tension if we adopt what seems to be the prevalent understanding of these two words today: that justice is punishing people, giving them what they deserve, whereas mercy is not punishing people, letting them off what they deserve. However, there is another sense to justice, which is present in the Old Testament and important for Paul. This refuses to see punishment as the goal of justice; instead, punishment is at most the means to justice. The goal of justice is to restore harmony and a right relationship. This is how the word 'just' is still used in music: when two notes are in a harmonious relationship.

In this way, God's mercy does not undo his justice or stand against it. God's mercy perfects his judgement, since it achieves the end to which justice strives. Mercy brings justice: harmony and the restoration of relationships.

Reflection by **Andrew Davison**

Continuous:
Genesis 45.1-15
Psalm 133

Related:
Isaiah 56.1,6-8
Psalm 67

Romans 11.1-2*a*, 29-32
Matthew 15.[10-20]21-28

Matthew 15.[10-20]21-28

'And her daughter was healed instantly' (v.28)

Another attempt to withdraw from the crowds and an encounter that disturbs us. Our sympathies are all with the woman, of course. She is a foreigner and a gentile. Her daughter is tormented and in her need she sees Jesus as the only grounds for hope, and so she shouts and keeps shouting and kneels and begs for mercy. We are impatient with the disciples who want to protect Jesus' retreat and their own privacy. We recoil even from the words of Jesus who seems to insult the woman and all her race.

The term 'dogs' (v.26) is softened a little, to be sure, when we know that the original refers to household pets – and young ones at that. 'Puppies' might be a better translation. There are strands of affection and respect in Jesus' first response. In the woman's reply there is boldness and wit as well as respect and faith.

The passage echoes in Jesus' life the stories of Elijah and Elisha, both of whom raise up the children of widows (1 Kings 17 and 2 Kings 4). In Elijah's case, the widow was also in the territory of Sidon. Both of the healing stories in Kings are elaborate and difficult. Jesus heals instantly, with just a word. Something greater than the greatest of the prophets is here.

Reflection by **Steven Croft**

Continuous:
Exodus 1.8 – 2.10
Psalm 124
Romans 12.1-8
Matthew 16.13-20

Proper 16

**Sunday between
21 & 27 August inclusive**

Exodus 1.8 – 2.10

*'... she got a papyrus basket for him ... put the child in it
and placed it among the reeds' (2.3)*

These words depict one of the most famous scenes in all of
history: the poignant, riveting drama of a vulnerable baby set
adrift on a river by his mother in a desperate bid to try to save
his life. The precariousness of the baby's destiny and very
survival has captured the imagination of millions for over two
and a half millennia.

The drama develops as three women, through a daring act of
unexpected compassion, make visible the hidden providence
of God and assure the baby's future. The biblical scholar
George Pixley has noted that this Egyptian 'den of death' is
still a place where God may find 'allies of life'. This is an
astonishing liberation, which later makes possible the
liberation of all Israel as Moses grows up to become their
pathway to freedom out of the bondage of the Egyptians.

The story has echoes of an 'ark' of life, ensuring the survival
and liberation of Noah and his family together with their
livestock. Somehow the deep taproots of Israel's story contain
possibilities of justice and freedom no matter what. The
people of Israel, as with the baby, have always been
vulnerable themselves and, so often on the brink of being
overcome by the waters of chaos, they still experience
unexpected redemption from the hidden hand of an invisible
God. There is always hope because there is always God – even
when there is no divine sign, only a sense of faith in a God
who mysteriously works within whatever happens.

Reflection by **David Moxon**

Related:
Isaiah 51.1-6
Psalm 138
Romans 12.1-8
Matthew 16.13-20

Proper 16

Isaiah 51.1-6

'Look to the rock from which you were hewn' (v.1)

There is great merit in living in the present, but sometimes it can blind us to the messages of the past and the potential of the future. Our culture is obsessed with scraping the jar of the present, living for today and consuming everything we can from it. We see how disastrous that policy can be when we look at the way we are exhausting the raw materials of the earth and yet expect to be immune from the effects of climate change.

Isaiah had a better plan. He drew on God's faithfulness in the past – 'Look to Abraham your father and to Sarah who bore you' (v.2) – in order to face the future with radiant confidence – 'my salvation will be for ever, and my deliverance will never be ended' (v.6). Here is a full time-frame in which we can rest secure. The God who holds the past also holds the future.

I've got to the age now where I notice in obituaries how old people were when they died, and suck in my breath when I see they were the same age as me. So it helps me if I remember that life isn't just a succession of greedy experiences but the steady outworking of God's faithfulness in my life, past, present and future. And at rock bottom there is rock.

Reflection by **John Pritchard**

Proper 16

Continuous:
Exodus 1.8 – 2.10
Psalm 124

Related:
Isaiah 51.1-6
Psalm 138

Romans 12.1-8
Matthew 16.13-20

Romans 12.1-8

'... be transformed by the renewing of your minds' (v.2)

Do not 'think of yourself more highly than you ought to think' (v.3). This is a recurrent theme throughout the Letter to the Romans, like a golden thread running through a tapestry. Until now, it has had a theological purpose, as part of an exploration of salvation, of grace and works, faith and the law. But we should not think of Paul as a theological writer in abstraction, as a theorist for whom the way we live is no concern. Since he likes rhetorical questions, we might pose one to Paul at this point: 'If salvation is by grace, does this render good living of no account?' Back would come his favourite response: 'By no means!'

The image of the body is a key to Paul's ethics. Taking the reality of the image of the body seriously changes everything. Caring for our fellow Christians is no longer a chore urged upon us by a commandment coming from outside. It becomes natural. It is as natural as loving our own body, since we are part of the Body of Christ. As we read in Ephesians (5.29), 'no one ever hates his own body'. That sentiment might seem a little over-optimistic, given today's typical unease of people with their bodies, but the point is clear. If we learn to see ourselves as part of the Body of Christ, then caring for our fellow members will come naturally.

Reflection by **Andrew Davison**

Continuous:
Exodus 1.8 – 2.10
Psalm 124

Related:
Isaiah 51.1-6
Psalm 138

Proper 16

Romans 12.1-8
Matthew 16.13-20

Matthew 16.13-20

'Who do you say that I am?' (v.15)

Practically everyone who came into contact with Jesus realized that there was something special about him. Who was he? Could he be a reincarnation of someone from the Jews' golden age of prophecy – maybe Jeremiah or Elijah (v.14)? Or perhaps John the Baptist had escaped Herod's prison despite all the rumours. If your own history and geography is the limit of your thinking, those were not unreasonable speculations.

However, Peter (or as he was known at the time, Simon) had spent a great deal of time in the company of Jesus. Like anyone who devotes themselves to Jesus over a sustained period, he was beginning to see things from God's point of view. To recognize Jesus as the Messiah was an extraordinary thing. To confess him as the Son of the Living God was beyond extraordinary (v.16).

It was a transformative moment for Peter. Like Abraham before him, he received a new name. Like Abraham he became known as 'the rock' (Isaiah 51.1-2). And like Abraham his act of faith enabled a new starting point in God's plan of salvation for all humankind.

'Look, I have set before you an open door, which no one is able to shut,' declared Jesus in a vision some decades later (Revelation 3.8). It was open because the keys were in safe hands (v.19). It's still open. Come in out of the cold.

Reflection by **Peter Graystone**

Proper 17

**Sunday between 28 August &
3 September inclusive**

Continuous:
Exodus 3.1-15
Psalm 105.1-6,23-26,45*b**
Romans 12.9-end
Matthew 16.21-end

Exodus 3.1-15

*'Who am I that I should go to Pharaoh, and bring the
Israelites out of Egypt?' (v.11)*

Moses, the rootless man, the alien, neither Egyptian nor
Hebrew, living in a foreign land, is about to find his true
identity – or, rather, to have it thrust upon him.

There is nothing in the story so far that suggests that Moses
knows the God of Abraham and Isaac. He recognizes the
numinous when he encounters it, but it terrifies him. And for
God to introduce himself to Moses, who doesn't know his
parents or his true family, as the God of his fathers, is perhaps
not tactful.

What's more, God gets straight down to business, telling
Moses how much he cares for the very people who have just
told Moses to get lost when he tried to help them. So, it is
very understandable that Moses should balk at God's simple
assumption that he can be put to work for a God and a people
he barely knows.

But there is a particular poignancy in the way Moses frames
his hesitation: 'Who am I?' he asks (v.11). Nothing in his life so
far has enabled him to answer that question to his own
satisfaction. He genuinely does not know who he is. God's
answer to him is, in effect, that identity is to be found in God
alone, God the great 'I am', source, creator and foundation
of all that is.

Reflection by **Jane Williams**

Related:
Jeremiah 15.15-21
Psalm 26.1-8
Romans 12.9-end
Matthew 16.21-end

Proper 17

Jeremiah 15.15-21

'Why is ... my wound incurable, refusing to be healed?'
(v.18)

Jeremiah accuses God in the strongest terms here. 'Truly, you are to me like a deceitful brook, like waters that fail' (v.18). This is the voice of one who feels desperately abandoned.

The prophet at this low point recalls for me the figure of Philoctetes from Greek legend – a Greek warrior-hero and the inheritor of Heracles' bow and arrows. Philoctetes receives an incurable wound from a snake bite. It festers and stinks so much that his former comrades set him ashore on the island of Lemnos, where he is left utterly alone. Like Jeremiah, all his memories of the joys and delights of earlier times turn to ashes in his mouth.

Philoctetes will one day be saved by the utilitarian calculations of the Greek army in their war against Troy. After some years they have to return to Lemnos because they need the bow and arrows in their war effort – and after some debate (and the intercession of one man more compassionate than the others), Philoctetes is taken too, and healed, and returned to the fellowship of his people.

Jeremiah does not have to wait for his hope of salvation; it is neither delayed nor utilitarian. Assurance comes quickly from the God he is accusing, 'I am with you to save you and deliver you' (v.20). Not because God wants something he has, but because God wants *him*.

Reflection by **Ben Quash**

Proper 17

Continuous:
Exodus 3.1-15
Psalm 105.1-6,23-26,45b*

Related:
Jeremiah 15.15-21
Psalm 26.1-8

Romans 12.9-end
Matthew 16.21-end

Romans 12.9-end

'... so far as it depends on you, live peaceably with all' (v.18)

These verses are the charter for Christian living. They are concentrated and they are lyrical. We will not find their equal anywhere in the Epistles.

Paul is not interested in suggesting cosmetic changes to the way we live, or patching up some other moral scheme. He urges us to a way of life flowing from a total transformation of how we see and evaluate everything – the 'renewal of your mind' spoken of in last Sunday's reading (Romans 12.2). The closing verses and his new way to treat enemies stand as an example. It could be seen as rather vindictive, with its 'heaping burning coals' (v.20), but we might hope that these are purifying coals (as in Isaiah 6) and not coals of torment. The behaviour he urges towards enemies represents a new way of living – a new logic, a new economy – which transcends the futility of tit for tat and overcomes evil with good.

Within the body of Christ we are to 'Rejoice with those who rejoice, weep with those who weep' (v.15). This follows precisely because of the insight that language of the body spells out. 'We, who are many, are one body in Christ, and individually we are members one of another' (Romans 12.5), we read last Sunday. Another's good is my good; well might I rejoice. Another's wound is my wound; well might I weep.

Reflection by **Andrew Davison**

Continuous:
Exodus 3.1-15
Psalm 105.1-6,23-26,45b*

Related:
Jeremiah 15.15-21
Psalm 26.1-8

Romans 12.9-end
Matthew 16.21-end

Matthew 16.21-end

'If any want to become my followers, let them ... take up their cross and follow me' (v.24)

R. S. Thomas in his poem 'Pilgrimages' says this: 'He is such a fast God, always ... leaving as we arrive.' It is an astonishing insight. As soon as we gain some understanding of who God is, God moves on ahead of us, confounding our conclusions, refusing to be pinned down.

'Do not cling to me' is what Jesus said to Mary Magdalene on the first Easter day. Do not think that human understanding can contain or constrain the mystery of God's presence. Therefore, as soon as Peter comes to his own astonishing conclusion that Jesus is not just a prophet, not just a great man, he is thrown backwards: this Messiah must suffer and die, and those who follow him must carry the same cross.

In one breath Peter is named as the rock upon which this house will be built; in the other he is revealed as the sand, the stumbling block, even Satan himself, upon which it will crumble. Well might we conclude that there is no profit in gaining this wealth of knowledge if it means losing our soul.

So we inch a bit further forward; we ask ourselves again: who can this Christ be? And as we are led into fresh revelations of God's presence, so we are also confronted by our own weakness and need. Like Peter, we are both rock and sand.

Reflection by **Stephen Cottrell**

Proper 18

Sunday between
4 & 10 September inclusive

Continuous:
Exodus 12.1-14
Psalm 149
Romans 13.8-end
Matthew 18.15-20

Exodus 12.1-14

'The blood shall be a sign for you' (v.13)

We hardly ever see blood. Not vivid, red, and spilled in front of us. Our slaughtering is sealed away from sight in abattoirs, the dreadful shedding of human blood glimpsed briefly in the distancing screen of a newscast. If we saw it for ourselves, then we would understand that 'the blood is the life' (Deuteronomy 12.23), we would know viscerally that this mysterious red fluid somehow carries the essence of a life itself. For that first Passover and the others that followed, the slaughter at twilight would have made all that clear. The Israelites entered fully into the paradox that it is only by the blood of another shed outwardly, that we are preserved, that our own blood might still course inwardly and give us life.

All this was a sign, and John the Baptist knew its meaning. 'Behold the Lamb of God' he said (John 1.29), for in Christ, the sign would be fulfilled. His blood, not on the lintels of houses, but shed on the cross, received in the wine of communion, would be our Passover and save us from the destroyer. However, the new covenant in Christ's blood is not, like the Exodus, a temporary rescue, but an invitation to fullness of life, to the banquet of the kingdom, so its sign is not bitter herbs, but wine. As George Herbert says in 'Agony':

> *'Love is that liquor sweet and most divine,*
> *Which my God feels as blood; but I, as wine'*

Reflection by **Malcolm Guite**

Related:
Ezekiel 33.7-11
Psalm 119.33-40
Romans 13.8-end
Matthew 18.15-20

Proper 18

Ezekiel 33.7-11

'... for why will you die, O house of Israel?' (v.11)

There are a lot of parallels between today's reading and Ezekiel's initial commissioning as God's prophet in Chapter 3. In both cases, God tells Ezekiel that he is to act as a sentinel, bearing a fearful responsibility for warning the people of what is about to happen. If he doesn't do his job, he will pay the price, but if he does, and the people choose to ignore him, then he is released from responsibility.

But here in Chapter 33, it sounds as though one set of warnings has already passed, and the people have not heeded their sentinel. For the first half of the chapter, there is no talk of what will happen to the righteous: it is as though God's sentinel cannot see anyone who deserves that name. The people who think of themselves as 'the righteous' seem to be treating righteousness as a sort of possession rather than as something that must be constantly practised.

Running through these verses is God's appeal: turn, turn away, turn back. There is real anguish as God cries, 'why will you die?' This is not what God wants, but what the people wilfully choose, over and over again.

God calls the people to turn around and walk in his way. But the people think God's 'way' is unfair. They want it to be theirs without the effort of the active daily choice to walk this 'way' with God.

Reflection by **Jane Williams**

Continuous:
Exodus 12.1-14
Psalm 149

Related:
Ezekiel 33.7-11
Psalm 119.33-40

Romans 13.8-end
Matthew 18.15-20

Romans 13.8-end

'Owe no one anything, except to love one another' (v.8)

Debt is the moral and spiritual topic of the hour. In the English of an earlier era, a person who owed someone else money was that person's 'bondsman': he or she was 'bonded'. We should find that abhorrent. On the other hand, mutual moral obligation – debts of kindness – bind a community together. Our preference today is for financial debt over moral debt. We do not like to be in the moral debt of others, but we consider financial debt to be perfectly natural. When such moral debts do exist, we prefer being owed to owing others.

For Christian theologians, the picture is the other way around, on both fronts. First, they have been deeply disturbed by financial debt but have seen moral debt as both natural (in a world where we all have to help each other through) and useful (since it forges bonds of gratitude and honour). 'Owe no one anything', wrote Paul, 'except to love one another' (v.8). This is the right sort of debt. Second, we typically take it far from well when others fail to fulfil their obligations to us. Christians, however, are supposed to pay attention to the debts owed to others (the debt to love them), but to sit very lightly to debts that others owe to them. This is spelt out in the Lord's Prayer, were we brave enough to translate it literally: 'we ourselves forgive everyone indebted to us'.

Reflection by **Andrew Davison**

Continuous:
Exodus 12.1-14
Psalm 149

Related:
Ezekiel 33.7-11
Psalm 119.33-40

Proper 18

Romans 13.8-end
Matthew 18.15-20

Matthew 18.15-20

'... point out the fault when the two of you are alone' (v.15)

In this passage, Jesus offers a blueprint for resolving conflict: first, go to the person alone; only if there is no resolution do we get a few others involved; only then should the conflict become widely known; and finally the broken relationship is acknowledged. In this approach we hear the view of the other person and perhaps realize that the fault lies not with them but with us – or, more often, with a combination of people and misunderstandings. The process starts in private, and it's far easier to acknowledge fault when it's done before only one or two people, thus avoiding public humiliation. Wisdom comes in honouring the position of the other person and avoiding gossiping and point scoring.

In the 6th century, Benedict wrote a rule for monks that incorporated Jesus' approach to conflict resolution. He was also at pains to avoid '*murmuratio*', or grumbling, which could undermine any community as surely as it undermined the Israelites, with their hardened hearts, wandering in the wilderness. Grumbling goes viral like a flashmob as people can gossip and plot over coffee and in cliques. The response for Jesus and Benedict is attentiveness. If someone upsets you, don't gossip about them but instead make time and space for them. Listen, understand and respond with love. If, finally, you have to acknowledge a broken relationship, you can do so knowing you worked for peace and reconciliation.

Reflection by **Paul Kennedy**

Proper 19

**Sunday between
11 & 17 September inclusive**

Continuous:
Exodus 14.19-end
Psalm 114 *or Canticle:*
Exodus 15.1b-11,20,21
Romans 14.1-12
Matthew 18.21-35

Exodus 14.19-end

'Israel saw the great work that the Lord did' (v.31)

The letter kills, but the Spirit gives life. Nowhere is that more true than in this life-giving story, whose 'letter' is so crowded with images of death. Read literally, and only literally, that picture of the Egyptians dead on the seashore in a story exalting one race over another is dark and repellant.

We do not stay with the dead letter, however. The death and resurrection of Jesus breathes new life and meaning into every story, especially this one. Exodus tells of rescue and redemption, but a local rescue, a small redemption, brief freedom soon squandered. The real triumph and the real glory were still to come.

That real Glory, that bigger story, is enacted and made effective in our baptism. It is the story of rescue from the deepest slavery, the slavery to sin; it celebrates the overthrow of the worst tyranny, the tyranny of death itself. Moses stood on dry land and held out his arm from a distance, but Christ, our new Moses, goes down with us into the deep waters of death and raises us to life in triumph. All of us, Egypt as well as Israel. We all go down into the waters of death, but we go down with Christ and we are all raised and saved with him.

'Israel saw the great work that the Lord did against the Egyptians', but we have seen the great work he does for all humanity.

Reflection by **Malcolm Guite**

Related:
Genesis 50.15-21
Psalm 103.[1-7]8-13*
Romans 14.1-12
Matthew 18.21-35

Genesis 50.15-21

'God intended it for good ...' (v.20)

God always has the last word. God is universal purpose, in whom we live and move and have our being, and yet we are free – what a paradox! In this final chapter of Genesis, we see, in a world of free and sometimes destructive choices, the weaving-together of so many frayed strands and ends. God is a master weaver who can even integrate torn and frazzled material into the design of a greater tapestry. God does not cause the damage or the straying of ends, but works with us nevertheless so that the overall pattern is not desecrated.

In this story, we see God achieve reconciliation through Joseph, working through the fear and guilt of his brothers beyond forgiveness to life and wellbeing. God is always behind the scene and invisible within the scene, yet is working at the green edge of the scene. God is majoring on goodness and mercy in an environment of freedom. In the words of Old Testament theologian Claus Westermann, God's plan 'is to bring the evil devised by the brothers to good effect'. Sin and the outcomes of sin can never have the last word: God and goodness are a majority.

As Irish poet and priest John O'Donohue once said: 'On the day when the weight deadens on your shoulders ... may a slow wind work these words of love around you, an invisible cloak to mind your life.'

Reflection by **David Moxon**

Proper 19

Continuous:
Exodus 14.19-end
Psalm 114 *or Canticle:*
Exodus 15.1b-11, 20,21

Related:
Genesis 50.15-21
Psalm 103.[1-7]8-13*

Romans 14.1-12
Matthew 18.21-35

Romans 14.1-12

'We do not live to ourselves, and we do not die to ourselves'
(v.7)

St Anthony of the Desert taught a theological truth of the first order when he said that 'our life and our death are with our neighbour'. We are not isolated individuals who might or might not choose to associate with others. We are communal by constitution. We are bound together by biology, language, culture and economics. If we 'live to ourselves', we are living a delusion, and a sad one at that. That anyone should 'die to ourselves' – which might mean dying alone – is one of the crowning tragedies of our social situation.

This sense of being bound together is the starting point for thinking about the Church. If there is commonality in a common birth, there is more still in a common redemption, and of being incorporated into the body of Christ. In a Church often wracked by divisions, this is a point to hold on to. We are joined together; our lives are intertwined. This is the primordial truth of ecclesiology; belonging together is God's gift, even if we might sometimes wish that it were not so. This is the necessary backdrop for being able to respect those who either exercise a greater sense of liberty than we would be comfortable with, or less. 'Those who eat must not despise those who abstain, and those who abstain must not pass judgement on those who eat' (v.3). The reason is Paul's favourite reason, because all rests on grace: 'for God has welcomed them'.

Reflection by **Andrew Davison**

Continuous:
Exodus 14.19-end
Psalm 114 *or Canticle:*
Exodus15.1b-11, 20,21

Related:
Genesis 50.15-21
Psalm 103.[1-7]8-13*

Romans 14.1-12
Matthew 18.21-35

Matthew 18.21-35

'... one who owed him ten thousand talents' (v.24)

Peter thinks he's generous in forgiving seven times, but it's mean according to Jesus' scale of 77 times (v.22) – or, in other words, so many times that it is impossible to keep track. Jesus tells a parable to demonstrate forgiveness where one who owed 10,000 talents is forgiven his debts – personal debts that, today, may not bail out a country's banking system, but do amount to perhaps £5bn! This is written during an extended eurozone crisis. Germany's leaders are clear that they cannot continually bail out countries that fail to get their finances in order. Greece has tried electing a government that pledged to withstand the austerity demanded. Can Germany forgive Greece's different financial principles? Can Greece listen to Germany's concerns without recalling the Nazi occupation of World War Two? Is it possible to forgive without counting the cost and feeling the weight of history?

Jesus says that forgiveness needs to be both experienced and lived out. The one forgiven the equivalent of multi-billion pound debts fails to forgive the one owing 100 denarii or 100 day's wages – a debt that, given time, could have been paid off. It's striking that as soon as there's a failure in living out forgiveness, there's also a failure in being forgiven. The first servant is dragged before the king, who condemns him to be tortured. So there does appear to be a limit to forgiveness. Not a numerical limit but a limit imposed in failing to live it out – forgive us our sins, as we forgive those who sin against us.

Reflection by **Paul Kennedy**

Proper 20

**Sunday between
18 & 24 September inclusive**

Continuous:
Exodus 16.2-15
Psalm 105.1-6,37-45*
Philippians 1.21-end
Matthew 20.1-16

Exodus 16.2-15

*'I will test them, whether they will follow my instruction
or not' (v.4)*

Why could God not just miraculously transport the Israelites from the Red Sea to the Jordan? Why must they make their way through the desert? Why can't God just give us now what we believe he wants to give us in the end?

The answer is simple: because we are not yet ready to receive it. In the Sinai Peninsula, a sweet, flaky substance is naturally produced by a species of plant lice; perhaps that is part of the background to this passage, with the miracle being the dependability of the supply. Israel has to learn how to accept daily bread from God's hand. If we read on to the end of the chapter, we discover that if the Israelites greedily try to get more, there will be just enough. If they run out of time and come home with little, there will be just enough too. If they try to hoard it so they can control the supply themselves, it rots away. Yet, on the sixth day, God gives them a double portion that can be preserved, so there can be Sabbath time.

God begins to prepare his people for journey's end by teaching them to keep time: beginning each day by recalling our utter dependence on him, creating a weekly rhythm in which one day is set aside to rest in his presence. Whose time are we keeping this week?

Reflection by **Jeremy Worthen**

Related:
Jonah 3.10 – 4.11
Psalm 145.1-8
Philippians 1.21-end
Matthew 20.1-16

Jonah 3.10 – 4.11

'Is it right for you to be angry?' (4.4,9)

We catch up with Jonah towards the end of his reluctant adventure. Having made a determined effort to scupper the preaching tour to Nineveh by heading off in the opposite direction (Jonah 1.3), he ends up in the unlikely habitat of a whale's belly (Jonah 1.17). Finally arriving in Nineveh, Jonah preaches a short sermon with a bad attitude. It is remarkably effective (input: five Hebrew words, outcome: 120,000 penitents), but to him this is a cause of dismay rather than joy. 'I knew you'd let them off', he complains (4.1-2).

One of the hardest things to swallow about the nature of grace is that it means God can, and will, show mercy to our enemies. It deconstructs our fantasy that God likes the people we do and dislikes those we dislike. Unfortunately, becoming a mature Christian is about grasping what it means in practice to say that God loves *all* people. For Jonah it manifests itself in the kind of petulant behaviour we would normally expect from a teenager: 'Yes, I'm right to be angry. Angry enough to die!' The way out of this standoff is the route we all have to take if we are to escape a narrow, self-referential view of God: seeing things through another pair of eyes. God encourages Jonah to assume the divine perspective with his penetrating challenge: 'Should I not be concerned about 120,000 persons … never mind all those animals?'

How might we enhance our understanding of grace by looking with different eyes at those we find difficult?

Reflection by **Helen Orchard**

Proper 20	*Continuous:*	*Related:*
	Exodus 16.2-15	Jonah 3.10 – 4.11
	Psalm 105.1-6,37-45*	Psalm 145.1-8

Philippians 1.21-end
Matthew 20.1-16

Philippians 1.21-end

'Only, live your life in a manner worthy of the gospel of Christ' (v.27)

One has to admire Paul's single-minded determination. He seems to be able to see everything that happens to him, for good or bad, even his own imprisonment at the hands of an oppressing power, as an opportunity to proclaim the gospel. That is his number one priority. Everything else that is happening to him, even the painful stuff of life, serves that one end. 'What does it matter?' (Philippians 1.18), he is even able to say. Paul had an almost reckless confidence in preaching the gospel that got him into a great deal of trouble.

Organizations and companies these days are encouraged to have a simple, clear vision statement that sums up what they are all about and tells their customers what they exist to do. If Paul had written a vision statement for himself, it might be something like this: 'To proclaim Christ'. Paul exhorts the Philippians likewise to live out their whole lives in a way that glorifies and honours Christ.

There are parts of the worldwide Church today where proclaiming Christ with the same boldness as Paul will land you in similar peril. For those of us fortunate enough not to live in contexts of real persecution, the danger might take another form. We might fail to develop that single-minded passion for proclaiming Christ. We might fail to make that our 'vision statement', not because of fear necessarily, not because it's too difficult, but because it's too easy.

Reflection by **Emma Ineson**

Continuous:
Exodus 16.2-15
Psalm 105.1-6,37-45*

Related:
Jonah 3.10 – 4.11
Psalm 145.1-8

Philippians 1.21-end
Matthew 20.1-16

Matthew 20.1-16

'... no one has hired us' (v.7)

We may feel that those 'idlers' who only worked one hour but got paid for the whole day were lucky, but I wonder how lucky they really were? The word for 'idle' here can simply mean unemployed. Were they lazy or just unfortunate men without work? Perhaps they weren't hired because they had a reputation as slackers, or maybe there was another reason: they were older, or slightly infirm, or disadvantaged in some way. One thing is certain: they want to work. When the landowner tells them to go to the vineyard, they go. They don't say 'There's only an hour left – we can't be bothered', or 'We'll get paid so little, it's not worth getting dirty for'. They go because they are desperate and they want to be employed, even if only for one hour.

Work gives us dignity and security, challenge and purpose, and to be without work can be soul-destroying. While those hired at first light have had to bear the heat of the day, those hired in early evening have borne the misery of unemployment and the insecurity of not knowing whether they would receive a wage at all. Seen from this perspective, the complaints of those who worked all day, secure in knowledge of a guaranteed income at the end of it, take on a different light.

Reflection by **Helen Orchard**

Proper 21

Sunday between 25 September
& 1 October inclusive

Continuous:
Exodus 17.1-7
Psalm 78.1-4,12-16*
Philippians 2.1-13
Matthew 21.23-32

Exodus 17.1-7

'Strike the rock, and water will come out of it' (v.6)

The difficulties in the desert continue. Despite the sweetened water at Marah, the springs of Elim, the quails and the manna in the wilderness of Sin – despite all these gifts, when they get to Rephidim and there is no water, the people argue and complain. On one level, it's understandable perhaps; after all, deserts are tough places, but the Israelites do seem to be severely lacking in gratitude!

God invites Moses to take his staff and to strike a rock. Water pours out. It's a powerful image; refreshing, life-giving water gushing out from what is hard and dry. The water was found there in the midst of the difficulty, not in some distant oasis.

'Strike the rock.' Sometimes the answer in the middle of a difficult or hard situation is not to search for refreshment elsewhere, but to seek – actively and determinedly – to find water right there. 'Striking the rock' may mean not giving up, it may mean going on loving and believing, it may mean seeking the best in your situation or in someone else. It certainly means prayer.

In the verses following today's passage, we read that 'whenever Moses held up his hand, Israel prevailed' (v.11); the raised hands of Moses are often seen as a symbol of prayer. Aaron and Hur supported his weary hands as the day wore on; it is good to be reminded of those who support us in prayer and by their love. We can't do it all by ourselves.

Reflection by **John Kiddle**

Related:
Ezekiel 18.1-4,25-end
Psalm 25.1-8
Philippians 2.1-13
Matthew 21.23-32

Proper 21

Ezekiel 18.1-4,25-end

'... get yourselves a new heart and a new spirit!' (v.31)

The first half of this chapter imagines a case where three generations of a family make different choices: to live consistently either righteously or wickedly. But now a more realistic scenario unfolds: what about people who have lived wrongly, but repent and try to improve? Or, alternatively, what about people who started well but then gave in to temptation? Which part of their lives will count?

God seems to reply that it is the final choice that counts. What is deliberately chosen, what we allow to give indelible shape to our lives, that is what leads us either towards life or towards death.

But that's not fair, the people whine. It's not very clear what their charge against God is. Is it unfair, in their eyes, because they expected God to honour his commitment to them, whether they kept their side of the bargain or not? Or is it unfair because some people might not get punished for the evil that they did, just because they repented? Again, we can hear echoes of Jesus' parables here: like the labourers in the vineyard who all get paid the same amount although some have worked harder than others (Matthew 20).

It seems we have a tendency to think God is unfair whenever his judgements don't come out just the way we want. Unless the verdict goes entirely in our direction, it's just not fair.

Reflection by **Jane Williams**

Proper 21	*Continuous:*	*Related:*
	Exodus 17.1-7	Ezekiel 18.1-4,25-end
	Psalm 78.1-4,12-16*	Psalm 25.1-8

Philippians 2.1-13
Matthew 21.23-32

Philippians 2.1-13

'... in humility regard others as better than yourselves' (v.3)

It's a funny thing, being humble. It's like a visual trick that you only see if you don't quite look at it. If you think you've mastered being humble, you probably haven't. If you start to feel proud about how humble you are, you're obviously not!

Humility is a much-misunderstood virtue. It is tempting to think that being humble is simply all about thinking badly about yourself in comparison with others. Here, Paul paints a picture of what it truly looks like to live a life of humility. And what it looks like – is Jesus. Jesus chose humility. He 'emptied himself' (v.7) and 'humbled himself' (v.8). Only because Jesus knew that he was 'in the form of God' (v.6) was he able to make the powerful choice to lay down his own heavenly status in order to become human.

Being humble is not putting yourself down. It's just not needing to promote yourself. The Christian writer C. S. Lewis said: 'The thing about a truly humble person is not that they think less of themselves, but that they think of themselves less.' Humility is not self-deprecation. It's not about being a doormat. It's not thinking of yourself as rubbish and awful. In fact, only those with a really strong, true, firm, accurate sense of their identity in Christ are able really to make the powerful choice to humble themselves. So perhaps becoming humble is something we can choose to do, and practise getting better at, following the way of Christ.

Reflection by **Emma Ineson**

Continuous:
Exodus 17.1-7
Psalm 78.1-4,12-16*

Related:
Ezekiel 18.1-4,25-end
Psalm 25.1-8

Philippians 2.1-13
Matthew 21.23-32

Matthew 21.23-32

'For John came to you in the way of righteousness and you did not believe him' (v.32)

We might entitle the second half of Matthew 21 as 'Jesus and the abominable no-men', because running through these verses is the Lord's impatience and even severity with things and people who fail to fulfil – and even resist and oppose – the purpose for which they are created. Love that is as urgent and real as the love of Jesus rejects everything and everybody who rejects it. This even includes the barren fig tree in the verses just before today's reading (vv.18-22). Love made fig trees to provide figs for hungry people, and they are useless when they don't.

Love gave John the Baptist to call Israel to repentance – and Jesus has no time for theoretical arguments about the source and nature of authority with those who resisted John's saving summons (vv.25-27).

It is all summed up in the parable at the end. These two sons could expect starring parts in *The Vicar of Dibley*! One starts by saying 'no, no, no', but repents into acting 'yes', while the other starts by saying 'yes, yes, yes', but ends by acting 'no'. On the showing of this passage, the latter is in acute danger of experiencing the impatient severity of Jesus, whereas the first son, who turns from 'no' to 'yes', from resistance to obedience, will find a place in the fields where God's abundant harvests grow.

Reflection by **Tom Smail**

Proper 22

**Sunday between
2 & 8 October inclusive**

Continuous:
Exodus 20.1-4,7-9,12-20
Psalm 19*
Philippians 3.4*b*-14
Matthew 21.33-end

Exodus 20.1-4,7-9,12-20

'Then God spoke all these words ...' (v.1)

The Ten Commandments. It would be hard, even in a secular culture, not to find some acknowledgement and appreciation of their ongoing influence. Even when translated into film and art, the abiding image of Moses-from-the-mountain, complete with tablets in hand and revealing the will of God to the Israelites, remains utterly iconic. Even in cartoons and comedy, there is the sense that these words from God, mediated through Moses, are to be obeyed. How else does one explain comedic quips such as 'the good news is, I beat him down to ten ... the bad news is, adultery is still in' (Dave Allen).

The Commandments are part of the rich and direct way in which God's will and purpose for humanity are revealed. What they actually represent is a distillation of how God expects us to relate to him, and to one another. These are the rules of life so far as God is concerned, the core curriculum for human flourishing. That they can be numbered on the fingers of our hands gives us some indication of God's sense of proportion. If we can simply live like this, all will be well.

There are many summaries of life and religion that are soundly descriptive. All faiths eat, pray and love – these things are at the heart of all major religions. But the Ten Commandments are not descriptive: they are prescriptive. These are God's biddings. They are not guidelines, advice or handy hints for better living. These commandments are simply to be obeyed as God's distilled wisdom for ordering human life and society.

Reflection by **Martyn Percy**

Related:
Isaiah 5.1-7
Psalm 80.8-16
Philippians 3.4*b*-14
Matthew 21.33-end

Isaiah 5.1-7

'My beloved had a vineyard' (v.1)

The singer Sinead O'Connor sings today's text, in a song called *If You Had a Vineyard*. She introduces the song by saying that, for her, Jerusalem refers to the Israelis and Judah refers to the Palestinians. She takes an ancient reading and places it in a contemporary context.

The vineyard of the Lord has always been a provocative parable; the story refers to God's people 'planted' in the promised land. They are to bear fruit; the hewed-out wine vat and best vines indicate the expectation of a good harvest. However, fruit is not borne, and Jerusalem and Judah are now invited to pass judgement on themselves.

God is present as the vineyard is established. In the introduction, cloud, smoke and fire are all Exodus symbols of God's presence. He gives the protection of shade and shelter but the Lord's people still turn to oppression and bloodshed. This is a parable of both unfruitfulness and unfaithfulness.

This parable challenges because it is easy to take God's blessings for granted and to forget that we, in turn, are to bless others. Both the Israelis and Palestinians, in Sinead's song, are blessed by having Abraham as their father and their home in the promised land. This blessing has led to violence, walls and blockades, she says. Today, let us consciously live as people blessed by God.

Reflection by **Paul Kennedy**

Proper 22

Continuous:
Exodus 20.1-4,7-9,12-20
Psalm 19*

Related:
Isaiah 5.1-7
Psalm 80.8-16

Philippians 3.4b-14
Matthew 21.33-end

Philippians 3.4b-14

'... whatever gains I had, these I have come to regard as loss because of Christ' (v.7)

Many of us spend a lot of time attempting to get our priorities right: juggling this with that, trying to work out whether *x* is more or less important than *y*, wondering whether we've got the balance right or whether we need to tweak them one more time.

As a young man, Paul was confident that his priorities were just right. He had a near-perfect CV: he had the right background and education, he had made the right choices at the right time and was highly motivated. His priorities were right, his background was secure, and he was poised ready to become a swiftly rising star. Then he met Christ, and his priorities were thrown into disarray. Paul uses strong language to say that what he thought were advantages were in fact disadvantages or loss (vv.7-8); what he was proud of before, he now recognized to be nothing more than dung, which is probably a better translation of 'rubbish' here (v.8).

The real priority was knowing Christ (vv.8,10), having a righteousness that came through Christ (v.9) and even sharing in his sufferings (v.10). Behind this priority, everything else faded into insignificance. We do not need to get our *priorities* right but our *priority* – Christ. The real answer is not to tweak the list, but to throw it out and start again with Christ at the top.

Reflection by **Paula Gooder**

Continuous:
Exodus 20.1-4,7-9,12-20
Psalm 19*

Related:
Isaiah 5.1-7
Psalm 80.8-16

Philippians 3.4b-14
Matthew 21.33-end

Matthew 21.33-end

'... this was the Lord's doing, and it is amazing in our eyes' (v.42)

Jesus scatters clues to his true identity like seeds on the soil, and still the religious leaders are slow to understand. At the climax to the parable of the tenants, Jesus quotes words from Psalm 118 (vv.22-23), beginning 'The stone that the builders rejected has become the cornerstone...'. And – at last! – 'When the chief priests and the Pharisees heard his parables, they realized that he was speaking about them' (v.45).

But this teaching is not just for the chief priests and the Pharisees. Throughout his ministry, Jesus has used both teaching and action to give clues to the true nature of his identity and mission, and most people – not just the religious leaders with their certainty and their vested interests – continued to misunderstand. Even those closest to Jesus, who most wanted to believe and understand – his disciples – Jesus chided for their inability to grasp his teaching (Matthew 15.16).

Throughout history, the Christian creeds have provided verbal snapshots, concise summaries of the content of our faith. But we have a problem if our use of them leads us to think that we know it all – in the way that the religious leaders of Jesus' time thought they knew – and that there is nothing more to be discovered about God and his dealings with humanity. Jesus' teaching continually urges his hearers to allow the boundaries of their thinking to be challenged and extended. How open are we to being surprised – 'amazed' – by God?

Reflection by **Barbara Mosse**

Proper 23
Sunday between
9 & 15 October inclusive

Continuous:
Exodus 32.1-14
Psalm 106.1-6,19-23*
Philippians 4.1-9
Matthew 22.1-14

Exodus 32.1-14

'Come, make gods for us ...' (v.1)

Because worship can take many forms, so can idolatry. Few today would be tempted to make an idol in the shape of an animal, and bow down and worship. Yet our cultural blindness can often lead us to affirm or benignly bless forces that we think serve us, but to which we are actually in bondage. For example, children who are exposed to relentless advertising for their foods of choice might turn away from vegetables, fruit and balanced diets in favour of snacks and foods high in fats. The result is obesity. A relentless focus on acquisitions and commodities may lead to children knowing what they want to have, but not what they want to be, in terms of vocations and careers.

Here, of course, we may discover that less is more – that by reducing choice, we enhance our enjoyment of ourselves and one another. But to appreciate this, some aspects of capitalism might have to be checked and challenged as not only unwise, but also probably sinful. The illusion of endless choice, and sating our desires, can quickly turn our gaze away from God and the needs of others.

Moses is exasperated by what he sees – among a people who have just been delivered from one captivity only to take up another without any pressure. But he pleads with God for time. He pleads for his people, and God 'changed his mind and let them live'. One can only assume that God already knows that those who consume materialism – very much the idolatry described – will end in being consumed by it. God gives them time, even though he knows they will fail. But he also knows he will still forgive.

Reflection by **Martyn Percy**

Related:
Isaiah 25.1-9
Psalm 23
Philippians 4.1-9
Matthew 22.1-14

Proper 23

Isaiah 25.1-9

'... let us be glad and rejoice in his salvation' (v.9)

It is not clear what city is being referred to in verse 2, but it symbolizes human greed and ruthlessness. As with the Tower of Babel, God has reduced it to ruins and revealed himself instead as a refuge to the poor (v.4).

This is a God who will overturn worldly structures of power and raise up the lowly. And what is really striking, in the midst of all this upheaval, is the wonderfully attractive vision of a new future we find in verses 6-9. In the Bible, such visions are always born out of exile or some kind of disorder: it's just when you might expect the people of God to be giving up hope, or turning in on themselves, that God seems to grant them amazing new visions of a renewed cosmos.

A Church that is strong and secure has little interest in nurturing such visions, but a Church that is facing an uncertain future can be precisely the seedbed for a new and compelling vision of how the world could be.

So now is a good time to ask yourself: what kind of vision do I have, and how can I help my local church to develop a vision, rooted in texts such as this, that will bring hope not just to the church itself but to all creation?

Reflection by **Gordon Mursell**

Continuous:
Exodus 32.1-14
Psalm 106.1-6,19-23*

Related:
Isaiah 25.1-9
Psalm 23

Philippians 4.1-9
Matthew 22.1-14

Philippians 4.1-9

'... help these women, for they have struggled beside me in the work of the gospel' (v.3)

It may be that a temporary disagreement between two leading women in the Philippian church was the occasion for this entire letter. It is certain that, from Paul's initial encounter with Lydia onwards, women played a leading role in the founding and growth of that church, and it is abundantly clear that Paul regarded them as partners in the gospel, not simply home-makers and hostesses.

Scholars suggest that women in Macedonia had a great deal more power and leverage in society than they did in, for example, Corinth, and it is extraordinary, given his background, that this was an aspect of Macedonian culture with which Paul seemed perfectly comfortable. Once more, the *kenosis* ('emptying out') of Christ is ongoing in his Body the Church, for Paul has cast aside his own pharisaical culture in order to know Christ. Not Christ the remembered Jewish man, but Christ alive, living and loving in these two gentile women. For, whatever their present disagreement, Paul knows that their final agreement will be 'in the Lord', for they are as surely 'in Christ' as he is and we are.

Perhaps only when we are prepared to 'forget what lies behind and strain forward to what lies ahead' (Philippians 3.13) as radically and readily as Paul did, will we, too, in our divided communion, eventually find our agreement in Christ.

Reflection by **Malcolm Guite**

Continuous:
Exodus 32.1-14
Psalm 106.1-6,19-23*

Related:
Isaiah 25.1-9
Psalm 23

Proper 23

Philippians 4.1-9
Matthew 22.1-14

Matthew 22.1-14

'... how did you get in here without a wedding robe?' (v.12)

The connection may not be immediately obvious, but Jesus here continues with the same thread of teaching begun in last Sunday's passage from Matthew 21. On a superficial reading, the story in this parable seems monstrously unfair: why go to the trouble of inviting someone to a wedding banquet, but then condemn them to punishment – simply because they were inappropriately dressed? We may find ourselves stumbling awkwardly over this parable, wishing it had been composed slightly differently!

Yet if it had been, a vital point would have been lost. Jesus is saying that it is not enough simply to accept an invitation and 'turn up'. The religious leaders of Jesus' time believed that they knew it all and there was nothing further to learn; they had 'turned up'. Jesus' words act as a warning to Christian readers not to fall into the same trap.

Much of Jesus' teaching points towards this end, and expresses the same truth in a variety of ways. Some seeds fall in shallow soil, where they shrivel because they have no root (Luke 8.6,13); the branches of the vine need pruning in order to bear fruit, but those that remain barren are removed and burned (John 15.1-16); the person who buries his talent loses even the little he originally had (Matthew 25.25,30). Yes – all are invited to the banquet, but the invitation is not to stagnation, but openness and growth.

Reflection by **Barbara Mosse**

Proper 24

**Sunday between
16 & 22 October inclusive**

Continuous:
Exodus 33.12-end
Psalm 99*
1 Thessalonians 1.1-10
Matthew 22.15-22

Exodus 33.12-end

'... show me your ways, so that I may know you' (v.13)

Today, we find the Israelites poised to leave Mount Sinai, and continue their journey. Yet even as the blessing of the Promised Land is anticipated, God reminds Moses of the need for his people to prepare. If God is to be met face to face by Moses, and on behalf of the Israelites, then preparation, obedience and readiness are required. Sins need to be set aside if God is to be truly encountered. Nothing can ultimately come between God's friendship and his pleasure in us (v.17). Yet plenty seems to hinder us – distractions, desires and sins clog up our relationships with one another, and with God. So the invitation today is to seek God's face, but by first setting aside all that hinders us from this.

Cranmer's majestic collect for purity in the Book of Common Prayer understood that a great deal of distraction, interference and sin is concealed inside us. Yet to God, all hearts are open – replete with their mixed emotions and motives. And all our desires are known too, with no secrets hidden. All of them are seen by the one who is returning. Yet the prayer continues in petition, 'cleanse the thoughts of our hearts by the inspiration of thy Holy Spirit'.

A prayer for the cleansing of desire seems an especially appropriate way to approach God. But it also captures something of the Israelites' own hope. That light can pierce the darkness and salvation overcome sin. Then we shall see: face to face.

Reflection by **Martyn Percy**

Related:
Isaiah 45.1-7
Psalm 96.1-9[10-13]
1 Thessalonians 1.1-10
Matthew 22.15-22

Proper 24

Isaiah 45.1-7

'Thus says the Lord to his anointed, to Cyrus' (v.1)

Cyrus? God's anointed? Come off it! Here was a non-Israelite, a man who worshipped idols and represented the occupying power, and yet God affords him the title of 'messiah' (anointed one), previously given to kings in the line of David. Cyrus is also described as God's 'shepherd' (Isaiah 44.28), the only person apart from David to be given these two titles before Jesus himself. Yet remarkably, under God, it was Cyrus, the pagan king of Persia, who allowed the exiles to return, Jerusalem to be rebuilt and the foundation stone of the Temple to be relaid.

For the Israelite exiles, the idea that God would use an idol-worshipping pagan to rescue them provokes a storm of protest (45.9-12) – they want to be choosy about their rescuer, even though beggars can't be choosers! When in our own communities, secular agencies or individuals with unconventional lives approach us wanting to help the Church, do we react with suspicion? Or do we ponder that God might just be using them as he did Cyrus?

God was not simply the tribal god of Israel, but the one true God of all the earth – 'I am the Lord, and there is no other' (v.5). If God can use world rulers who may not even know him to be agents of his purposes, how might that inspire us to pray for the leaders of today's global powers – China, Russia, India and the United States?

Reflection by **Mark Ireland**

Proper 24

Continuous:
Exodus 33.12-end
Psalm 99*

Related:
Isaiah 45.1-7
Psalm 96.1-9[10-13]
1 Thessalonians 1.1-10
Matthew 22.15-22

1 Thessalonians 1.1-10

*'... you turned to God from idols, to serve a living
and true God' (v.9)*

The first letter to the Thessalonians is probably the earliest of Paul's letters, written less than 20 years after the death of Jesus. It puts us in touch with the beginnings of Christianity as a distinct movement, a mission with a new message. Here is the freshness of Paul's passion for the gospel, his energy and excitement spilling over as he writes to these early gentile Christians.

The heart of the Thessalonians' conversion experience is the rejection of idols (v.9). Their embrace of Christianity has been at considerable cost. They have suffered persecution (v.6). They will also have become alienated from society in a more general way. In the ancient world, social relationships, patronage and networks of belonging often revolved around associations linked to pagan temples. Paul rejoices that his new converts have resisted this social pressure and become strong in the Christian virtues of faith, love and hope (v.3). Paul sees the significance of these virtues in the light of future expectation. They are waiting for the Lord's coming.

As we, from our different perspective, wait for the Lord's coming each Advent, this letter can nudge us towards a spiritual reality check. What are the idols from which we still need to turn? How is the Holy Spirit leading us towards the living and true God?

Reflection by **Angela Tilby**

Continuous:
Exodus 33.12-end
Psalm 99*

Related:
Isaiah 45.1-7
Psalm 96.1-9[10-13]
1 Thessalonians 1.1-10
Matthew 22.15-22

Proper 24

Matthew 22.15-22

'Give ... to the emperor the things that are the emperor's, and to God the things that are God's' (v.21)

Some commentators have pointed to this passage as giving an indication that Jesus advocates a separation of Church and state. But this apparent dualism is occasioned by a very specific context; for Matthew, the kingdom of God represented by Jesus embraces the whole of life and does not split it into factions. The specific occasion here forms part of a series of controversies initiated by the Pharisees in the hope of trapping Jesus into saying something that could be judged to be either blasphemous or heretical. They have already decided to kill him (Matthew 12.14); a successful entrapment here would give that decision a veneer of justification.

As with everything that Jesus said, however, his words here point to levels of meaning beyond their original purpose. They succeed in providing an unanswerable response to the guile of the Pharisees, but they also give his hearers a further indication of the truth of his identity and mission. These are *not* the words of a revolutionary who intends to restore the kingdom of Israel by force, as so many of his followers wanted and expected him to do. Rather, Jesus speaks as one content to give the authorities their due, and to preach his subversive message of God's love and forgiveness within the established social order. It poses a challenge equally valid today, encouraging us to seek God in and through *all* our relationships: within families, communities, and in society as a whole.

Reflection by **Barbara Mosse**

Proper 25

**Sunday between
23 & 29 October inclusive**

Continuous:
Deuteronomy 34.1-12
Psalm 90.1-6,13-17*
1 Thessalonians 2.1-8
Matthew 22.34-end

Deuteronomy 34.1-12

'I have let you see it with your eyes' (v.4)

If this scripture offers us a 'mountain-top moment', then it is one of poignancy and heartbreak as well as hope and vision. In some ways the best commentary on it is another, more recent mountain-top moment. In a famous speech, Martin Luther King told his followers that God had allowed him to go up the mountain. He added: 'I've looked over ... I've seen the Promised Land. I may not get there with you. But ... we, as a people, will get to the Promised Land.' With these words, shortly before his assassination, he offered a most direct and inspiring interpretation of this moment in the story of Moses and his people, the story of another group of former slaves seeking liberty together.

Deuteronomy's heart-breaking, and yet inspiring, coda to the story of Moses, the man of vision who enables a whole people to reach a place he cannot reach himself, sets out the essence of 'vision' as a gift. To climb the mountain, to see beyond the usual horizon and to communicate the vision even if you cannot at present fulfil it, these are the very gifts we need in the leaders of any faith community. Not practicality, not routine, not the prudent calculation of likelihoods, but vision. The practicality and the prudence come into place once we have the vision, and they help us to achieve it, but without vision, the people perish.

Reflection by **Malcolm Guite**

Related:
Leviticus 19.1-2,15-18
Psalm 1
1 Thessalonians 2.1-8
Matthew 22.34-end

Leviticus 19.1-2,15-18

'You shall be holy' (v.2)

Holiness doesn't always have a good press. We think it's beyond our reach. People who claim to be holy risk being shown up as hypocrites. This passage is towards the beginning of a section of Leviticus known as the 'holiness code' (chapters 17–26). Much of this code is what we might call 'preached law'. It's not so much a legal code as one long encouragement to put God's commandments into practice in daily life. Its purpose is to show that our faith should reach into the small details and hidden corners of our lives.

Many of the commandments found here are not new. The first verses of today's reading contain three of the ten in Exodus 20. But two things are distinctive here. The first is the reasons given. God's people are called not just to do what God says but to reflect God's very nature: 'You shall be holy, for I the Lord your God am holy' (v.2). The refrain that runs through this needs expanding a little. '(You should be like this because) I am the Lord (your God)'. Belonging to the Lord creates responsibilities as well as privileges.

The second distinctive element, which I love, are the practical touches that run through the holiness code. These are the bits that call for imaginative interpretation today: not many of us will glean fields or measure cloth today. How are we to fulfil these commandments?

Reflection by **Steven Croft**

243

Continuous: *Related:*
Deuteronomy 34.1-12   Leviticus 19.1-2,15-18
Psalm 90.1-6,13-17*   Psalm 1
1 Thessalonians 2.1-8
Matthew 22.34-end

1 Thessalonians 2.1-8

'... like a nurse tenderly caring for her own children' (v.7)

What a fragile and homely image of the work of the great apostle – 'like a nurse'. It's not how we usually think of Paul, but it seems to be how he thinks of himself with regard to his ministry at Thessalonica. It's a very pragmatic, ordinary description. It's more about getting a job done than about any kind of self-advancement. In a way, John the Baptist did a similar thing when he marked himself out simply as 'a voice crying in the wilderness'. He was a messenger with a message to deliver. Two of the greatest leaders of our faith – self-styled as the wet-nurse and the messenger.

There is something hinted at here that may point to a kind of liberation for us, for we often care far too deeply about how we are labelled. We find ourselves labouring under the heavy yoke of our own false self, with its insistent hungers and cravings for self-enlargement, for grandeur. We want labels that match to that false self's demands.

Yet what we sense in Paul and John is freedom. In one sense, it was irrelevant what they were. They had a job to do, that's all. The false self gets swallowed up by the greatness of the demands of gospel of the kingdom. And the result of that can only be joy!

Reflection by **Sue Hope**

Continuous: *Related:*
Deuteronomy 34.1-12   Leviticus 19.1-2,15-18
Psalm 90.1-6,13-17*   Psalm 1
     1 Thessalonians 2.1-8
     Matthew 22.34-end

Proper 25

Matthew 22.34-end

'You shall love the Lord your God with all your heart ...'
(v.37)

The Pharisees' challenge to Jesus continues. In response, Jesus takes the love principle first expounded in the Sermon on the Mount (Matthew 5) and stresses again its central importance to the life of discipleship. And, as so often happens with Jesus, his answers are double-hinged. As Tom Wright puts it: 'Jesus' answer was so traditional that nobody could challenge him on it, and so deeply searching that everyone else would be challenged by it' (*Matthew for Everyone*, Part 2, p. 93).

So where is the challenge for us? The Greek word for 'love' (*agape*) is here used to refer to both love of God and love of neighbour. The priority is to love God with all the deepest God-given capacities of our being, but there is to be no either/or about this love. From a true love of God must flow love of neighbour: it cannot be otherwise, because both 'loves' are of the same substance. Any supposed love of God that denies or despises the neighbour has no place in this understanding, in which Jesus has extended the interpretation of 'neighbour' to include our 'enemy' (Matthew 5.43-44).

It is up to each one of us, under God and in the particular life circumstances in which we find ourselves, to work out how best this dual commandment can be lived. Only if the love of God has priority will it then be possible to love our neighbour as ourselves.

Reflection by **Barbara Mosse**

Last Sunday after Trinity

if observed as Bible Sunday

Nehemiah 8.1-4a[5-6] 8-12
Psalm 119.9-16
Colossians 3.12-17
Matthew 24.30-35

Nehemiah 8.1-4a[5-6] 8-12

*'This day is holy to the Lord your God;
do not mourn or weep' (v.9)*

Have you noticed how God often uses new Christians to infuse renewed hope and zeal into our fellowships and worship services? 'Baby' Christians often radiate a wellspring of joy that appears unquenchable, reminding us that 'for God all things are possible' (Matthew 19.26). Often their enthusiasm challenges our joyfulness (or lack thereof) and encourages us to re-dedicate ourselves to God in humble adoration.

Today's reading makes a powerful and faithful proclamation in acknowledging the ability of God's word to break yokes, while evoking tears of repentance *and* joy. Often those who are new in Christ help us recognize just how complacent our relationship with him has become, or how we may have drifted away from God's divine plan for us. Ezra's encouraging words, 'do not mourn' affirm God's forgiveness.

Perhaps this is why the gospel holds such importance in worship and evangelism. God's word gently reminds us of his love and our sinful frailties. It pierces our hearts, brings repentance, gives ongoing reassurance and allows us to move closer to God. Then, as we learn to accept God's will for our lives, those tears of repentance vanish. They are swept away by joyous celebration as we come to recognize how God's protective arm has faithfully been at work in our lives, ever present, guiding and drawing us towards reconciliation.

Reflection by **Rosalyn Murphy**

Nehemiah 8.1-4a[5-6] 8-12
Psalm 119.9-16
Colossians 3.12-17
Matthew 24.30-35

Last Sunday after Trinity

Colossians 3.12-17

'... let the peace of Christ rule in your hearts' (v.15)

Earlier in this chapter, Paul declares: 'you have stripped off the old self with its practices and have clothed yourselves with the new self' (vv.9-10). Building on this image, Paul now urges the Colossians to clothe themselves with 'compassion, kindness, humility, meekness, and patience' (v.12). Such clothing is possible because of God's first love for them: they are his 'chosen ones' and, as such, must forgive one another just as they have been forgiven. The ultimate 'garment' is love (v.14), which works in people's lives to bring healing and balance to relationships, in both family and the wider society, and enables the peace of Christ to rule their hearts (v.15).

How easy do we find it to let the peace of Christ rule in our hearts? For most of the time, I suspect, we're too full of wayward desires and contrary motives to get anything but fleeting glimpses of the wonderful reality Paul was writing about. During a conversation between Thich Nhat Hanh and Thomas Merton in 1966, the Buddhist monk said, 'We don't teach meditation to the young monks. They are not ready for it until they stop slamming doors.'

In what ways do we 'slam doors'? What might be the motives that drive us to do so? A starting point, perhaps, would be to acknowledge that we do experience flashpoints of ego-centred anger, and then to offer that acknowledgement to God. This then opens us up to receive the precious gift of Christ's peace, with its potential to bring healing within ourselves, our families and communities.

Reflection by **Barbara Mosse**

Last Sunday after Trinity

Nehemiah 8.1-4a[5-6] 8-12
Psalm 119.9-16
Colossians 3.12-17
Matthew 24.30-35

Matthew 24.30-35

'... you know that he is near' (v.33)

There are things to learn about the past, the future and the present in these words of Jesus.

Four decades after he said them, Jerusalem was under siege. In 70 AD the Jews who were defending it were conquered, the city sacked and the Temple destroyed. Jesus had been correct that catastrophe would occur within a generation (v.34). The Roman army's victory was so overwhelming that a commemorative monument was built. The Arch of Titus still stands today on the Via Sacra in Rome. The Emperor Domitian erected it as a sign for his times: 'Behold and learn!'

However, Christians throughout the centuries have also taken courage from these verses that Jesus will return, this time not in humility but with triumphant glory (v.30). Those whose earthly life has been characterized by suffering and poverty long for that day of justice. Those who have oppressed fellow humans and disdained the ways of God will greet with dismay that day of judgement. 'Watch and pray!' (Luke 21.36).

And what of the present? Life would be so much easier if we knew when Jesus will return, but revealing that to us was never his intention. Leaves bud, unfurl and fall year after year, and it's easy to lose heart. But that very fact should keep reminding us that God will be faithful to his promise, said Jesus (v.32). Today the world needs Jesus to return more than ever. 'Read the signs of the times!'

Reflection by **Peter Graystone**

Revelation 7.9-17
Psalm 34.1-10
1 John 3.1-3
Matthew 5.1-12

All Saints' Day

1 November *Principal Feast*
*(Sunday between 30 October & 5 November
if this is kept as All Saints' Sunday)*

Revelation 7.9-end

'... a great multitude that no one could count' (v.9)

In Chapter 7 of Revelation, John's vision looks first back and then forward to introduce the theme of final redemption. In the first half of the chapter, he refers back to the salvation of the saints. The servants of God are marked on the foreheads to show that they belong to God. This is the meaning of their baptism. They have been bought by God, transferred to God's ownership.

At first glance the redeemed servants of God – the 144,000 (v.4) – look like a representative group modelled on the tribes that make up Israel. But looking forward ('after this I looked...', v.9), John also sees the redeemed saints as a worldwide community so large that they cannot be counted. This indicates that, though in some sense believers are representatives of the whole of humanity, the final scope of salvation is unlimited. The multitude is seen in heaven, joining the worship of heaven alongside the angels, the elders and the living energies of God.

The dialogue with 'one of the elders' (v.13) reinforces the point that earthly suffering is part of the vocation of those who follow the Lamb. We may feel we do not suffer much compared to those who are persecuted. We should nevertheless consider how our baptismal faith is strengthening and sustaining us to cope with the sufferings that inevitably come our way in the course of life.

Reflection by **Angela Tilby**

All Saints' Day

Revelation 7.9-end
Psalm 34.1-10
I John 3.1-3
Matthew 5.1-12

1 John 3.1-3

'... what we will be has not yet been revealed' (v.2)

The very first chapter of this epistle – the First Letter of John – begins by celebrating what has been revealed in Christ: 'We declare to you what was from the beginning, what we have heard, what we have seen with our eyes, what we have looked at and touched with our hands, concerning the word of life – this life was revealed, and we have seen it' (1 John 1.1-2). It is all in the past tense. It is all about the 'givens' of revelation that help us to orientate ourselves in the present moment. They are vital points by which we steer.

Yet two chapters later, the emphasis has shifted to the future, to 'what has not yet been revealed'. This is a crucial reminder that the Christian life is not all about the 'given'; it must be radically open to what is yet to be 'found'.

There can be something off-puttingly complacent about a Christianity that thinks it has the answer to everything already, so that in any new situation all it has to do is to root around in its bundle of 'givens' in order to produce just the right answer for just the right occasion, all ready-made. But, as all the saints have known, the God who has stocked our backpacks for the journey also places things up ahead of us on the road – and both the givens and the founds are equally 'of God'.

Reflection by **Ben Quash**

Revelation 7.9-end
Psalm 34.1-10
1 John 3.1-3
Matthew 5.1-12

Matthew 5.1-12

'Blessed are the poor in spirit' (v.3)

A plain reading of the Beatitudes could lead to a degree of scepticism. As a matter of common experience, those who mourn are not always comforted, and the merciful sometimes get a mouthful rather than receiving mercy. So what was Jesus saying? Was it a set of high standards to make us raise our game? Was it a new law so impossible to keep that we would have to turn to grace instead? Or was it something else again?

In a world where so many values are topsy-turvy, it's not surprising that when truth arrives, we think it's upside down. The Beatitudes leave us floundering because they're so bewilderingly different. Jesus is putting before us the values of a new world, the upside-down world that's actually the right way up. He's not just encouraging us to try harder; he's telling us to be born again, to come alive to the new creation that's already bubbling up beneath the surface everywhere. We just have to release it, claim it and live it.

When I look at my own life, it seems like a comedy of errors; there's not much sign of the new creation. But appearance and reality are often confused. There are signs of that upside-down kingdom breaking through the concrete in our world time and again, in astonishing feats of forgiveness, gifts of generosity, selfless caring, commitment to justice, love of neighbour and of enemy. This good news would flood the world if it could only get heard. As we celebrate All Saints' Day, what could we do that would demonstrate that upside-down new world in our actions today?

Reflection by **John Pritchard**

Fourth Sunday before Advent

**Sunday between 30 October &
5 November inclusive** *(For use if the
Feast of All Saints is celebrated on 1 November)*

Micah 3.5-end
Psalm 43*
1 Thessalonians 2.9-13
Matthew 24.1-14

Micah 3.5-end

'But as for me, I am filled with power...' (v.8)

Micah directs his excoriating words towards the rulers and the prophets who abuse their power and position. Rulers, prophets and priests have sold out their integrity for money. The rulers have become oppressors. Religious leaders have become more greedy than godly (v.5). These prophets do not convey a message form the Lord; rather they say messages to please people who pay them money.

These prophets are going to be judged. They will face darkness (v.6) – they will not be given a vision or revelation from God. They will be disgraced and shamed because they will not have any answers from God. God will judge those who have corrupted their prophetic office for personal gain.

When Micah offers the message of God, he is risking his own life. He tells the uncomfortable truth in spite of the opposition from the people he is speaking to. He does not fall for the normal route of pleasing people with what they want to hear but speaks what they need to hear from God. He is not going to be paid by his people for this job but is filled with power and the spirit of the Lord.

The temptation to please those who meet the ministry costs is real for many ministers of the Gospel. The congregation might expect to be uplifted and comforted, not to be scolded by the minister. How might we preach and hear the 'offensive' side of the Gospel in faithfulness to God?

Reflection by **John Perumbalath**

Micah 3.5-end
Psalm 43*
1 Thessalonians 2.9-13
Matthew 24.1-14

Fourth Sunday before Advent

1 Thessalonians 2.9-13

'... God's word, which is also at work in you believers' (v.13)

If you're a breadmaker, you'll know that yeast has the most amazing properties. It *looks* rather odd – nondescript even – but as soon as it is mixed with sugar and warmed with water, it starts reacting, bubbling up – and once it's added to the flour, you can feel the difference. Suddenly the flour comes alive – because the yeast is a living organism.

The word of God works very like yeast. It's alive with energy and power: it has effect. Paul writes of God's word, 'which is also at work – *energetai* – in you believers' (v.13). The life of God is activating in them, bubbling with creativity and bearing joy as its gift. And this divine word, closely identified with Jesus who is *the* Word, undergoes a similar process to that of yeast for the energy to be released. Paul employs the term '*akoese*' as a clue to this process – meaning hearing, obeying, taking in, admitting. The Thessalonians had to *receive* the word of the Gospel into themselves, to take it in – you could say, to give way, to surrender to it. The result is lift-off into life, with all its divine energy and fullness.

The same divine energy can be active, now, deep down in us, hidden in our own breathings, by faith, generating strength for today.

Reflection by **Sue Hope**

Fourth Sunday before Advent

Micah 3.5-end
Psalm 43*
I Thessalonians 2.9-13
Matthew 24.1-14

Matthew 24.1-14

'What will be the sign of your coming and of the end of the age?' (v.3)

The fascination of the disciples with the temple buildings and Jesus' alarming observation concerning their fate usher in a section of Matthew's Gospel known as the 'Little Apocalypse', climaxing with the coming of the Son of Man (vv.30-31). It should perhaps be no surprise that the disciples' first concern, on hearing Jesus' prediction of the temple's destruction, should be about how and when this would be fulfilled. Rather than give them a direct answer, Jesus responds with a warning: 'Beware that no one leads you astray. For many will come in my name, saying, "I am the Messiah!" and they will lead many astray' (vv.4-5).

Jesus' catalogue of 'wars and rumours of wars' (v.6) has struck a consistent note of alarm in the human psyche from Jesus' time right up to the present day. Despite Jesus' warnings that 'the end is not yet', every historical epoch including our own has produced its own crop of end-time prophets declaring that theirs was the age in which these things were finally to be fulfilled.

Our awareness of these resonances can leave us in an uncomfortable place of tension. Aware of the turmoil in our world, we are asked to note the working-out of the pattern of events Jesus describes as they evolve in our own time. But we are warned against using them as any kind of accurate predictor of that which still remains hidden within the mystery of God.

Reflection by **Barbara Mosse**

Amos 5.18-24
Psalm 70
1 Thessalonians 4.13-end
Matthew 25.1-13

Third Sunday before Advent

**Sunday between
6 & 12 November inclusive**

Amos 5.18-24

'... let justice roll down like waters' (v.24)

Worship and lifestyle must stay connected. If they are ever detached, then there will be a massive distortion in Christian faith. We are meant to bring into our worship and prayer all that concerns us in life, and go from our worship and our prayers to live better, stronger and more distinctive lives in the world. A Christian disciple dances in the continual rhythm of worship and mission. Yet when the link is broken, what is otherwise good becomes twisted.

Amos names this distortion. Worship in the northern kingdom has become detached from life, a separated and sealed compartment. The 'day of the Lord' (vv.18,20) refers to the great Autumn Festival. This Festival has become simply an excuse for a great feast, for a concert, for a spectacular show. The meaning has been lost. The Festival was meant to draw the Israelites back to their roots, to the values of justice and righteousness, to care for the poor and the outsider, to their vocation in the world. But it has become empty words and gestures: there is nothing at the centre.

For that reason, the Lord's day will be much more about judgement than joy. For that reason, Amos articulates the same Lord's deep dissatisfaction with empty worship: take away the noise of your songs. For that reason, as the Israelites pray for rain at the Festival, Amos names God's deep longing for justice and righteousness to flow among God's people.

Reflection by **Steven Croft**

255

Third Sunday before Advent

Amos 5.18-24
Psalm 70
1 Thessalonians 4.13-end
Matthew 25.1-13

1 Thessalonians 4.13-end

'God will bring with him those who have died' (v.14)

There was anxiety in the church at Thessalonica. Some of the believers had died. When Jesus returned to 'take up' those who were waiting for him, would those who had already died be left behind? What was the status of their death? Were they to be excluded from God's future because death had come before that great day for which they were waiting?

Paul writes to reassure them but also to enlarge their vision. And he does so by a strange and wonderful contrast. He refers twice to those who have died as *ton koimomenon* – 'those who have fallen asleep' (vv.13,15). Between these two references, he embeds an ancient credal statement: 'We believe that Jesus died and rose again.' But the word he uses for *his* death is nothing to do with sleep. It's a terrible word. It suggests the decomposition of the body and final annihilation. It is redolent with bleak despair.

The inference is clear. There's a different quality between the death that Jesus died and the death of the believer. They may be biologically similar, but one is total and final, while the other is not ultimately death at all – only sleeping. The latter is dependent upon the former – and upon the cataclysmic fact that Jesus burst the bonds of that terrible death to rise again.

Reflection by **Sue Hope**

Amos 5.18-24
Psalm 70
1 Thessalonians 4.13-end
Matthew 25.1-13

Third Sunday before Advent

Matthew 25.1-13

'... but the wise took flasks of oil with their lamps' (v.4)

The parable of the wise and foolish bridesmaids is not the only context in which Jesus refers to himself as a bridegroom. Earlier in Matthew's Gospel Jesus makes a direct self-identification, when he is asked by the disciples of John the Baptist why his own disciples do not fast (Matthew 9.15). The link with the coming of the Son of Man referred to in the previous chapter is clear, and we are viewing the final return of Jesus through yet another lens.

So the parable is about the coming of the kingdom of God and the return of Jesus. The bridesmaids represent the Church. All have lamps and oil; all sleep when the coming of the bridegroom is delayed. But only five have equipped themselves with sufficient oil to last until his arrival; the others are insufficiently prepared. There is a potential for confusion here, as elsewhere Jesus tells his hearers not to worry about the future – what they will eat, drink or wear – 'for tomorrow will bring worries of its own' (Matthew 6.34).

However, the contradiction is apparent, rather than real. In Matthew 6, Jesus was concerned with the kind of anxious hoarding and fretting about the future that reveals a basic lack of trust in God's ability to provide. But here, he is addressing the need for Christians to 'keep calm and carry on' – to persist doggedly in faith, hope and trust, year after year, however long the 'bridegroom' is delayed.

Reflection by **Barbara Mosse**

Second Sunday before Advent

**Sunday between
13 & 19 November inclusive**

Zephaniah 1.7,12-end
Psalm 90.1-8[9-11]12*
1 Thessalonians 5.1-11
Matthew 25.14-30

Zephaniah 1.7,12-18

'... the people who rest complacently on their dregs' (v.12)

Zephaniah is great-great-grandson of King Hezekiah, who secured the kingdom of Judah against the Assyrians, but whose death marked the start of a period of inexorable decline. Zephaniah himself is one generation away from exile.

All around him, the prophet sees complacency. The atmosphere before the great festival ('The day of the Lord', v.7) is not unlike the two weeks before Christmas in our own day. Lots of rushing around, visiting the merchants in the different quarters of Jerusalem, planning the festivities.

The prophet's task is to speak words of challenge and judgement in a complacent and superficial world. There are eternal truths and realities beneath all the turmoil of life. All we see will ultimately come to an end. God's grace and reality endure for ever.

The heart of the challenge is at verse 12. Zephaniah describes the people as those 'who rest complacently on their dregs'. Laziness and apathy have taken a deep hold on the soul of Judah. People have stopped striving for holiness. They have stopped believing that faith makes a difference. They are less than they could be.

Zephaniah's call is to speak the word of God to awaken the conscience of the nation from torpor and idleness – the sin the saints have called *'accidie'*. Zephaniah is the enemy of apathy. Will we take up his mantle?

Reflection by **Steven Croft**

Zephaniah 1.7,12-end
Psalm 90.1-8[9-11]12*
1 Thessalonians 5.1-11
Matthew 25.14-30

Second Sunday before Advent

1 Thessalonians 5.1-11

'... let us keep awake and be sober' (v.6)

Paul doesn't waste time on the question of when the Lord may return. He points out that only one thing can be known about it precisely – that it will take the world by surprise. Nevertheless, the reality of 'that day' is vital to the health of the Christian community. It's vital because it shifts our perspective. It's like looking at the human story as a painting that has been given a new frame – and the beauty and artfulness of the frame begin to have an effect on how we see the picture.

Living without seeing the framework means we live in some senses blindly, in the dark. 'Let us eat, drink and be merry, for tomorrow we die.' We might have goals, but they are bound by the limits of our own short-sightedness. When we gaze at the framework, however, we undergo a paradigm shift. Goals that may have seemed important lose their urgency. Our focus changes and resets.

That's why Paul reminds the Thessalonians to be *gregoromen* – watchful, wakeful, aware – not forgetting what they are for and about. 'Watchful vigilance' works like a doorkeeper. It stands ready to open the door to the Lord, who, from time to time in the course of our ordinary day, visits us – a foretaste of that greater advent for which we wait.

Reflection by **Sue Hope**

Second Sunday before Advent

Zephaniah 1.7,12-end
Psalm 90.1-8[9-11]12*
1 Thessalonians 5.1-11
Matthew 25.14-30

Matthew 25.14-30

*'… I was afraid, and I went and hid your talent
in the ground' (v.25)*

This familiar parable is about the distribution and use of God's gifts. It chimes in well with contemporary Christianity and its strong interest in the gifts of the Spirit. However, the talents here are not specifically spiritual but refer to everything God gives us, by nature or by grace, to the skilled worker or perceptive parent as much as to the penetrating prophet.

The distribution of the gifts is unequal, but those who concentrate on a few things they are good at are valued just as much as those whose stretch is wider and can take on more.

The test for all of us alike is not about how many gifts we have – that is God's business – but about how we use them, which is very much ours. Gifts are not badges of spiritual status to be collected; they are tools for furthering God's purposes, and we are judged on how much profit we have made for our master, who is both the world's creator and the world's redeemer. As creator, he has given a multiplicity of gifts so that the potentialities of his creation may be realized; as redeemer, he has given other gifts so that his gospel may be spread.

Reflection by **Tom Smail**

Ezekiel 34.11-16,20-24
Psalm 95.1-7*
Ephesians 1.15-end
Matthew 25.31-end

Christ the King

The Sunday next before Advent
Sunday between
20 & 26 November inclusive

Ezekiel 34.11-16,20-24

'I will judge between sheep and sheep' (v.22)

The first half of Ezekiel Chapter 34 is a searing indictment of the leaders of God's people, who have served their own interests and taken no thought for their flock at all. God promises that he himself will replace the worthless shepherds, and search out his scattered sheep and bring them safely home (vv.11-16). Remind you of anything?

In the second part of the chapter, we get more New Testament echoes. God now turns his attention from the iniquities of the shepherds to those of the sheep. The sheep can't blame everything on their leaders: their own personal responsibility remains, and God will judge between sheep and sheep, between rams and goats. We see the effect of badly shepherded sheep, where the strong and the greedy take what they want and leave bare fields and muddy water for the weak. Was this passage in Jesus' mind when he told the parable of the sheep and the goats, which we also read about this Sunday (Matthew 25.31-46)?

As so often in the message of the prophets, and indeed in Jesus' message, peace, prosperity and the reign of God are linked with justice and care for the poor. The sheep of God's pasture, under the watchful, loving eye of God's shepherd, all have equal access to pasture, water and care. God's people cannot come to this place of safety and plenty on any other terms than justice for all.

Reflection by **Jane Williams**

Christ the King

The Sunday next before Advent

Ezekiel 34.11-16,20-24
Psalm 95.1-7*
Ephesians 1.15-end
Matthew 25.31-end

Ephesians 1.15-end

'God put this power to work in Christ' (v.20)

It sometimes seems that Christianity and power are incompatible: Jesus is an outsider of no account – 'so small, not a king at all', as Pilate sings in the musical *Jesus Christ Superstar*. This Messiah's first followers have no more than two swords (Luke 22.38).

Nietzsche called Christianity a religion for slaves. Perhaps it is for the best, for it is difficult for those who get earthly power to resist the temptation to lord it over the rest. But that should not be so among us, if we recall the one who came 'not to be served but to serve' (Mark 10.42-45). Not among us, if we know where true power lies – and what it is.

The only true power is of God. It is 'immeasurably great' (v.19) and it is at work 'in Christ' (v.20). The exaltation of Christ (vv.20-23), above and beyond any name that is or could be named, above even the angelic heavenly beings ('rules', 'authorities', 'dominions', 'powers'), is the fulfilment of God's plan for creation.

God intended human beings to be 'crowned with glory and honour' and have 'all things under their feet' (Psalm 8.5-6). But, of course, we blew it. Christ the king can fill the empty place of power, for he alone has proved that he knows how to exercise it. Beware all imitations.

Reflection by **Jeff Astley**

Ezekiel 34.11-16,20-24
Psalm 95.1-7*
Ephesians 1.15-end
Matthew 25.31-end

Christ the King

The Sunday next before Advent

Matthew 25.31-end

'... he will separate people ... as a shepherd separates the sheep from the goats' (v.32)

The specific point of this parable is often missed. It is about how the Son of Man at his coming will reach his verdict on 'the nations' – the peoples who do not know the God of Israel, still less his Messiah. The judgement on them is based on their treatment of 'the least of these who are members of my family' (v.40). They do not know Christ, but they will have Christ's people among them; if, like Saul of Tarsus, they persecute them, they are persecuting Christ, but if they serve them, they are unknowingly serving Christ.

If those who do not know him are judged by how well they treat those whom he loves, how much more will be expected of those who do know him and know also how much he loves not just his believing people but the whole of humanity in their needs and miseries?

The bother is that, when we judge ourselves by that measure, the dividing line that, in the story, runs so cleanly between the accepted sheep and the rejected goats often seems to run through the middle of our lives, so that we are on both sides at once – goatish sheep or sheepish goats!

Reflection by **Tom Smail**

I Kings 8.22-30
or Revelation 21.9-14
Psalm 122
Hebrews 12.18-24
Matthew 21.12-16

1 Kings 8.22-30

'... that your eyes may be open night and day towards this house' (v.29)

This was one of the great days of Israel's life. The Ark of the Covenant, that vital symbol of national identity and unity, is brought up the hill from the city of David and placed with great solemnity in the inner sanctuary. Solomon rises to the occasion with a prayer of dedication that praises God for his faithfulness to his promise (v.24) while at the same time recognizing that Israel has a matching responsibility to remain faithful to God. (The seeds of tragedy are already being planted.)

Solomon poses the problem that afflicts all shrines: 'But will God indeed dwell on the earth?' (v.27). How can you place infinity in a pint pot? The answer is that the temple is not meant to limit the infinite God, but it does allow faithful people to pray in or towards a place of supreme significance, while God is still 'in heaven your dwelling place' (v.30).

God gives us many aids and artefacts for our Christian journey – special places, special people, forms of worship, books and practices of prayer. These are wonderful gifts in the toolbag of discipleship, but they are clunky and inflexible tools at best. We do well to remember that everything is provisional, apart from God.

Reflection by **John Pritchard**

1 Kings 8.22-30
or **Revelation 21.9-14**
Psalm 122
Hebrews 12.18-24
Matthew 21.12-16

Revelation 21.9-14

*'[And he] showed me the holy city Jerusalem coming down
out of heaven from God' (v.10)*

The descent of the heavenly city is described in all its glorious detail, from the vantage point of the seer who has been transported 'in the spirit' to a high mountain. The city comes down from God – it has no human origin. This contrasts with Rome and earlier constructions of human pride, Babel and Babylon. The city 'has the glory of God' in its radiance, beauty and order. The twelve foundations are based in recent history, the faithfulness of the twelve apostles of the Lamb.

The details of the city's constrction are not original to Revelation; they echo a number of Old Testament passages, in particular the temple vision of Ezekiel 40. The connection between the city and the temple is reinforced by the depiction of the city as a perfect cube unlike any earthly city. (The inner sanctuary of the Jerusalem temple, the Holy of Holies, was a cube.) The city is built out of precious stones and metals. The stones echo the detail of the priestly vestments in Exodus 28, showing that the city is now the embodiment of holiness.

This, then, is God's design for humanity's ultimate happiness. All that is precious and beautiful is brought together in harmony, and the whole is suffused with the glory of God. We cannot create the holy city, but we can be faithful in our daily lives to the point where we begin to reflect its radiance.

Reflection by **Angela Tilby**

Dedication Festival

I Kings 8.22-30
or Revelation 21.9-14
Psalm 122
Hebrews 12.18-24
Matthew 21.12-16

Hebrews 12.18-24

'But you have come ... to the city of the living God' (v.22)

There are two different understandings of religion here. One is theatrical: exhilarating and frightening in equal measures. Its essence is an exciting *experience*, with a beginning and an end. It may be a communal experience, and people leave it awed and shaken, but they are not fundamentally changed.

The other is religion of daily holiness, whose mirror image is the vision of the heavenly Jerusalem, where the rejoicing hosts of heaven and earth live with God. The practices of this religion are designed to build parallels here and now with what we long for in the future.

So this religion values, above all, those virtues that build trust and fellowship. It abhors above all those vices that cause bitterness, suspicion and division.

These two pictures of religion do not have to be complete alternatives. Hebrews reminds us that our God is indeed a 'consuming fire', real, potent and all-consuming. But this God is not just a source of exciting personal experiences for us, but the God of the whole world. To serve this God is to be drawn out of ourselves, and our own interesting religious urges, into God's purposes for creation. Our faith is not just for us, but to help us build a community that will be at home in 'the city of the living God'.

Reflection by **Jane Williams**

I Kings 8.22-30
or Revelation 21.9-14
Psalm 122
Hebrews 12.18-24
Matthew 21.12-16

Matthew 21.12-16

'... a house of prayer' (v.13)

It's extremely difficult to make a sermon on the Old Testament prophets so memorable that people are still talking about it after their coffee and biscuits. Believe me, I've tried! Jesus managed it spectacularly by climaxing his sermon with a rampage through the building in which all the furniture was overturned. Unforgettable, even twenty centuries later.

However, we are more familiar with his visual aid than with his words. He was preaching about how the glorious vision of Isaiah 56.7, 'my house shall be called a house of prayer,' had deteriorated into the miserable mess of Jeremiah 7.11, 'a den of robbers'.

The passage in Isaiah is about how God's intention has always been that his salvation should cascade beyond the Jews so that people of all the nations of the world should be caught up his grace. The Court of the Gentiles in the Jerusalem Temple was there precisely so that foreigners could encounter God's love and mercy. What did Jesus find there? Not a place of welcome for gentiles, outsiders and strangers, but an exorbitantly expensive market in temple essentials for insiders.

Any building dedicated to the glory of Jesus Christ needs to be a place where people who are unfamiliar or awkward find a loving welcome. One in which only the religious feel at home needs a dramatic overhaul. But when that happens, healing and new vision are the beautiful results (v.14).

Reflection by **Peter Graystone**

Harvest Thanksgiving

Deuteronomy 8.7-18
or Deuteronomy 28.1-14
Psalm 65
2 Corinthians 9.6-end
Luke 12.16-30 *or* Luke 17.11-19

Deuteronomy 8.7-18

'But remember the Lord your God ...' (v.18)

The people of God are called to lead a life of thanksgiving and gratitude in the land the Lord has given them. However, Moses realizes that, in prosperity, their sense of self-sufficiency will lead them to push God aside (v.17). They will possibly believe they are autonomous and self-fulfilling individuals, whose fortunes are in their own hands.

This is a good depiction of our society, believers included. If we achieve something, we attribute it to our talents and brains. If we fail to achieve, we have just been unlucky or the victims of our circumstances. God has little to do with what we do or what happens to us.

What we need to do is 'remember' or 'not forget' (vv.11,14, 18,19). Remember the source of your abundance, the Lord your God. Remember your days of scarcity and struggle. Remember how you reached here. Such memory helps us to be thankful and grateful to God.

Just thanking God for the abundance we enjoy is not enough. It would seem self-centred – we thank God that we have too much while others have less than enough. The gratitude that God expects involves keeping his commandments (v.11). A greater part of the commandments is about how we treat each other and show compassion to the needy. So remember not only your God and your past but today's less fortunate people too. Thanksgiving is not just thanking God for our abundance; it is about God's generous provision for all.

Reflection by **John Perumbalath**

Deuteronomy 8.7-18
or **Deuteronomy 28.1-14**
Psalm 65
2 Corinthians 9.6-end
Luke 12.16-30 *or* Luke 17.11-19

Harvest Thanksgiving

Deuteronomy 28.1-14

'The Lord will command the blessing' (v.8)

There is something awesome, even terrifying, about the pronouncement of a solemn blessing – or a curse. Today's reading envisages the dramatic performance of a covenant-renewal service on the threshold of the Promised Land, where God's people heard the terms of their commitment to the Lord stipulated with all the gravity of a binding corporate contract.

From childhood days, I remember the spine-tingling impact of the final blessing in church. These were not just idle words. Something primal and mysterious was being uttered, with power to transform all that would unfold in the world outside. 'And the blessing of God Almighty ...' Words of benediction convey, for believers, this transformative power. Often lyrical and poetic, they evoke a new world of beauty and fulfilment. Against the tediousness of everyday information and instruction, words of blessing re-awaken the soul.

Blessings speak of divine abundance. Today's liturgy promises a comprehensive grace: blessings in the city, and in the field; blessings of the womb, and of the flock; blessings of the harvest, and of the hearth – a generous outpouring of creativity and life (vv.3-6). These could be magic formulae, mere wishful thinking, but the theological authenticity of a blessing is anchored in moral and spiritual relationships – not only with the God who is the source of all blessing, but also with our neighbours in his covenant community. It would be a poor and lonely world indeed without blessings.

Reflection by **Margaret Whipp**

269

Harvest Thanksgiving

Deuteronomy 8.7-18
or Deuteronomy 28.1-14
Psalm 65
2 Corinthians 9.6-end
Luke 12.16-30 *or* Luke 17.11-19

2 Corinthians 9.6-end
'God loves a cheerful giver' (v. 7)

The use of money is a litmus test of faith and discipleship. Paul's injunctions here are the product of mature reflection on the 'collection for the saints'. His theology draws on the biblical imagery of harvesting, which encompasses both the abundant provision of God the Creator and the human responsibility to labour in sowing and reaping.

The most obvious principle is that the scale of reaping reflects the intensity of sowing. Generosity in response to God's grace brings rich returns. Like the teaching of Jesus on trusting God to provide (Matthew 6.25-33), this raises difficult questions about what God is doing and what can be expected of people in situations of poverty and destitution. Nevertheless, it is integral to the gospel that our trust in God should be expressed in free and sacrificial giving according to our means – not grudgingly or dutifully, but thoughtfully and cheerfully.

It is God who provides the means of life, not only supplying the seed but also multiplying the fruits of giving in a 'harvest of righteousness' that overflows in good works. In the background is the Jewish understanding of blessing, enfolding God and his people in a cycle of giving and thanksgiving, centred on Christ as the ultimate gift.

Reflection by **Christopher Jones**

Deuteronomy 8.7-18
or Deuteronomy 28.1-14
Psalm 65
2 Corinthians 9.6-end
Luke 12.16-30 *or* Luke 17.11-19

Harvest Thanksgiving

Luke 12.16-30

'... do not keep striving for what you are to eat and ... drink, and do not keep worrying' (v.29)

A loud cry from Christ to free us from the burden of worry! This cry could not be more relevant today as we live in a world consumed by the rush to earn and to spend.

Two thousand years since God journeyed to our world and preached in our streets, his words still resonate with our busy-ness to obtain the latest technology, to drive a faster car, to live in a bigger house filled with more of everything – except faith, love and justice.

But Jesus is not just talking about material things – the larger barns and the stockpiles of grain and goods of verse 18. He knows that there will always be crises in our lives, but no crisis has ever been averted or ended through fear and worry. If we worry, then we think we are facing life on our own. We are not alone, and this is the message that Jesus wants us to understand. The words of Christ deserve a pause so that we can think about the contrast between what is truly essential and what actually dominates our lives.

To be citizens of the kingdom of God, we need to take a decision – a decision to shed our worry and fear and take on the cloak of Christ, giving him the reign over our lives and freeing us to live an abundant life with him and with each other.

Reflection by **Nadim Nassar**

Harvest Thanksgiving

Deuteronomy 8.7-18
or Deuteronomy 28.1-14
Psalm 65
2 Corinthians 9.6-15
Luke 12.16-30 *or* **Luke 17.11-19**

Luke 17.11-19

*'Then one of them, when he saw that he was healed,
turned back ... and thanked him.' (vv.15-16)*

We've all neglected to communicate our thanks at times, so
we can empathize with the nine lepers. Preoccupied with their
healing, perhaps they couldn't wait to be declared 'disease
free'. However, by not turning back, they miss the deep shared
joy of giving praise to God, and having their lives enriched by
Jesus' delight in their wholeness.

The nine Jews should have acknowledged God's goodness,
but instead the recognition comes from an unlikely person –
a Samaritan. As an outcast, this unclean foreigner is not
entitled to anything from anyone. Jesus, however, is
interested not in 'entitlement' but in 'gift'. In the Samaritan's
loving response we see the rare expression of gratitude as he
recognizes that the true source of this gift of healing is God.
His gratitude prompts a precious moment of personal
encounter with Jesus, for whom his thanks is a gift.

By acknowledging that all we have and are is God's gift, we
start to dismantle the culture of entitlement that subtly
undermines our capacity for contentment. Gratitude, welling
up from the heart, fosters humility in us and deepens our
relationship with God. Scripture reminds us 'in every thing
give thanks' (1 Thessalonians 5.18, AV). There is no more
appropriate time to do this than at Harvest Thanksgiving, but
a regular review of the grace of God at work in the events of
every day – however small or difficult they may seem – is a
valuable spiritual practice available to us all.

Reflection by **Sue Pickering**

REFLECTIONS FOR DAILY PRAYER

If you enjoyed *Reflections for Sundays (Year A)*, why not consider enhancing your spiritual journey through the rich landscape of the Church's year with *Reflections for Daily Prayer*, the Church of England's popular daily prayer companion.

Covering Monday to Saturday each week, *Reflections for Daily Prayer* offers stimulating and accessible reflections on a Bible reading from the lectionary for *Common Worship: Morning Prayer*. Thousands of readers value the creative insights, scholarship and pastoral wisdom offered by our team of experienced writers.

Each day includes:

- full lectionary details for Morning Prayer
- a reflection on one of the Bible readings
- a Collect for the day.

This book also contains:

- a simple form of Morning Prayer, with seasonal variations, for use throughout the year
- a short form of Night Prayer (also known as Compline)
- a guide to the practice of daily prayer by John Pritchard
- a simple introduction to contemplative reading of the Bible from Stephen Cottrell.

Each annual volume contains reflections for an entire year starting in Advent and is published each year in the preceding May.

For more information about Reflections for Daily Prayer, visit our website: www.dailyprayer.org.uk

REFLECTIONS FOR DAILY PRAYER

App

Make Bible study and reflection a part of your routine wherever you go with the Reflections for Daily Prayer App for Apple and Android devices.

Download the app for free from the App Store (Apple devices) or Google Play (Android devices) and receive a week's worth of reflections free. Then purchase a monthly, three-monthly or annual subscription to receive up-to-date content.

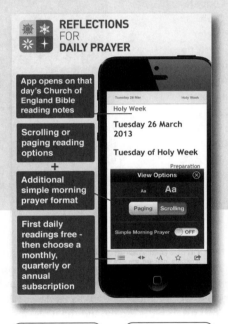

REFLECTIONS ON THE **PSALMS**

Reflections on the Psalms provides original and insightful meditations on each of the Bible's 150 Psalms, from the same experienced team of distinguished writers that have made *Reflections for Daily Prayer* so successful. The author team comprises:

Ian Adams
Christopher Cocksworth
Joanna Collicutt
Gillian Cooper
Steven Croft
Paula Gooder
Peter Graystone
Malcolm Guite
Helen-Ann Hartley
Barbara Mosse
Mark Oakley
Martyn Percy
John Pritchard
Ben Quash
John Sentamu
Angela Tilby
Lucy Winkett
Jeremy Worthen

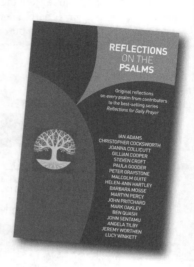

Each reflection is accompanied by its corresponding Psalm refrain and prayer from the *Common Worship Psalter*, making this a valuable resource for personal or devotional use. Specially written introductions by Paula Gooder and Steven Croft explore the Psalms and the Bible and the Psalms in the life of the Church.

£14.99 • 192 pages
ISBN 978 0 7151 4490 9

Also available in Kindle and epub formats

Resources for Daily Prayer

Common Worship: Daily Prayer

The official daily office of the Church of England,
Common Worship: Daily Prayer is a rich collection of
devotional material that will enable those
wanting to enrich their quiet times to develop
a regular pattern of prayer. It includes:

- Prayer During the Day
- Forms of Penitence
- Morning and Evening Prayer
- Night Prayer (Compline)
- Collects and Refrains
- Canticles
- Complete Psalter

896 pages • with 6 ribbons • 202 x 125mm

Hardback	978 0 7151 2199 3	**£22.50**
Soft cased	978 0 7151 2178 8	**£27.50**
Bonded leather	978 0 7151 2277 8	**£50.00**

Time to Pray

This compact, soft-case volume offers two simple,
shorter offices from *Common Worship: Daily Prayer*.
It is an ideal introduction to a more structured personal
devotional time, or can be used as a lighter, portable
daily office for those on the move.

Time to Pray includes:

- Prayer During the Day
  (for every day of the week)
- Night Prayer
- Selected Psalms

£12.99 • 112 pages • Soft case
ISBN 978 0 7151 2122 1

Order now at **www.chpublishing.co.uk**
or via **Norwich Books and Music**
Telephone **(01603) 785923**
E-mail **orders@norwichbooksandmusic.co.uk**